# Web Development with Node and Express

*Ethan Brown*

Beijing · Cambridge · Farnham · Köln · Sebastopol · Tokyo

**Web Development with Node and Express**

by Ethan Brown

Copyright © 2014 Ethan Brown. All rights reserved.

Printed in the United States of America.

Published by O'Reilly Media, Inc., 1005 Gravenstein Highway North, Sebastopol, CA 95472.

O'Reilly books may be purchased for educational, business, or sales promotional use. Online editions are also available for most titles (*http://safaribooksonline.com*). For more information, contact our corporate/institutional sales department: 800-998-9938 or *corporate@oreilly.com*.

| | |
|---|---|
| **Editors:** Simon St. Laurent and Brian Anderson | **Indexer:** Ellen Troutman Zaig |
| **Production Editor:** Matthew Hacker | **Cover Designer:** Karen Montgomery |
| **Copyeditor:** Linley Dolby | **Interior Designer:** David Futato |
| **Proofreader:** Rachel Monaghan | **Illustrator:** Rebecca Demarest |

July 2014:      First Edition

**Revision History for the First Edition:**

2014-06-27:   First release

2015-07-17:   Second release

See *http://oreilly.com/catalog/errata.csp?isbn=9781491949306* for release details.

ISBN: 978-1-491-94930-6

[LSI]

*This book is dedicated to my family:*

*My father, Tom, who gave me a love of engineering; my mother, Ann, who gave me a love of writing; and my sister, Meris, who has been a constant companion.*

# Table of Contents

Foreword. . . . . . . . . . . . . . . . . . . . . . . . . . . . . . . . . . . . . . . . . . . . . . . . . . . . . . . . . . . . . . . . . . . . . . . xiii

Preface. . . . . . . . . . . . . . . . . . . . . . . . . . . . . . . . . . . . . . . . . . . . . . . . . . . . . . . . . . . . . . . . . . . . . . . . xv

1. Introducing Express. . . . . . . . . . . . . . . . . . . . . . . . . . . . . . . . . . . . . . . . . . . . . . . . . . . . . . . . . . . 1
    The JavaScript Revolution                                           1
    Introducing Express                                                 2
    A Brief History of Express                                          4
    Upgrading to Express 4.0                                            4
    Node: A New Kind of Web Server                                      5
    The Node Ecosystem                                                  6
    Licensing                                                           7

2. Getting Started with Node. . . . . . . . . . . . . . . . . . . . . . . . . . . . . . . . . . . . . . . . . . . . . . . . . . . . 9
    Getting Node                                                        9
    Using the Terminal                                                 10
    Editors                                                            11
    npm                                                                12
    A Simple Web Server with Node                                      13
        Hello World                                                    14
        Event-Driven Programming                                      14
        Routing                                                       15
        Serving Static Resources                                      15
    Onward to Express                                                  17

3. Saving Time with Express. . . . . . . . . . . . . . . . . . . . . . . . . . . . . . . . . . . . . . . . . . . . . . . . . . . . 19
    Scaffolding                                                        19
    The Meadowlark Travel Website                                      20
    Initial Steps                                                      20
        Views and Layouts                                             24

Static Files and Views                                                           26
Dynamic Content in Views                                                         27
Conclusion                                                                       28

4. Tidying Up. . . . . . . . . . . . . . . . . . . . . . . . . . . . . . . . . . . . . . . . . . . . . . . . . . . . .  29
Best Practices                                                                   29
Version Control                                                                  30
How to Use Git with This Book                                                    31
    If You're Following Along by Doing It Yourself                               31
    If You're Following Along by Using the Official Repository                   32
npm Packages                                                                     33
Project Metadata                                                                 34
Node Modules                                                                     35

5. Quality Assurance. . . . . . . . . . . . . . . . . . . . . . . . . . . . . . . . . . . . . . . . . . . . . . .  37
QA: Is It Worth It?                                                              38
Logic Versus Presentation                                                        39
The Types of Tests                                                               39
Overview of QA Techniques                                                        40
Running Your Server                                                              40
Page Testing                                                                     41
Cross-Page Testing                                                               44
Logic Testing                                                                    48
Linting                                                                          49
Link Checking                                                                    49
Automating with Grunt                                                            50
Continuous Integration (CI)                                                      52

6. The Request and Response Objects. . . . . . . . . . . . . . . . . . . . . . . . . . . . . . . . . .  55
The Parts of a URL                                                              55
HTTP Request Methods                                                             56
Request Headers                                                                  57
Response Headers                                                                 57
Internet Media Types                                                             58
Request Body                                                                     58
Parameters                                                                       59
The Request Object                                                               59
The Response Object                                                              61
Getting More Information                                                         62
Boiling It Down                                                                  63
    Rendering Content                                                            63
    Processing Forms                                                             65

Providing an API                                                          66

7. Templating with Handlebars. . . . . . . . . . . . . . . . . . . . . . . . . . . . . . . . . . . . . . . . . . . . .  69
   There Are No Absolute Rules Except This One                            70
   Choosing a Template Engine                                             71
   Jade: A Different Approach                                             71
   Handlebars Basics                                                      73
      Comments                                                            74
      Blocks                                                              74
      Server-Side Templates                                              76
      Views and Layouts                                                  76
      Using Layouts (or Not) in Express                                  78
      Partials                                                            79
      Sections                                                            81
      Perfecting Your Templates                                           82
      Client-Side Handlebars                                             83
   Conclusion                                                             85

8. Form Handling. . . . . . . . . . . . . . . . . . . . . . . . . . . . . . . . . . . . . . . . . . . . . . . . . . . . . . . .  87
   Sending Client Data to the Server                                      87
   HTML Forms                                                             87
   Encoding                                                               88
   Different Approaches to Form Handling                                  89
   Form Handling with Express                                             91
   Handling AJAX Forms                                                    92
   File Uploads                                                           95
   jQuery File Upload                                                     97

9. Cookies and Sessions. . . . . . . . . . . . . . . . . . . . . . . . . . . . . . . . . . . . . . . . . . . . . . . . .  101
   Externalizing Credentials                                            102
   Cookies in Express                                                    103
   Examining Cookies                                                     105
   Sessions                                                              105
      Memory Stores                                                      105
      Using Sessions                                                     107
   Using Sessions to Implement Flash Messages                            107
   What to Use Sessions For                                              109

10. Middleware. . . . . . . . . . . . . . . . . . . . . . . . . . . . . . . . . . . . . . . . . . . . . . . . . . . . . . . .  111
   Common Middleware                                                     116
   Third-Party Middleware                                                118

**11. Sending Email**.................................................. 119

SMTP, MSAs, and MTAs                                      119
Receiving Email                                          120
Email Headers                                            120
Email Formats                                            121
HTML Email                                               121
Nodemailer                                               122
   Sending Mail                           123
   Sending Mail to Multiple Recipients    123
Better Options for Bulk Email                            124
Sending HTML Email                                       124
   Images in HTML Email                   125
   Using Views to Send HTML Email         126
   Encapsulating Email Functionality      128
Email as a Site Monitoring Tool                          129

**12. Production Concerns**.......................................... 131

Execution Environments                                   131
Environment-Specific Configuration                       132
Scaling Your Website                                     133
   Scaling Out with App Clusters          134
   Handling Uncaught Exceptions           137
   Scaling Out with Multiple Servers      140
Monitoring Your Website                                  141
   Third-Party Uptime Monitors            141
   Application Failures                   142
Stress Testing                                           142

**13. Persistence**.................................................. 145

Filesystem Persistence                                   145
Cloud Persistence                                        147
Database Persistence                                     148
   A Note on Performance                  148
   Setting Up MongoDB                     149
   Mongoose                               149
   Database Connections with Mongoose     150
   Creating Schemas and Models            151
   Seeding Initial Data                   152
   Retrieving Data                        153
   Adding Data                            154
   Using MongoDB for Session Storage      156

**14. Routing.** . . . . . . . . . . . . . . . . . . . . . . . . . . . . . . . . . . . . . . . . . . . . . . **159**
Routes and SEO                                                      161
Subdomains                                                         161
Route Handlers Are Middleware                                       162
Route Paths and Regular Expressions                                 164
Route Parameters                                                    164
Organizing Routes                                                  165
Declaring Routes in a Module                                        166
Grouping Handlers Logically                                         167
Automatically Rendering Views                                       168
Other Approaches to Route Organization                              169

**15. REST APIs and JSON.** . . . . . . . . . . . . . . . . . . . . . . . . . . . . . . . . . . . . . . . **171**
JSON and XML                                                       172
Our API                                                            172
API Error Reporting                                                173
Cross-Origin Resource Sharing (CORS)                                174
Our Data Store                                                     175
Our Tests                                                          175
Using Express to Provide an API                                     177
Using a REST Plugin                                                 178
Using a Subdomain                                                  180

**16. Static Content.** . . . . . . . . . . . . . . . . . . . . . . . . . . . . . . . . . . . . . . . . . . . **183**
Performance Considerations                                          184
Future-Proofing Your Website                                        184
Static Mapping                                                  185
Static Resources in Views                                       187
Static Resources in CSS                                         187
Static Resources in Server-Side JavaScript                          189
Static Resources in Client-Side JavaScript                          189
Serving Static Resources                                            191
Changing Your Static Content                                        192
Bundling and Minification                                           192
Skipping Bundling and Minification in Development Mode          195
A Note on Third-Party Libraries                                     197
QA                                                                 197
Summary                                                            199

**17. Implementing MVC in Express.** . . . . . . . . . . . . . . . . . . . . . . . . . . . . . . . . . **201**
Models                                                             202
View Models                                                        203

    Controllers                                                              205

Controllers                                                      205
Conclusion                                                      207

**18. Security**. . . . . . . . . . . . . . . . . . . . . . . . . . . . . . . . . . . . . . . . . . . . . . . . . . . . . . . . . . . . . . **209**
HTTPS                                                          209
   Generating Your Own Certificate                            210
   Using a Free Certificate Authority                          211
   Purchasing a Certificate                                    212
   Enabling HTTPS for Your Express App                         214
   A Note on Ports                                             215
   HTTPS and Proxies                                           216
Cross-Site Request Forgery                                      217
Authentication                                                  218
   Authentication Versus Authorization                         218
   The Problem with Passwords                                  219
   Third-Party Authentication                                  219
   Storing Users in Your Database                              220
   Authentication Versus Registration and the User Experience  221
   Passport                                                    222
   Role-Based Authorization                                    231
   Adding Additional Authentication Providers                  233
Conclusion                                                      234

**19. Integrating with Third-Party APIs**. . . . . . . . . . . . . . . . . . . . . . . . . . . . . . . . . . . . . . **235**
Social Media                                                    235
   Social Media Plugins and Site Performance                   235
   Searching for Tweets                                        236
   Rendering Tweets                                            239
Geocoding                                                       243
   Geocoding with Google                                       243
   Geocoding Your Data                                         244
   Displaying a Map                                            247
   Improving Client-Side Performance                           249
Weather Data                                                    250
Conclusion                                                      252

**20. Debugging**. . . . . . . . . . . . . . . . . . . . . . . . . . . . . . . . . . . . . . . . . . . . . . . . . . . . . . . . . . . **253**
The First Principle of Debugging                                253
Take Advantage of REPL and the Console                         254
Using Node's Built-in Debugger                                 255
Node Inspector                                                  255
Debugging Asynchronous Functions                               259

Debugging Express                                                       259

21. **Going Live**. . . . . . . . . . . . . . . . . . . . . . . . . . . . . . . . . . . . . . . . . . . . . . **263**
    Domain Registration and Hosting                                     263
       Domain Name System                                               264
       Security                                                         264
       Top-Level Domains                                                265
       Subdomains                                                       266
       Nameservers                                                      267
       Hosting                                                          268
       Deployment                                                       271
    Conclusion                                                          274

22. **Maintenance**. . . . . . . . . . . . . . . . . . . . . . . . . . . . . . . . . . . . . . . . . . . . **275**
    The Principles of Maintenance                                       275
       Have a Longevity Plan                                            275
       Use Source Control                                               277
       Use an Issue Tracker                                             277
       Exercise Good Hygiene                                            277
       Don't Procrastinate                                              278
       Do Routine QA Checks                                             278
       Monitor Analytics                                                279
       Optimize Performance                                             279
       Prioritize Lead Tracking                                         279
       Prevent "Invisible" Failures                                     281
    Code Reuse and Refactoring                                          281
       Private npm Registry                                             282
       Middleware                                                       283
    Conclusion                                                          285

23. **Additional Resources**. . . . . . . . . . . . . . . . . . . . . . . . . . . . . . . . . . . . **287**
    Online Documentation                                               287
    Periodicals                                                        288
    Stack Overflow                                                     288
    Contributing to Express                                            290
    Conclusion                                                         292

**Index**. . . . . . . . . . . . . . . . . . . . . . . . . . . . . . . . . . . . . . . . . . . . . . . . . . . . . **293**

# Foreword

The combination of JavaScript, Node, and Express is an ideal choice for web teams that want a powerful, quick-to-deploy technology stack that is widely respected in the development community and large enterprises alike.

Building great web applications and finding great web developers isn't easy. Great apps require great functionality, user experience, and business impact: delivered, deployed, and supported quickly and cost effectively. The lower total cost of ownership and faster time-to-market that Express provides is critical in the business world. If you are a web developer, you have to use at least some JavaScript. But you also have the option of using a *lot* of it. In this book, Ethan Brown shows you that you can use a lot of it, and it's not that hard thanks to Node and Express.

Node and Express are like machine guns that deliver upon the silver-bullet promise of JavaScript.

JavaScript is the most universally accepted language for client-side scripting. Unlike Flash, it's supported by all major web browsers. It's the fundamental technology behind many of the attractive animations and transitions you see on the Web. In fact, it's almost impossible not to utilize JavaScript if you want to achieve modern client-side functionality.

One problem with JavaScript is that it has always been vulnerable to sloppy programming. The Node ecosystem is changing that by providing frameworks, libraries, and tools that speed up development and encourage good coding habits. This helps us bring better apps to market faster.

We now have a great programming language that is supported by large enterprises, is easy-to-use, is designed for modern browsers, and is supplemented with great frameworks and libraries on both client-side and server-side. I call that revolutionary.

—Steve Rosenbaum
*President and CEO, Pop Art, Inc.*

# Preface

## Who This Book Is For

Clearly, this book is for programmers who want to create web applications (traditional websites, RESTful APIs, or anything in between) using JavaScript, Node, and Express. One of the exciting aspects of Node development is that it has attracted a whole new audience of programmers. The accessibility and flexibility of JavaScript has attracted self-taught programmers from all over the world. At no time in the history of computer science has programming been so accessible. The number and quality of online resources for learning to program (and getting help when you get stuck) is truly astonishing and inspiring. So to those new (possibly self-taught) programmers, I welcome you.

Then, of course, there are the programmers like me, who have been around for a while. Like many programmers of my era, I started off with assembler and BASIC, and went through Pascal, C++, Perl, Java, PHP, Ruby, C, C#, and JavaScript. At university, I was exposed to more niche languages such as ML, LISP, and PROLOG. Many of these languages are near and dear to my heart, but in none of these languages do I see so much promise as I do in JavaScript. So I am also writing this book for programmers like myself, who have a lot of experience, and perhaps a more philosophical outlook on specific technologies.

No experience with Node is necessary, but you should have some experience with Java-Script. If you're new to programming, I recommend Codecademy (*http://www.codecademy.com/tracks/javascript*). If you're an experienced programmer, I recommend Douglas Crockford's *JavaScript: The Good Parts* (O'Reilly). The examples in this book can be used with any system that Node works on (which covers Windows, OS X, and

Linux). The examples are geared toward command-line (terminal) users, so you should have some familiarity with your system's terminal.

Most important, this book is for programmers who are excited. Excited about the future of the Internet, and want to be part of it. Excited about learning new things, new techniques, and new ways of looking at web development. If, dear reader, you are not excited, I hope you will be by the time you reach the end of this book....

## How This Book Is Organized

Chapters 1 and 2 will introduce you to Node and Express and some of the tools you'll be using throughout the book. In Chapters 3 and 4, you start using Express and build the skeleton of a sample website that will be used as a running example throughout the rest of the book.

Chapter 5 discusses testing and QA, and Chapter 6 covers some of Node's more important constructs and how they are extended and used by Express. Chapter 7 covers templating (using Handlebars), which lays the foundation of building useful websites with Express. Chapters 8 and 9 cover cookies, sessions, and form handlers, rounding out the things you need to know to build basic functional websites with Express.

Chapter 10 delves into "middleware," a concept central to Connect (one of Express's major components). Chapter 11 explains how to use middleware to send email from the server and discusses security and layout issues inherent to email.

Chapter 12 offers a preview into production concerns. Even though, at this stage in the book, you don't have all the information you need to build a production-ready website, thinking about production now can save you from major headaches in the future.

Chapter 13 is about persistence, with a focus on MongoDB (one of the leading document databases).

Chapter 14 gets into the details of routing with Express (how URLs are mapped to content), and Chapter 15 takes a diversion into writing APIs with Express. Chapter 16 covers the details of serving static content, with a focus on maximizing performance. Chapter 17 reviews the popular model-view-controller (MVC) paradigm, and how it fits into Express.

Chapter 18 discusses security: how to build authentication and authorization into your app (with a focus on using a third-party authentication provider), as well as how to run your site over HTTPS.

Chapter 19 explains how to integrate with third-party services. Examples used are Twitter, Google Maps, and Weather Underground.

Chapters 20 and 21 get you ready for the big day: your site launch. They cover debugging, so you can root out any defects before launch, and the process of going live. Chapter 22 talks about the next important (and oft-neglected) phase: maintenance.

The book concludes with Chapter 23, which points you to additional resources, should you want to further your education about Node and Express, and where you can go to get help.

# Example Website

Starting in Chapter 3, a running example will be used throughout the book: the Meadowlark Travel website. Just having gotten back from a trip to Lisbon, I have travel on my mind, so the example website I have chosen is for a fictional travel company in my home state of Oregon (the Western Meadowlark is the state bird of Oregon). Meadowlark Travel allows travelers to connect to local "amateur tour guides," and partners with companies offering bike and scooter rentals and local tours. In addition, it maintains a database of local attractions, complete with history and location-aware services.

Like any pedagogical example, the Meadowlark Travel website is contrived, but it is an example that covers many of the challenges facing real-world websites: third-party component integration, geolocation, ecommerce, performance, and security.

As the focus on this book is backend infrastructure, the example website will not be complete; it merely serves as a fictional example of a real-world website to provide depth and context to the examples. Presumably, you are working on your own website, and you can use the Meadowlark Travel example as a template for it.

# Conventions Used in This Book

The following typographical conventions are used in this book:

*Italic*
> Indicates new terms, URLs, email addresses, filenames, and file extensions.

`Constant width`
> Used for program listings, as well as within paragraphs to refer to program elements such as variable or function names, databases, data types, environment variables, statements, and keywords.

**`Constant width bold`**
> Shows commands or other text that should be typed literally by the user.

*`Constant width italic`*
> Shows text that should be replaced with user-supplied values or by values determined by context.

This element signifies a tip or suggestion.

 This element signifies a general note.

 This element indicates a warning or caution.

## Using Code Examples

Supplemental material (code examples, exercises, etc.) is available for download at *https://github.com/EthanRBrown/web-development-with-node-and-express.*

This book is here to help you get your job done. In general, if example code is offered with this book, you may use it in your programs and documentation. You do not need to contact us for permission unless you're reproducing a significant portion of the code. For example, writing a program that uses several chunks of code from this book does not require permission. Selling or distributing a CD-ROM of examples from O'Reilly books does require permission. Answering a question by citing this book and quoting example code does not require permission. Incorporating a significant amount of example code from this book into your product's documentation does require permission.

We appreciate, but do not require, attribution. An attribution usually includes the title, author, publisher, and ISBN. For example: "*Web Development with Node and Express* by Ethan Brown (O'Reilly). Copyright 2014 Ethan Brown, 978-1-491-94930-6."

If you feel your use of code examples falls outside fair use or the permission given above, feel free to contact us at *permissions@oreilly.com.*

## Safari® Books Online

 *Safari Books Online* is an on-demand digital library that delivers expert content in both book and video form from the world's leading authors in technology and business.

Technology professionals, software developers, web designers, and business and creative professionals use Safari Books Online as their primary resource for research, problem solving, learning, and certification training.

Safari Books Online offers a range of plans and pricing for enterprise, government, education, and individuals.

Members have access to thousands of books, training videos, and prepublication manuscripts in one fully searchable database from publishers like O'Reilly Media, Prentice Hall Professional, Addison-Wesley Professional, Microsoft Press, Sams, Que, Peachpit Press, Focal Press, Cisco Press, John Wiley & Sons, Syngress, Morgan Kaufmann, IBM Redbooks, Packt, Adobe Press, FT Press, Apress, Manning, New Riders, McGraw-Hill, Jones & Bartlett, Course Technology, and hundreds more. For more information about Safari Books Online, please visit us online.

# How to Contact Us

Please address comments and questions concerning this book to the publisher:

O'Reilly Media, Inc.
1005 Gravenstein Highway North
Sebastopol, CA 95472
800-998-9938 (in the United States or Canada)
707-829-0515 (international or local)
707-829-0104 (fax)

We have a web page for this book, where we list errata, examples, and any additional information. You can access this page at *http://bit.ly/web_dev_node_express*.

To comment or ask technical questions about this book, send email to *bookquestions@oreilly.com*.

For more information about our books, courses, conferences, and news, see our website at *http://www.oreilly.com*.

Find us on Facebook: *http://facebook.com/oreilly*

Follow us on Twitter: *http://twitter.com/oreillymedia*

Watch us on YouTube: *http://www.youtube.com/oreillymedia*

# Acknowledgments

So many people in my life have played a part in making this book a reality: it would not have been possible without the influence of all the people who have touched my life and made me who I am today.

I would like to start out by thanking everyone at Pop Art: not only has my time at Pop Art given me a renewed passion for engineering, but I have learned so much from everyone there, and without their support, this book would not exist. I am grateful to Steve Rosenbaum for creating an inspiring place to work, and to Del Olds for bringing me on board, making me feel welcome, and being an honorable leader. Thanks to Paul Inman for his unwavering support and inspiring attitude toward engineering, and Tony Alferez for his warm support and for helping me carve out time for writing without impacting Pop Art. Finally, thanks to all the great engineers I have worked with, who keep me on my toes: John Skelton, Dylan Hallstrom, Greg Yung, Quinn Michaels, and CJ Stritzel.

Zach Mason, thank you for being an inspiration to me. This book may be no *The Lost Books of the Odyssey*, but it is *mine*, and I don't know if I would have been so bold without your example.

I owe everything to my family. I couldn't have wished for a better, more loving education than the one they gave me, and I see their exceptional parenting reflected in my sister too.

Many thanks to Simon St. Laurent for giving me this opportunity, and to Brian Anderson for his steady and encouraging editing. Thanks to everyone at O'Reilly for their dedication and passion. Thanks to Jennifer Pierce, Mike Wilson, Ray Villalobos, and Eric Elliot for their thorough and constructive technical reviews.

Katy Roberts and Hanna Nelson provided invaluable feedback and advice on my "over the transom" proposal that made this book possible. Thank you both so much! Thanks to Chris Cowell-Shah for his excellent feedback on the QA chapter.

Lastly, thanks to my dear friends, without whom I surely would have gone insane. Byron Clayton, Mark Booth, Katy Roberts, and Sarah Lewis, you are the best group of friends a man could ask for. And thanks to Vickey and Judy, just for being who they are. I love you all.

# CHAPTER 1

# Introducing Express

## The JavaScript Revolution

Before I introduce the main subject of this book, it is important to provide a little background and historical context, and that means talking about JavaScript and Node.

The age of JavaScript is truly upon us. From its humble beginnings as a client-side scripting language, not only has it become completely ubiquitous on the client side, but its use as a server-side language has finally taken off too, thanks to Node.

The promise of an all-JavaScript technology stack is clear: no more context switching! No longer do you have to switch mental gears from JavaScript to PHP, C#, Ruby, or Python (or any other server-side language). Furthermore, it empowers frontend engineers to make the jump to server-side programming. This is not to say that server-side programming is strictly about the language: there's still a lot to learn. With JavaScript, though, at least the language won't be a barrier.

This book is for all those who see the promise of the JavaScript technology stack. Perhaps you are a frontend engineer looking to extend your experience into backend development. Perhaps you're an experienced backend developer like myself who is looking to JavaScript as a viable alternative to entrenched server-side languages.

If you've been a software engineer for as long as I have, you have seen many languages, frameworks, and APIs come into vogue. Some have taken off, and some have faded into obsolescence. You probably take pride in your ability to rapidly learn new languages, new systems. Every new language you come across feels a little more familiar: you recognize a bit here from a language you learned in college, a bit there from that job you had a few years ago. It feels good to have that kind of perspective, certainly, but it's also wearying. Sometimes you want to just *get something done*, without having to learn a whole new technology or dust off skills you haven't used in months or years.

JavaScript may seem, at first, an unlikely champion. I sympathize, believe me. If you told me three years ago that I would not only come to think of JavaScript as my language of choice, but also write a book about it, I would have told you you were crazy. I had all the usual prejudices against JavaScript: I thought it was a "toy" language. Something for amateurs and dilettantes to mangle and abuse. To be fair, JavaScript did lower the bar for amateurs, and there was a lot of questionable JavaScript out there, which did not help the language's reputation. To turn a popular saying on its head, "Hate the player, not the game."

It is unfortunate that people suffer this prejudice against JavaScript: it has prevented people from discovering how powerful, flexible, and elegant the language is. Many people are just now starting to take JavaScript seriously, even though the language as we know it now has been around since 1996 (although many of its more attractive features were added in 2005).

By picking up this book, you are probably free of that prejudice: either because, like me, you have gotten past it, or because you never had it in the first place. In either case, you are fortunate, and I look forward to introducing you to Express, a technology made possible by a delightful and surprising language.

In 2009, years after people had started to realize the power and expressiveness of JavaScript as a browser scripting language, Ryan Dahl saw JavaScript's potential as a server-side language, and Node was born. This was a fertile time for Internet technology. Ruby (and Ruby on Rails) took some great ideas from academic computer science, combined them with some new ideas of its own, and showed the world a quicker way to build websites and web applications. Microsoft, in a valiant effort to become relevant in the Internet age, did amazing things with .NET and learned not only from Ruby and JavaScript, but also from Java's mistakes, while borrowing heavily from the halls of academia.

It is an exciting time to be involved in Internet technology. Everywhere, there are amazing new ideas (or amazing old ideas revitalized). The spirit of innovation and excitement is greater now than it has been in many years.

# Introducing Express

The Express website describes Express as "a minimal and flexible node.js web application framework, providing a robust set of features for building single and multipage and hybrid web applications." What does that really mean, though? Let's break that description down:

*Minimal*

This is one of the most appealing aspects of Express. Many times, framework developers forget that usually "less is more." The Express philosophy is to provide the *minimal* layer between your brain and the server. That doesn't mean that it's not robust, or that it doesn't have enough useful features. It means that it gets in your way less, allowing you full expression of your ideas, while at the same time providing something useful.

*Flexible*

Another key aspect of the Express philosophy is that Express is extensible. Express provides you a very minimal framework, and you can add in different parts of Express functionality as needed, replacing whatever doesn't meet your needs. This is a breath of fresh air. So many frameworks give you *everything*, leaving you with a bloated, mysterious, and complex project before you've even written a single line of code. Very often, the first task is to waste time carving off unneeded functionality, or replacing the functionality that doesn't meet requirements. Express takes the opposite approach, allowing you to add what you need when you need it.

*Web application framework*

Here's where semantics starts to get tricky. What's a web application? Does that mean you can't build a website or web pages with Express? No, a website *is* a web application, and a web page *is* a web application. But a web application can be more: it can provide functionality to *other* web applications (among other things). In general, "app" is used to signify something that has functionality: it's not just a static collection of content (though that is a very simple example of a web app). While there is currently a distinction between an "app" (something that runs natively on your device) and a "web page" (something that is served to your device over the network), that distinction is getting blurrier, thanks to projects like PhoneGap, as well as Microsoft's move to allow HTML5 applications on the desktop, as if they were native applications. It's easy to imagine that in a few years, there won't be a distinction between an app and a website.

*Single-page web applications*

Single-page web applications are a relatively new idea. Instead of a website requiring a network request every time the user navigates to a different page, a single-page web application downloads the entire site (or a good chunk of it) to the client's browser. After that initial download, navigation is faster because there is little or no communication with the server. Single-page application development is facilitated by the use of popular frameworks such as Angular or Ember, which Express is happy to serve up.

*Multipage and hybrid web applications*

Multipage web applications are a more traditional approach to websites. Each page on a website is provided by a separate request to the server. Just because this approach is more traditional does not mean it is not without merit or that single-page applications are somehow better. There are simply more options now, and you can decide what parts of your content should be delivered as a single-page app, and what parts should be delivered via individual requests. "Hybrid" describes sites that utilize both of these approaches.

If you're still feeling confused about what Express actually *is*, don't worry: sometimes it's much easier to just start using something to understand what it is, and this book will get you started building web applications with Express.

## A Brief History of Express

Express's creator, TJ Holowaychuk, describes Express as a web framework inspired by Sinatra, which is a web framework based on Ruby. It is no surprise that Express borrows from a framework built on Ruby: Ruby spawned a wealth of great approaches to web development, aimed at making web development faster, more efficient, and more maintainable.

As much as Express was inspired by Sinatra, it is also deeply intertwined with Connect, a "plugin" library for Node. Connect coined the term "middleware" to describe pluggable Node modules that can handle web requests to varying degrees. Up until version 4.0, Express bundled Connect; in version 4.0, Connect (and all middleware except `static`) was removed to allow these middleware to be updated independently.

Express underwent a fairly substantial rewrite between 2.x and 3.0, then again between 3.x and 4.0. This book will focus on version 4.0.

## Upgrading to Express 4.0

If you already have some experience with Express 3.0, you'll be happy to learn that upgrading to Express 4.0 is pretty painless. If you're new to Express, you can skip this section. Here are the high points for those with Express 3.0 experience:

- Connect has been removed from Express, so with the exception of the `static` middleware, you will need to install the appropriate packages (namely, `connect`). At the same time, Connect has been moving some of its middleware into their own packages, so you might have to do some searching on npm to figure out where your middleware went.

- `body-parser` is now its own package, which no longer includes the `multipart` middleware, closing a major security hole. It's now safe to use the `body-parser` middleware.

- You no longer have to link the Express router into your application. So you should remove `app.use(app.router)` from your existing Express 3.0 apps.

- `app.configure` was removed; simply replace calls to this method by examining `app.get(env)` (using either a `switch` statement or `if` statements).

For more details, see the official migration guide (*http://bit.ly/1pkw80L*).

Express is an open source project and continues to be primarily developed and maintained by TJ Holowaychuk.

# Node: A New Kind of Web Server

In a way, Node has a lot in common with other popular web servers, like Microsoft's Internet Information Services (IIS) or Apache. What is more interesting, though, is how it differs, so let's start there.

Much like Express, Node's approach to webservers is very minimal. Unlike IIS or Apache, which a person can spend many years mastering, Node is very easy to set up and configure. That is not to say that tuning Node servers for maximum performance in a production setting is a trivial matter: it's just that the configuration options are simpler and more straightforward.

Another major difference between Node and more traditional web servers is that Node is single threaded. At first blush, this may seem like a step backward. As it turns out, it is a stroke of genius. Single threading vastly simplifies the business of writing web apps, and if you need the performance of a multithreaded app, you can simply spin up more instances of Node, and you will effectively have the performance benefits of multithreading. The astute reader is probably thinking this sounds like smoke and mirrors. After all, isn't multithreading through server parallelism (as opposed to app parallelism) simply moving the complexity around, not eliminating it? Perhaps, but in my experience, it has moved the complexity to exactly where it should be. Furthermore, with the growing popularity of cloud computing and treating servers as generic commodities, this approach makes a lot more sense. IIS and Apache are powerful indeed, and they are designed to squeeze the very last drop of performance out of today's powerful hardware. That comes at a cost, though: they require considerable expertise to set up and tune to achieve that performance.

In terms of the way apps are written, Node apps have more in common with PHP or Ruby apps than .NET or Java apps. While the JavaScript engine that Node uses (Google's V8) does compile JavaScript to native machine code (much like C or C++), it does so transparently,[1] so from the user's perspective, it behaves like a purely interpreted language. Not having a separate compile step reduces maintenance and deployment hassles: all you have to do is update a JavaScript file, and your changes will automatically be available.

---

1. Often called "Just in Time" (JIT) compilation.

Another compelling benefit of Node apps is that Node is incredibly platform independent. It's not the first or only platform-independent server technology, but platform independence is really more of a spectrum than a binary proposition. For example, you can run .NET apps on a Linux server thanks to Mono, but it's a painful endeavor. Likewise, you can run PHP apps on a Windows server, but it is not generally as easy to set up as it is on a Linux machine. Node, on the other hand, is a snap to set up on all the major operating systems (Windows, OS X, and Linux) and enables easy collaboration. Among website design teams, a mix of PCs and Macs is quite common. Certain platforms, like .NET, introduce challenges for frontend developers and designers, who often use Macs, which has a huge impact on collaboration and efficiency. The idea of being able to spin up a functioning server on any operating system in a matter of minutes (or even seconds!) is a dream come true.

## The Node Ecosystem

Node, of course, lies at the heart of the stack. It's the software that enables JavaScript to run on the server, uncoupled from a browser, which in turn allows frameworks written in JavaScript (like Express) to be used. Another important component is the database, which will be covered in more depth in Chapter 13. All but the simplest of web apps will need a database, and there are databases that are more at home in the Node ecosystem than others.

It is unsurprising that database interfaces are available for all the major relational databases (MySQL, MariaDB, PostgreSQL, Oracle, SQL Server): it would be foolish to neglect those established behemoths. However, the advent of Node development has revitalized a new approach to database storage: the so-called "NoSQL" databases. It's not always helpful to define something as what it's *not*, so we'll add that these NoSQL databases might be more properly called "document databases" or "key/value pair databases." They provide a conceptually simpler approach to data storage. There are many, but MongoDB is one of the frontrunners, and the one we will be using in this book.

Because building a functional website depends on multiple pieces of technology, acronyms have been spawned to describe the "stack" that a website is built on. For example, the combination of Linux, Apache, MySQL, and PHP is referred to as the *LAMP* stack. Valeri Karpov, an engineer at MongoDB, coined the acronym *MEAN*: Mongo, Express, Angular, and Node. While it's certainly catchy, it is limiting: there are so many choices for databases and application frameworks that "MEAN" doesn't capture the diversity of the ecosystem (it also leaves out what I believe is an important component: templating engines).

Coining an inclusive acronym is an interesting exercise. The indispensable component, of course, is Node. While there are other server-side JavaScript containers, Node is emerging as the dominant one. Express, also, is not the only web app framework available, though it is close to Node in its dominance. The two other components that are usually essential for web app development are a database server and a templating engine (a templating engine provides what PHP, JSP, or Razor provides naturally: the ability to seamlessly combine code and markup output). For these last two components, there aren't as many clear frontrunners, and this is where I believe it's a disservice to be restrictive.

What ties all these technologies together is JavaScript, so in an effort to be inclusive, I will be referring to the "JavaScript stack." For the purposes of this book, that means Node, Express, and MongoDB.

# Licensing

When developing Node applications, you may find yourself having to pay more attention to licensing than you ever have before (I certainly have). One of the beauties of the Node ecosystem is the vast array of packages available to you. However, each of those packages carries its own licensing, and worse, each package may depend on other packages, meaning that understanding the licensing of the various parts of the app you've written can be tricky.

However, there is some good news. One of the most popular licenses for Node packages is the MIT license, which is painlessly permissive, allowing you to do *almost* anything you want, including use the package in closed source software. However, you shouldn't just assume every package you use is MIT licensed.

 There are several packages available in npm that will try to figure out the licenses of each dependency in your project. Search npm for license-sniffer or license-spelunker.

While MIT is the most common license you will encounter, you may also see the following licenses:

*GNU General Public License (GPL)*
> The GPL is a very popular open source license that has been cleverly crafted to keep software free. That means if you use GPL-licensed code in your project, your project must *also* be GPL licensed. Naturally, this means your project can't be closed source.

*Apache 2.0*
> This license, like MIT, allows you to use a different license for your project, including a closed source license. You must, however, include notice of components that use the Apache 2.0 license.

*Berkeley Software Distribution (BSD)*

Similar to Apache, this license allows you to use whatever license you wish for your project, as long as you include notice of the BSD-licensed components.

 Software is sometimes *dual licensed* (licensed under two different licenses). A very common reason for doing this is to allow the software to be used in both GPL projects and projects with more permissive licensing. (For a component to be used in GPL software, the component must be GPL licensed.) This is a licensing scheme I often employ with my own projects: dual licensing with GPL and MIT.

Lastly, if you find yourself writing your own packages, you should be a good citizen and pick a license for your package, and document it correctly. There is nothing more frustrating to a developer than using someone's package and having to dig around in the source to determine the licensing or, worse, find that it isn't licensed at all.

# CHAPTER 2

# Getting Started with Node

If you don't have any experience with Node, this chapter is for you. Understanding Express and its usefulness requires a basic understanding of Node. If you already have experience building web apps with Node, feel free to skip this chapter. In this chapter, we will be building a very minimal web server with Node; in the next chapter, we will see how to do the same thing with Express.

## Getting Node

Getting Node installed on your system couldn't be easier. The Node team has gone to great lengths to make sure the installation process is simple and straightforward on all major platforms.

The installation is so simple, as a matter of fact, that it can be summed up in three simple steps:

1. Go to the Node home page (*http://nodejs.org*).
2. Click the big green button that says INSTALL.
3. Follow instructions.

For Windows and OS X, an installer will be downloaded that walks you through the process. For Linux, you will probably be up and running more quickly if you use a package manager (*https://github.com/joyent/node/wiki/Installing-Node.js-via-package-manager*).

 If you're a Linux user and you do want to use a package manager, make sure you follow the instructions in the aforementioned web page. Many Linux distributions will install an extremely old version of Node if you don't add the appropriate package repository.

You can also download a standalone installer (*http://nodejs.org/download*), which can be helpful if you are distributing Node to your organization.

If you have trouble building Node, or for some reason you would like to build Node from scratch, please refer to the official installation instructions (*http://bit.ly/node_installation*).

## Using the Terminal

I'm an unrepentant fan of the power and productivity of using a terminal (also called a "console" or "command prompt"). Throughout this book, all examples will assume you're using a terminal. If you're not friends with your terminal, I highly recommend you spend some time familiarizing yourself with your terminal of choice. Many of the utilities in this book have corresponding GUI interfaces, so if you're dead set against using a terminal, you have options, but you will have to find your own way.

If you're on OS X or Linux, you have a wealth of venerable shells (the terminal command interpreter) to choose from. The most popular by far is bash, though zsh has its adherents. The main reason I gravitate toward bash (other than long familiarity) is ubiquity. Sit down in front of any Unix-based computer, and 99% of the time, the default shell will be bash.

If you're a Windows user, things aren't quite so rosy. Microsoft has never been particularly interested in providing a pleasant terminal experience, so you'll have to do a little more work. Git helpfully includes a "Git bash" shell, which provides a Unix-like terminal experience (it only has a small subset of the normally available Unix command-line utilities, but it's a useful subset). While Git bash provides you with a minimal bash shell, it's still using the built-in Windows console application, which leads to an exercise in frustration (even simple functionality like resizing a console window, selecting text, cutting, and pasting is unintuitive and awkward). For this reason, I recommend installing a more sophisticated terminal such as Console2 (*http://bit.ly/Console_2*) or Con-Emu (*http://bit.ly/Con-Emu*). For Windows power users—especially for .NET developers or for hardcore Windows systems or network administrators—there is another option: Microsoft's own PowerShell. PowerShell lives up to its name: people do remarkable things with it, and a skilled PowerShell user could give a Unix command-line guru a run for their money. However, if you move between OS X/Linux and Windows, I still recommend sticking with Git bash for the consistency it provides.

Another option, if you're a Windows user, is virtualization. With the power and architecture of modern computers, the performance of virtual machines (VMs) is practically indistinguishable from actual machines. I've had great luck with Oracle's free Virtual-Box, and Windows 8 offers VM support built in. With cloud-based file storage, such as Dropbox, and the easy bridging of VM storage to host storage, virtualizing is looking more attractive all the time. Instead of using Git bash as a bandage on Windows's lackluster console support, consider using a Linux VM for development. If you find the UI isn't as smooth as you would like, you could use a terminal application, such as PuTTY (*http://www.putty.org*), which is what I often do.

Finally, no matter what sytem you're on, there's the excellent Codio (*https://codio.com*). Codio is a website that will spin up a new Linux instance for every project you have and provide an IDE and command line, with Node already installed. It's extremely easy to use and is a great way to get started very quickly with Node.

When you specify the -g (global) option when installing npm packages, they are installed in a subdirectory of your Windows home directory. I've found that a lot of these packages don't perform well if there are spaces in your username (my username used to be "Ethan Brown," and now it's "ethan.brown"). For your sanity, I recommend choosing a Windows username without a space in it. If you already have such a username, it's advisable to create a new user, and then transfer your files over to the new account: trying to rename your Windows home directory is possible but fraught with danger.

Once you've settled on a shell that makes you happy, I recommend you spend some time getting to know the basics. There are many wonderful tutorials on the Internet, and you'll save yourself a lot of headaches later on by learning a little now. At minimum, you should know how to navigate directories; copy, move, and delete files; and break out of a command-line program (usually Ctrl-C). If you want to become a terminal ninja, I encourage you to learn how to search for text in files, search for files and directories, chain commands together (the old "Unix philosophy"), and redirect output.

On many Unix-like systems, Ctrl-S has a special meaning: it will "freeze" the terminal (this was once used to pause output quickly scrolling past). Since this is such a common shortcut for Save, it's very easy to unthinkingly press, which leads to a very confusing situation for most people (this happens to me more often than I care to admit). To unfreeze the terminal, simply hit Ctrl-Q. So if you're ever confounded by a terminal that seems to have suddenly frozen, try pressing Ctrl-Q and see if it releases it.

# Editors

Few topics inspire such heated debate among programmers as the choice of editors, and for good reason: the editor is your primary tool. My editor of choice is vi[1] (or an editor

---

1. These days, vi is essentially synonymous with vim (vi improved). On most systems, vi is aliased to vim, but I usually type vim to make sure I'm using vim.

that has a vi mode). vi isn't for everyone (my coworkers constantly roll their eyes at me when I tell them how easy it would be to do what they're doing in vi), but finding a powerful editor and learning to use it will significantly increase your productivity and, dare I say it, enjoyment. One of the reasons I particularly like vi (though hardly the most important reason) is that like bash, it is ubiquitous. If you have access to a Unix system (Cygwin included), vi is there for you. Many popular editors (even Microsoft Visual Studio!) have a vi mode. Once you get used to it, it's hard to imagine using anything else. vi is a hard road at first, but the payoff is worth it.

If, like me, you see the value in being familiar with an editor that's available anywhere, your other option is Emacs. Emacs and I have never quite gotten on (and usually you're either an Emacs person or a vi person), but I absolutely respect the power and flexibility that Emacs provides. If vi's modal editing approach isn't for you, I would encourage you to look into Emacs.

While knowing a console editor (like vi or Emacs) can come in incredibly handy, you may still want a more modern editor. Some of my frontend colleagues swear by Coda, and I trust their opinion. Unfortunately, Coda is available only on OS X. Sublime Text is a modern and powerful editor that also has an excellent vi mode, and it's available on Windows, Linux, and OS X.

On Windows, there are some fine free options out there. TextPad and Notepad++ both have their supporters. They're both capable editors, and you can't beat the price. If you're a Windows user, don't overlook Visual Studio as a JavaScript editor: it's remarkably capable, and has one of the best JavaScript autocomplete engines of any editor. You can download Visual Studio Express from Microsoft for free.

# npm

npm is the ubiquitous package manager for Node packages (and is how we'll get and install Express). In the wry tradition of PHP, GNU, WINE, and others, "npm" is not an acronym (which is why it isn't capitalized); rather, it is a recursive abbreviation for "npm is not an acronym."

Broadly speaking, a package manager's two primary responsibilities are installing packages and managing dependencies. npm is a fast, capable, and painless package manager, which I feel is in large part responsible for the rapid growth and diversity of the Node ecosystem.

npm is installed when you install Node, so if you followed the steps listed earlier, you've already got it. So let's get to work!

The primary command you'll be using with npm (unsurprisingly), is `install`. For example, to install Grunt (a popular JavaScript task runner), you would issue the following command (on the console):

```
npm install -g grunt-cli
```

The `-g` flag tells npm to install the package *globally*, meaning it's available globally on the system. This distinction will become clearer when we cover the *package.json* files. For now, the rule of thumb is that JavaScript utilities (like Grunt) will generally be installed globally, whereas packages that are specific to your web app or project will not.

 Unlike languages like Python—which underwent a major language change from 2.0 to 3.0, necessitating a way to easily switch between different environments—the Node platform is new enough that it is likely that you should always be running the latest version of Node. However, if you do find yourself needing to support multiple version of Node, there is a project, nvm (*https://github.com/creationix/ nvm*), that allows you to switch environments.

# A Simple Web Server with Node

If you've ever built a static HTML website before, or are coming from a PHP or ASP background, you're probably used to the idea of the web server (Apache or IIS, for example) serving your static files so that a browser can view them over the network. For example, if you create the file *about.html*, and put it in the proper directory, you can then navigate to *http://localhost/about.html*. Depending on your web server configuration, you might even be able to omit the *.html*, but the relationship between URL and filename is clear: the web server simply knows where the file is on the computer, and serves it to the browser.

 *localhost*, as the name implies, refers to the computer you're on. This is a common alias for the IPv4 loopback address 127.0.0.1, or the IPv6 loopback address ::1. You will often see 127.0.0.1 used instead, but I will be using *localhost* in this book. If you're using a remote computer (using SSH, for example), keep in mind that browsing to *localhost* will not connect to that computer.

Node offers a different paradigm than that of a traditional web server: the app that you write *is* the web server. Node simply provides the framework for you to build a web server.

"But I don't want to write a web server," you might be saying! It's a natural response: you want to be writing an app, not a web server. However, Node makes the business of writing this web server a simple affair (just a few lines, even) and the control you gain over your application in return is more than worth it.

So let's get to it. You've installed Node, you've made friends with the terminal, and now you're ready to go.

## Hello World

I've always found it unfortunate that the canonical introductory programming example is the uninspired message "Hello World." However, it seems almost sacrilegious at this point to fly in the face of such ponderous tradition, so we'll start there, and then move on to something more interesting.

In your favorite editor, create a file called *helloWorld.js*:

```
var http = require('http');

http.createServer(function(req,res){
        res.writeHead(200, { 'Content-Type': 'text/plain' });
        res.end('Hello world!');
}).listen(3000);

console.log('Server started on localhost:3000; press Ctrl-C to terminate....');
```

Make sure you are in the same directory as *helloWorld.js*, and type **node hello World.js**. Then open up a browser and navigate to *http://localhost:3000*, and voilà! Your first web server. This particular one doesn't serve HTML; rather, it just transmits the message "Hello world!" in plaintext to your browser. If you want, you can experiment with sending HTML instead: just change `text/plain` to `text/html` and change `'Hello world!'` to a string containing valid HTML. I didn't demonstrate that, because I try to avoid writing HTML inside JavaScript for reasons that will be discussed in more detail in Chapter 7.

## Event-Driven Programming

The core philosophy behind Node is that of *event-driven programming*. What that means for you, the programmer, is that you have to understand what events are available to you and how to respond to them. Many people are introduced to event-driven programming by implementing a user interface: the user clicks on something, and you handle the "click event." It's a good metaphor, because it's understood that the programmer has no control over when, or if, the user is going to click something, so event-driven programming is really quite intuitive. It can be a little harder to make the conceptual leap to responding to events on the server, but the principle is the same.

In the previous code example, the event is implicit: the event that's being handled is an HTTP request. The `http.createServer` method takes a function as an argument; that function will be invoked every time an HTTP request is made. Our simple program just sets the content type to plaintext and sends the string "Hello world!"

# Routing

Routing refers to the mechanism for serving the client the content it has asked for. For web-based client/server applications, the client specifies the desired content in the URL; specifically, the path and querystring (the parts of a URL will be discussed in more detail in Chapter 6).

Let's expand our "Hello world!" example to do something more interesting. Let's serve a really minimal website consisting of a home page, an About page, and a Not Found page. For now, we'll stick with our previous example and just serve plaintext instead of HTML:

```
var http = require('http');

http.createServer(function(req,res){
        // normalize url by removing querystring, optional
        // trailing slash, and making it lowercase
        var path = req.url.replace(/\/?(?:\?.*)?$/, '').toLowerCase();
        switch(path) {
                case '':
                        res.writeHead(200, { 'Content-Type': 'text/plain' });
                        res.end('Homepage');
                        break;
                case '/about':
                        res.writeHead(200, { 'Content-Type': 'text/plain' });
                        res.end('About');
                        break;
                default:
                        res.writeHead(404, { 'Content-Type': 'text/plain' });
                        res.end('Not Found');
                        break;
        }
}).listen(3000);

console.log('Server started on localhost:3000; press Ctrl-C to terminate....');
```

If you run this, you'll find you can now browse to the home page (*http://localhost:3000*) and the About page (*http://localhost:3000/about*). Any querystrings will be ignored (so *http://localhost:3000/?foo=bar* will serve the home page), and any other URL (*http://localhost:3000/foo*) will serve the Not Found page.

# Serving Static Resources

Now that we've got some simple routing working, let's serve some real HTML and a logo image. These are called "static resources" because they don't change (as opposed to, for example, a stock ticker: every time you reload the page, the stock prices change).

Serving static resources with Node is suitable for development and small projects, but for larger projects, you will probably want to use a proxy server such as Nginx or a CDN to serve static resources. See Chapter 16 for more information.

If you've worked with Apache or IIS, you're probably used to just creating an HTML file, navigating to it, and having it delivered to the browser automatically. Node doesn't work like that: we're going to have to do the work of opening the file, reading it, and then sending its contents along to the browser. So let's create a directory in our project called *public* (why we don't call it *static* will become evident in the next chapter). In that directory, we'll create *home.html, about.html, 404.html*, a subdirectory called *img*, and an image called *img/logo.jpg*. I'll leave that up to you: if you're reading this book, you probably know how to write an HTML file and find an image. In your HTML files, reference the logo thusly: `<img src="/img/logo.jpg" alt="logo">`.

Now modify *helloWorld.js*:

```
var http = require('http'),
        fs = require('fs');

function serveStaticFile(res, path, contentType, responseCode) {
        if(!responseCode) responseCode = 200;
        fs.readFile(__dirname + path, function(err,data) {
                if(err) {
                        res.writeHead(500, { 'Content-Type': 'text/plain' });
                        res.end('500 - Internal Error');
                } else {
                        res.writeHead(responseCode,
                                { 'Content-Type': contentType });
                        res.end(data);
                }
        });
}

http.createServer(function(req,res){
        // normalize url by removing querystring, optional
        // trailing slash, and making lowercase
        var path = req.url.replace(/\/?(?:\?.*)?$/, '')
                .toLowerCase();
        switch(path) {
                case '':
                        serveStaticFile(res, '/public/home.html', 'text/html');
                        break;
                case '/about':
                        serveStaticFile(res, '/public/about.html', 'text/html');
                        break;
                case '/img/logo.jpg':
                        serveStaticFile(res, '/public/img/logo.jpg',
```

```
                    'image/jpeg');
                break;
        default:
                serveStaticFile(res, '/public/404.html', 'text/html',
                    404);
                break;
    }
}).listen(3000);

console.log('Server started on localhost:3000; press Ctrl-C to terminate....');
```

In this example, we're being pretty unimaginative with our routing. If you navigate to *http://localhost:3000/about*, the *public/about.html* file is served. You could change the route to be anything you want, and change the file to be anything you want. For example, if you had a different About page for each day of the week, you could have files *public/about_mon.html*, *public/about_tue.html*, and so on, and provide logic in your routing to serve the appropriate page when the user navigates to *http://localhost:3000/about*.

Note we've created a helper function, `serveStaticFile`, that's doing the bulk of the work. `fs.readFile` is an asynchronous method for reading files. There is a synchronous version of that function, `fs.readFileSync`, but the sooner you start thinking asynchronously, the better. The function is simple: it calls `fs.readFile` to read the contents of the specified file. `fs.readFile` executes the callback function when the file has been read; if the file didn't exist or there were permissions issues reading the file, the `err` variable is set, and the function returns an HTTP status code of 500 indicating a server error. If the file is read successfully, the file is sent to the client with the specified response code and content type. Response codes will be discussed in more detail in Chapter 6.

`__dirname` will resolve to the directory the executing script resides in. So if your script resides in */home/sites/app.js*, `__dirname` will resolve to */home/sites*. It's a good idea to use this handy global whenever possible. Failing to do so can cause hard-to-diagnose errors if you run your app from a different directory.

# Onward to Express

So far, Node probably doesn't seem that impressive to you. We've basically replicated what Apache or IIS do for you automatically, but now you have some insight into how Node does things and how much control you have. We haven't done anything particularly impressive, but you can see how we could use this as a jumping-off point to do more sophisticated things. If we continued down this road, writing more and more sophisticated Node applications, you might very well end up with something that re-sembles Express....

Fortunately, we don't have to: Express already exists, and it saves you from implementing a lot of time-consuming infrastructure. So now that we've gotten a little Node experience under our belt, we're ready to jump into learning Express.

# CHAPTER 3

# Saving Time with Express

In Chapter 2, you learned how to create a simple web server using only Node. In this chapter, we will recreate that server using Express. This will provide a jumping-off point for the rest of the content of this book and introduce you to the basics of Express.

## Scaffolding

Scaffolding is not a new idea, but many people (myself included) were introduced to the concept by Ruby. The idea is simple: most projects require a certain amount of so-called "boilerplate" code, and who wants to recreate that code every time you begin a new project? A simple way is to create a rough skeleton of a project, and every time you need a new project, you just copy this skeleton, or template.

Ruby on Rails took this concept one step further by providing a program that would automatically generate scaffolding for you. The advantage of this approach is that it could generate a more sophisticated framework than just selecting from a collection of templates.

Express has taken a page from Ruby on Rails and provided a utility to generate scaffolding to start your Express project.

While the Express scaffolding utility is useful, it currently doesn't generate the framework I will be recommending in this book. In particular, it doesn't provide support for my templating language of choice (Handlebars), and it also doesn't follow some of the naming conventions I prefer (though that is easy enough to fix).

While we won't be using the scaffolding utility, I encourage you to take a look at it once you've finished the book: by then you'll be armed with everything you need to know to evaluate whether the scaffolding it generates is useful for you.

Boilerplate is also useful for the actual HTML that will be delivered to the client. I recommend the excellent HTML5 Boilerplate. It generates a great blank slate for an

HTML5 website. Recently, HTML5 Boilerplate (*http://bit.ly/boiler_plate*) has added the ability to generate a custom build. One of the custom build options includes Twitter Bootstrap, a frontend framework I highly recommend. We'll be using a Bootstrap-based custom build in Chapter 7 to provide a responsive, modern HTML5 website.

## The Meadowlark Travel Website

Throughout this book, we'll be using a running example: a fictional website for Meadowlark Travel, a company offering services for people visiting the great state of Oregon. If you're more interested in creating a REST application, have no fear: the Meadowlark Travel website will expose REST services in addition to serving a functional website.

## Initial Steps

Start by creating a new directory for your project: this will be the root directory for your project. In this book, whenever we refer to the "project directory," "app directory," or "project root," we're referring to this directory.

 You'll probably want to keep your web app files separate from all the other files that usually accompany a project, such as meeting notes, documentation, etc. For that reason, I recommend making your project root a subdirectory of your project directory. For example, for the Meadowlark Travel website, I might keep the project in *~/projects/meadowlark*, and the project root in *~/projects/meadowlark/site*.

npm manages project dependencies—as well as metadata about the project—in a file called *package.json*. The easiest way to create this file is to run `npm init`: it will ask you a series of questions and generate a *package.json* file to get you started (for the "entry point" question, use *meadowlark.js* or the name of your project).

 Every time you run npm, you'll get warnings unless you provide a repository URL in *package.json*, and a nonempty *README.md* file. The metadata in the *package.json* file is really only necessary if you're planning on publishing to the npm repository, but squelching npm warnings is worth the small effort.

The first step will be installing Express. Run the following npm command:

```
npm install --save express
```

Running `npm install` will install the named package(s) in the *node_modules* directory. If you specify the `--save` flag, it will update the *package.json* file. Since the *node_modules* dirctory can be regenerated at any time with npm, we will not save it in our repository. To ensure we don't accidentally add it to our repository, we create a file called *.gitignore*:

```
# ignore packages installed by npm
node_modules

# put any other files you don't want to check in here,
# such as .DS_Store (OSX), *.bak, etc.
```

Now create a file called *meadowlark.js*. This will be our project's entry point. Throughout the book, we will simply be referring to this file as the "app file":

```
var express = require('express');

var app = express();

app.set('port', process.env.PORT || 3000);

// custom 404 page
app.use(function(req, res){
        res.type('text/plain');
        res.status(404);
        res.send('404 - Not Found');
});

// custom 500 page
app.use(function(err, req, res, next){
        console.error(err.stack);
        res.type('text/plain');
        res.status(500);
        res.send('500 - Server Error');
});

app.listen(app.get('port'), function(){
  console.log( 'Express started on http://localhost:' +
    app.get('port') + '; press Ctrl-C to terminate.' );
});
```

 Many tutorials, as well as the Express scaffolding generator, encourage you to name your primary file *app.js* (or sometimes *index.js* or *server.js*). Unless you're using a hosting service or deployment system that requires your main application file to have a specific name, I don't feel there's a compelling reason to do this, and I prefer to name the primary file after the project. Anyone who's ever stared at a bunch of editor tabs that all say "index.html" will immediately see the wisdom of this. npm init will default to *index.js*; if you use a different name for your application file, make sure to update the main property in *package.json*.

You now have a minimal Express server. You can start the server (node meadow lark.js), and navigate to *http://localhost:3000*. The result will be disappointing: you haven't provided Express with any routes, so it will simply give you a generic 404 page indicating that the page doesn't exist.

Note how we specify the port that we want our application to run on: app.set(*port*, process.env.PORT || 3000). This allows us to override the port by setting an environment value before you start the server. If your app isn't running on port 3000 when you run this example, check to see if your PORT environment variable is set.

I highly recommend getting a browser plugin that shows you the status code of the HTTP request as well as any redirects that took place. It will make it easier to spot redirect issues in your code, or incorrect status codes, which are often overlooked. For Chrome, Ayima's Redirect Path works wonderfully. In most browsers, you can see the status code in the Network section of the developer tools.

Let's add some routes for the home page and an About page. Before the 404 handler, we'll add two new routes:

```
app.get('/', function(req, res){
        res.type('text/plain');
        res.send('Meadowlark Travel');
});
app.get('/about', function(req, res){
        res.type('text/plain');
        res.send('About Meadowlark Travel');
});

// custom 404 page
app.use(function(req, res, next){
        res.type('text/plain');
        res.status(404);
        res.send('404 - Not Found');
});
```

app.get is the method by which we're adding routes. In the Express documentation, you will see app.VERB. This doesn't mean that there's literally a method called VERB; it's just a placeholder for your (lowercased) HTTP verbs ("get" and "post" being the most common). This method takes two parameters: a path and a function.

The path is what defines the route. Note that app.VERB does the heavy lifting for you: by default, it doesn't care about the case or trailing slash, and it doesn't consider the querystring when performing the match. So the route for the About page will work for */about, /About, /about/, /about?foo=bar, /about/?foo=bar*, etc.

The function you provide will get invoked when the route is matched. The parameters passed to that function are the request and response objects, which we'll learn more about in Chapter 6. For now, we're just returning plaintext with a status code of 200 (Express defaults to a status code of 200—you don't have to specify it explicitly).

Instead of using Node's low-level res.end, we're switching to using Express's extension, res.send. We are also replacing Node's res.writeHead with res.set and res.status. Express is also providing us a convenience method, res.type, which sets the Content-Type header. While it's still possible to use res.writeHead and res.end, it isn't necessary or recommended.

Note that our custom 404 and 500 pages must be handled slightly differently. Instead of using app.get, it is using app.use. app.use is the method by which Express adds *middleware*. We'll be covering middleware in more depth in Chapter 10, but for now, you can think of this as a catch-all handler for anything that didn't get matched by a route. This brings us to a very important point: *in Express, the order in which routes and middleware are added is significant.* If we put the 404 handler above the routes, the home page and About page would stop working: instead, those URLs would result in a 404. Right now, our routes are pretty simple, but they also support wildcards, which can lead to problems with ordering. For example, what if we wanted to add subpages to About, such as */about/contact* and */about/directions*? The following will not work as expected:

```
app.get('/about*',function(req,res){
        // send content....
})
app.get('/about/contact',function(req,res){
        // send content....
})
app.get('/about/directions',function(req,res){
        // send content....
})
```

In this example, the /about/contact and /about/directions handlers will never be matched because the first handler uses a wildcard in its path: /about*.

Express can distinguish between the 404 and 500 handlers by the number of arguments their callback functions take. Error routes will be covered in depth in Chapters 10 and 12.

Now you can start the server again, and see that there's a functioning home page and About page.

So far, we haven't done anything that couldn't be done just as easily without Express, but already Express is providing us some functionality that isn't immediately obvious. Remember in the previous chapter how we had to normalize req.url to determine what resource was being requested? We had to manually strip off the querystring and the trailing slash, and convert to lowercase. Express's router is now handling those details for us automatically. While it may not seem like a large thing now, it's only scratching the surface of what Express's router is capable of.

## Views and Layouts

If you're familiar with the "model-view-controller" paradigm, then the concept of a view will be no stranger to you. Essentially, a view is what gets delivered to the user. In the case of a website, that usually means HTML, though you could also deliver a PNG or a PDF, or anything that can be rendered by the client. For our purposes, we will consider views to be HTML.

Where a view differs from a static resource (like an image or CSS file) is that a view doesn't necessarily have to be static: the HTML can be constructed on the fly to provide a customized page for each request.

Express supports many different view engines that provide different levels of abstraction. Express gives some preference to a view engine called *Jade* (which is no surprise, because it is also the brainchild of TJ Holowaychuk). The approach Jade takes is very minimal: what you write doesn't resemble HTML at all, which certainly represents a lot less typing: no more angle brackets or closing tags. The Jade engine then takes that and converts it to HTML.

Jade is very appealing, but that level of abstraction comes at a cost. If you're a frontend developer, you have to understand HTML and understand it well, even if you're actually writing your views in Jade. Most frontend developers I know are uncomfortable with the idea of their primary markup language being abstracted away. For this reason, I am recommending the use of another, less abstract templating framework called *Handlebars*. Handlebars (which is based on the popular language-independent templating language Mustache) doesn't attempt to abstract away HTML for you: you write HTML with special tags that allow Handlebars to inject content.

To provide Handlebars support, we'll use Eric Ferraiuolo's `express-handlebars` package. In your project directory, execute:

```
npm install --save express-handlebars
```

Then in *meadowlark.js*, add the following lines after the app has been created:

```
var app = express();

// set up handlebars view engine
var handlebars = require('express-handlebars')
        .create({ defaultLayout:'main' });
app.engine('handlebars', handlebars.engine);
app.set('view engine', 'handlebars');
```

This creates a view engine and configures Express to use it by default. Now create a directory called *views* that has a subdirectory called *layouts*. If you're an experienced web developer, you're probably already comfortable with the concepts of *layouts* (sometimes called "master pages"). When you build a website, there's a certain amount of HTML that's the same—or very close to the same—on every page. Not only does it become tedious to rewrite all that repetitive code for every page, it creates a potential maintenance nightmare: if you want to change something on every page, you have to change *all* the files. Layouts free you from this, providing a common framework for all the pages on your site.

So let's create a template for our site. Create a file called *views/layouts/main.handlebars*:

```
<!doctype html>
<html>
<head>
    <title>Meadowlark Travel</title>
</head>
<body>
    {{{body}}}
</body>
</html>
```

The only thing that you probably haven't seen before is this: {{{body}}}. This expression will be replaced with the HTML for each view. When we created the Handlebars instance, note we specified the default layout (defaultLayout: 'main'). That means that unless you specify otherwise, this is the layout that will be used for any view.

Now let's create view pages for our home page, *views/home.handlebars*:

```
<h1>Welcome to Meadowlark Travel</h1>
```

Then our About page, *views/about.handlebars*:

```
<h1>About Meadowlark Travel</h1>
```

Then our Not Found page, *views/404.handlebars*:

```
<h1>404 - Not Found</h1>
```

And finally our Server Error page, *views/500.handlebars*:

```
<h1>500 - Server Error</h1>
```

You probably want your editor to associate *.handlebars* and *.hbs* (another common extension for Handlebars files) with HTML, to enable syntax highlighting and other editor features. For vim, you can add the line au BufNewFile,BufRead *.handlebars set file type=html to your *~/.vimrc* file. For other editors, consult your documentation.

Now that we've got some views set up, we have to replace our old routes with new routes that use these views:

```
app.get('/', function(req, res) {
        res.render('home');
});
app.get('/about', function(req, res) {
        res.render('about');
});

// 404 catch-all handler (middleware)
app.use(function(req, res, next){
        res.status(404);
        res.render('404');
});

// 500 error handler (middleware)
app.use(function(err, req, res, next){
        console.error(err.stack);
        res.status(500);
        res.render('500');
});
```

Note that we no longer have to specify the content type or status code: the view engine will return a content type of text/html and a status code of 200 by default. In the catch-all handler, which provides our custom 404 page, and the 500 handler, we have to set the status code explicitly.

If you start your server and check out the home or About page, you'll see that the views have been rendered. If you examine the source, you'll see that the boilerplate HTML from *views/layouts/main.handlebars* is there.

## Static Files and Views

Express relies on a *middleware* to handle static files and views. Middleware is a concept that will be covered in more detail in Chapter 10. For now, it's sufficient to know that middleware provides modularization, making it easier to handle requests.

The static middleware allows you to designate one or more directories as containing static resources that are simply to be delivered to the client without any special handling. This is where you would put things like images, CSS files, and client-side JavaScript files.

In your project directory, create a subdirectory called *public* (we call it *public* because anything in this directory will be served to the client without question). Then, before you declare any routes, you'll add the static middleware:

```
app.use(express.static(__dirname + '/public'));
```

The static middleware has the same effect as creating a route for each static file you want to deliver that renders a file and returns it to the client. So let's create an *img* subdirectory inside *public*, and put our *logo.png* file in there.

Now we can simply reference */img/logo.png* (note, we do not specify `public`; that directory is invisible to the client), and the `static` middleware will serve that file, setting the content type appropriately. Now let's modify our layout so that our logo appears on every page:

```
<body>
        <header><img src="/img/logo.png" alt="Meadowlark Travel Logo"></header>
        {{{body}}}
</body>
```

 The `<header>` element was introduced in HTML5 to provide additional semantic information about content that appears at the top of the page, such as logos, title text, or navigation.

## Dynamic Content in Views

Views aren't simply a complicated way to deliver static HTML (though they can certainly do that as well). The real power of views is that they can contain dynamic information.

Let's say that on the About page, we want to deliver a "virtual fortune cookie." In our *meadowlark.js* file, we define an array of fortune cookies:

```
var fortunes = [
        "Conquer your fears or they will conquer you.",
        "Rivers need springs.",
        "Do not fear what you don't know.",
        "You will have a pleasant surprise.",
        "Whenever possible, keep it simple.",
];
```

Modify the view (*/views/about.handlebars*) to display a fortune:

```
<h1>About Meadowlark Travel</h1>

<p>Your fortune for the day:</p>
<blockquote>{{fortune}}</blockquote>
```

Now modify the route */about* to deliver the random fortune cookie:

```
app.get('/about', function(req, res){
        var randomFortune =
                fortunes[Math.floor(Math.random() * fortunes.length)];
        res.render('about', { fortune: randomFortune });
});
```

Now if you restart the server and load the */about* page, you'll see a random fortune. Templating is incredibly useful, and we will be covering it in depth in Chapter 7.

## Conclusion

We've created a very basic website with Express. Even though it's simple, it contains all the seeds we need for a full-featured website. In the next chapter, we'll be crossing our *t*s and dotting our *i*s in preparation for adding more advanced functionality.

# Tidying Up

In the last two chapters, we were just experimenting: dipping our toes into the waters, so to speak. Before we proceed to more complex functionality, we're going to do some housekeeping and build some good habits into our work.

In this chapter, we'll start our Meadowlark Travel project in earnest. Before we start building the website itself, though, we're going to make sure we have the tools we need to produce a high-quality product.

The running example in this book is not necessarily one you have to follow. If you're anxious to build your own website, you could follow the framework of the running example, but modify it accordingly so that by the time you finish this book, you could have a finished website!

## Best Practices

The phrase "best practices" is one you hear thrown around a lot these days, and it means that you should "do things right" and not cut corners (we'll talk about what this means specifically in a moment). No doubt you've heard the engineering adage that your options are "fast," "cheap," and "good," and you can pick any two. The thing that's always bothered me about this model is that it doesn't take into account the *accrual value* of doing things correctly. The first time you do something correctly, it may take five times as long to do it as it would have to do it quick and dirty. The second time, though, it's only going to take three times as long. By the time you've done it correctly a dozen times, you'll be doing it almost as fast as the quick and dirty way.

I had a fencing coach who would always remind us that practice doesn't make perfect: practice makes *permanent*. That is, if you do something over and over again, eventually it will become automatic, rote. That is true, but it says nothing about the quality of the thing you are practicing. If you practice bad habits, then bad habits become rote. Instead, you should follow the rule that *perfect* practice makes perfect. In that spirit, I encourage you to follow the rest of the examples in this book as if you were making a real-live website, as if your reputation and remuneration were depending on the quality of the outcome. Use this book to not only learn new skills, but to practice building good habits.

The practices we will be focusing on are version control and QA. In this chapter, we'll be discussing version control, and we'll discuss QA in the next chapter.

# Version Control

Hopefully I don't have to convince you of the value of version control (if I did, that might take a whole book itself). Broadly speaking, version control offers these benefits:

*Documentation*

Being able to go back through the history of a project to see the decisions that were made and the order in which components were developed can be valuable documentation. Having a technical history of your project can be quite useful.

*Attribution*

If you work on a team, attribution can be hugely important. Whenever you find something in code that is opaque or questionable, knowing who made that change can save you many hours. It could be that the comments associated with the change are sufficient to answer your questions, and if not, you'll know who to talk to.

*Experimentation*

A good version control system enables experimentation. You can go off on a tangent, trying something new, without fear of affecting the stability of your project. If the experiment is successful, you can fold it back into the project, and if it is not successful, you can abandon it.

Years ago, I made the switch to distributed version control systems (DVCS). I narrowed my choices down to Git and Mercurial, and went with Git, due to its ubiquity and flexibility. Both are excellent and free version control systems, and I recommend you use one of them. In this book, we will be using Git, but you are welcome to substitute Mercurial (or another version control system altogether).

If you are unfamiliar with Git, I recommend Jon Loeliger's excellent *Version Control with Git* (O'Reilly). Also, Code School has a nice introductory course on Git (*http://try.github.io*).

# How to Use Git with This Book

First, make sure you have Git. Type `git --version`. If it doesn't respond with a version number, you'll need to install Git. See the Git documentation (*http://git-scm.com*) for installation instructions.

There are two ways to follow along with the examples in this book. One is to type out the examples yourself, and follow along with the Git commands. The other is to clone the Git repository I am using for all of the examples and check out the associated tags for each example. Some people learn better by typing out examples, while some prefer to just see and run the changes without having to type it all in.

## If You're Following Along by Doing It Yourself

We've already got a very rough framework for our project: some views, a layout, a logo, a main application file, and a *package.json* file. Let's go ahead and create a Git repository and add all those files.

First, we go to the project directory and create a Git repository there:

```
git init
```

Now before we add all the files, we'll create a *.gitignore* file to help prevent us from accidentally adding things we don't want to add. Create a text file called *.gitignore* in your project directory in which you can add any files or directories you want Git to ignore by default (one per line). It also supports wildcards. For example, if your editor creates backup files with a tilde at the end (like *meadowlark.js~*), you might put *\*~* in the *.gitignore* file. If you're on a Mac, you'll want to put `.DS_Store` in there. You'll also want to put `node_modules` in there (for reasons that will be discussed soon). So for now, the file might look like this:

```
node_modules
*~
.DS_Store
```

 Entries in the *.gitignore* file also apply to subdirectories. So if you put *\*~* in the *.gitignore* in the project root, all such backup files will be ignored even if they are in subdirectories.

Now we can add all of our existing files. There are many ways to do this in Git. I generally favor `git add -A`, which is the most sweeping of all the variants. If you are new to Git, I recommend you either add files one by one (`git add meadowlark.js`, for example) if you only want to commit one or two files, or `git add -A` if you want to add all of your changes (including any files you might have deleted). Since we want to add all the work we've already done, we'll use:

```
git add -A
```

 Newcomers to Git are commonly confused by the `git add` command: it adds *changes*, not files. So if you've modified *meadowlark.js*, and then you type `git add meadowlark.js`, what you're really doing is adding the changes you've made.

Git has a "staging area," where changes go when you run `git add`. So the changes we've added haven't actually been committed yet, but they're ready to go. To commit the changes, use `git commit`:

```
git commit -m "Initial commit."
```

The `-m "Initial commit."` allows you to write a message associated with this commit. Git won't even let you make a commit without a message, and for good reason. Always strive to make meaningful commit messages: they should briefly but concisely describe the work you've done.

## If You're Following Along by Using the Official Repository

To get the official repository for this book, run `git clone`:

```
git clone https://github.com/EthanRBrown/web-development-with-node-and-express
```

This repository has a directory for each chapter that contains code samples. For example, the source code for this chapter can be found in the `ch04` directory. These directories represent the *end* of the chapter. That is, when you finish this chapter, you can see the finished code in the `ch04` directory. For chapters where there's a significant divergence, there may be additional directories, such as `ch08-jquery-file-upload`, which will be noted in the chapter text.

As this book is updated and improved, the repository will also be updated, and when it is, I will add a version tag so you can check out a version of the repository that corresponds to the version of the book you're reading now. The current version of the repository is 1.5.1. If you have an older version of this book, and you wish to see the latest changes and improvements to the code samples, you can check out the most current version: just be warned that the repository samples will be different than what you read here.

In the first version of this book, I took a different approach with the repository, with a linear history as if you were developing an increasingly sophisticated project. While this approach pleasantly mirrored the way a project in the real world might develop, it caused a lot of headache, both for me and my readers. As npm packages changed, the code samples would change, and short of rewriting the entire history of the repo, there was no good way to update the repository, or note the changes in the text. While the chapter-per-directory approach is more artificial, it allows the text to be synced more closely with the repository, and also enables easier community contribution.

If at any point you want to experiment, keep in mind that the tag you have checked out puts you in what Git calls a "detached HEAD" state. While you are free to edit any files, it is unsafe to commit anything you do without creating a branch first. So if you do want to base an experimental branch off of a tag, simply create a new branch and check it out, which you can do with one command: `git checkout -b experiment` (where `experiment` is the name of your branch; you can use whatever you want). Then you can safely edit and commit on that branch as much as you want.

# npm Packages

The npm packages that your project relies on reside in a directory called *node_modules* (it's unfortunate that this is called *node_modules* and not *npm_packages*, as Node modules are a related but different concept). Feel free to explore that directory to satisfy your curiosity or to debug your program, but you should never modify any code in this directory. In addition to that being bad practice, all of your changes could easily be undone by npm. If you need to make a modification to a package your project depends on, the correct course of action would be to create your own fork of the project. If you do go this route, and you feel that your improvements would be useful to others, congratulations: you're now involved in an open source project! You can submit your changes, and if they meet the project standards, they'll be included in the official package. Contributing to existing packages and creating customized builds is beyond the scope of this book, but there is a vibrant community of developers out there to help you if you want to contribute to existing packages.

The purpose of the *package.json* file is twofold: to describe your project and to list dependencies. Go ahead and look at your *package.json* file now. You should see something like this (the exact version numbers will probably be different, as these packages get updated often):

```
{
  "dependencies": {
    "express": "^4.12.3",
    "express-handlebars": "^2.0.1"
  }
}
```

Right now, our *package.json* file contains only information about dependencies. The caret (^) in front of the package versions indicates that any version that starts with the specified version number—up to the next major version number—will work. For example, this *package.json* indicates that any version of Express that starts with 4.0.0 will work, so 4.0.1 and 4.9.9 would both work, but 3.4.7 would not, nor would 5.0.0. This is the default version specificity when you use npm install --save, and is generally a pretty safe bet. The consequence of this approach is that if you want to move up to a newer version, you will have to edit the file to specify the new version. Generally, that's a good thing because it prevents changes in dependencies from breaking your project without your knowing about it. Version numbers in npm are parsed by a component called "semver" (for "semantic versioner"). If you want more information about versioning in npm, consult the semver documentation (*https://www.npmjs.org/doc/misc/semver.html*).

Since the *package.json* file lists all the dependencies, the *node_modules* directory is really a derived artifact. That is, if you were to delete it, all you would have to do to get the project working again would be to run npm install, which will recreate the directory and put all the necessary dependencies in it. It is for this reason that I recommend putting node_modules in your *.gitignore* file, and not including it in source control. However, some people feel that your repository should contain everything necessary to run the project, and prefer to keep node_modules in source control. I find that this is "noise" in the repository, and I prefer to omit it.

Whenever you use a Node module in your project, you should make sure it's listed as a dependency in *package.json*. If you fail to do this, npm will be unable to construct the right dependencies, and when another developer checks out the project (or when you do on a different computer), the correct dependencies won't be installed, which negates the value of a package manager.

# Project Metadata

The other purpose of the *package.json* file is to store project metadata, such as the name of the project, authors, license information, and so on. If you use npm init to initially create your *package.json* file, it will populate the file with the necessary fields for you, and you can update them at any time. If you intend to make your project available on npm or GitHub, this metadata becomes critical. If you would like more information about the fields in *package.json*, see the *package.json* documentation (*https://npmjs.org/doc/json.html*). The other important piece of metadata is the *README.md* file. This file can be a handy place to describe the overall architecture of the website, as well as any critical information that someone new to the project might need. It is in a text-based wiki format called Markdown. Refer to the Markdown documentation (*http://daring fireball.net/projects/markdown*) for more information.

# Node Modules

As mentioned earlier, Node modules and npm packages are related but different concepts. Node modules, as the name implies, offer a mechanism for modularization and encapsulation. npm packages provide a standardized scheme for storing, versioning, and referencing projects (which are not restricted to modules). For example, we import Express itself as a module in our main application file:

```
var express = require('express');
```

require is a Node function for importing a module. By default, Node looks for modules in the directory *node_modules* (it should be no surprise, then, that there's an *express* directory inside of *node_modules*). However, Node also provides a mechanism for creating your own modules (you should never create your own modules in the *node_modules* directory). Let's see how we can modularize the fortune cookie functionality we implemented in the previous chapter.

First let's create a directory to store our modules. You can call it whatever you want, but *lib* (short for "library") is a common choice. In that folder, create a file called *fortune.js*:

```
var fortuneCookies = [
        "Conquer your fears or they will conquer you.",
        "Rivers need springs.",
        "Do not fear what you don't know.",
        "You will have a pleasant surprise.",
        "Whenever possible, keep it simple.",
];

exports.getFortune = function() {
        var idx = Math.floor(Math.random() * fortuneCookies.length);
        return fortuneCookies[idx];
};
```

The important thing to note here is the use of the global variable exports. If you want something to be visible outside of the module, you have to add it to exports. In this example, the function getFortune will be available from outside this module, but our array fortuneCookies will be *completely hidden*. This is a good thing: encapsulation allows for less error-prone and fragile code.

There are several ways to export functionality from a module. We will be covering different methods throughout the book and summarizing them in Chapter 22.

Now in *meadowlark.js*, we can remove the `fortuneCookies` array (though there would be no harm in leaving it: it can't conflict in any way with the array with the same name defined in *lib/fortune.js*). It is traditional (but not required) to specify imports at the top of the file, so at the top of the *meadowlark.js* file, add the following line:

```
var fortune = require('./lib/fortune.js');
```

Note that we prefix our module name with `./`. This signals to Node that it should not look for the module in the *node_modules* directory; if we omitted that prefix, this would fail.

Now in our route for the About page, we can utilize the `getFortune` method from our module:

```
app.get('/about', function(req, res) {
        res.render('about', { fortune: fortune.getFortune() } );
});
```

If you're following along, let's commit those changes:

```
git add -A
git commit -m "Moved 'fortune cookie' functionality into module."
```

Or if you're using the official repository, you can see the changes in this tag:

```
git checkout ch04
```

You will find modules to be a very powerful and easy way to encapsulate functionality, which will improve the overall design and maintainability of your project, as well as make testing easier. Refer to the official Node module documentation (*http://nodejs.org/ api/modules.html*) for more information.

# CHAPTER 5

# Quality Assurance

*Quality assurance*: it's a phrase that is prone to send shivers down the spines of developers—which is unfortunate. After all, don't you want to make quality software? Of course you do. So it's not the end goal that's the sticking point: it's the politics of the matter. I've found that there are two common situations that arise in web development:

*Large or well-funded organizations*

There's usually a QA department and, unfortunately, an adversarial relationship springs up between QA and development. This is the worst thing that can happen. Both departments are playing on the same team, for the same goal, but QA often defines success as finding more bugs, while development defines success as generating fewer bugs, and that serves as the basis for conflict and competition.

*Small organizations and organizations on a budget*

Often, there is no QA department; the development staff is expected to serve the dual role of establishing QA and developing software. This is not a ridiculous stretch of the imagination or a conflict of interest. However, QA is a very different discipline than development, and it attracts different personalities and talents. This is not an impossible situation, and certainly there are developers out there who have the QA mindset, but when deadlines loom, it's usually QA that gets the short shrift, to the project's detriment.

With most real-world endeavors, multiple skills are required, and increasingly, it's harder to be an expert in all of those skills. However, some competency in the areas for which you are not directly responsible will make you more valuable to the team and make the team function more effectively. A developer acquiring QA skills offers a great example: these two disciplines are so tightly intertwined that cross-disciplinary understanding is extremely valuable.

There is also a movement to merge the roles of QA and development, making developers responsible for QA. In this paradigm, software engineers who specialize in QA act almost as consultants to developers, helping them build QA into their development workflow. Whether QA roles are divided or integrated, it is clear that understanding QA is beneficial to developers.

This book is not for QA professionals; it is aimed at developers. So my goal is not to make you a QA expert, but to give you some experience in that area. If your organization has a dedicated QA staff, it will make it easier for you to communicate and collaborate with them. If you do not, it will give you a starting point to establishing a comprehensive QA plan for your project.

# QA: Is It Worth It?

QA can be expensive—sometimes *very* expensive. So is it worth it? It's a complicated formula with complicated inputs. Most organizations operate on some kind of "return on investment" model. If you spend money, you must expect to receive at least as much money in return (preferably more). With QA, though, the relationship can be muddy. A well-established and well-regarded product, for example, may be able to get by with quality issues for longer than a new and unknown project. Obviously, no one *wants* to produce a low-quality product, but the pressures in technology are high. Time-to-market can be critical, and sometimes it's better to come to market with something that's less than perfect than to come to market with the perfect product two months later.

In web development, quality can be broken down into four dimensions:

*Reach*

> Reach refers to the market penetration of your product: the number of people viewing your website or using your service. There's a direct correlation between reach and profitability: the more people who visit the website, the more people who buy the product or service. From a development perspective, search engine optimization (SEO) will have the biggest impact on reach, which is why we will be including SEO in our QA plan.

*Functionality*

> Once people are visiting your site or using your service, the quality of your site's functionality will have a large impact on user retention: a site that works as advertised is more likely to drive return visits than one that isn't. Unlike the other dimensions, functionality testing can often be automated.

*Usability*

> Where functionality is concerned with functional correctness, usability evaluates human-computer interaction (HCI). The fundamental question is, "Is the functionality delivered in a way that is useful to the target audience?" This often translates to, "Is it easy to use?" though the pursuit of ease can often oppose flexibility or power: what seems easy to a programmer might be different than what seems easy to a nontechnical consumer. In other words, you must consider your

target audience when assessing usability. Since a fundamental input to a usability measurement is a user, usability is not usually something that can be automated. However, user testing should be included in your QA plan.

*Aesthetics*
Aesthetics is the most subjective of the four dimensions and is therefore the least relevant to development. While there are few development concerns when it comes to your site's aesthetics, routine reviews of your site's aesthetics should be part of your QA plan. Show your site to a representative sample audience, and find out if it feels dated or does not invoke the desired response. Keep in mind that aesthetics is time sensitive (aesthetic standards shift over time) and audience specific (what appeals to one audience may be completely uninteresting to another).

While all four dimensions should be addressed in your QA plan, functionality testing and SEO can be tested automatically during development, so that will be the focus of this chapter.

# Logic Versus Presentation

Broadly speaking, in your website, there are two "realms": *logic* (often called "business logic," a term I eschew because of its bias toward commercial endeavor) and *presentation*. You can think of your website's logic existing in kind of a pure intellectual domain. For example, in our Meadowlark Travel scenario, there might be a rule that a customer must possess a valid driver's license before renting a scooter. This is a very simple data-based rule: for every scooter reservation, the user needs a valid driver's license. The *presentation* of this is disconnected. Perhaps it's just a checkbox on the final form of the order page, or perhaps the customer has to provide a valid driver's license number, which is validated by Meadowlark Travel. It's an important distinction, because things should be as clear and simple as possible in the logic domain, whereas the presentation can be as complicated or as simple as it needs to be. The presentation is also subject to usability and aesthetic concerns, where the business domain is not.

Whenever possible, you should seek a clear delineation between your logic and presentation. There are many ways to do that, and in this book, we will be focusing on encapsulating logic in JavaScript modules. Presentation, on the other hand, will be a combination of HTML, CSS, multimedia, JavaScript, and frontend libraries like jQuery.

# The Types of Tests

The type of testing we will be considering in this book falls into two broad categories: unit testing and integration testing (I am considering "system testing" to be a type of integration testing). Unit testing is very fine-grained, testing single components to make sure they function properly, whereas integration testing tests the interaction between multiple components, or even the whole system.

In general, unit testing is more useful and appropriate for logic testing (although we will see some instances where it is used in presentation code as well). Integration testing is useful in both realms.

## Overview of QA Techniques

In this book, we will be using the following techniques and software to accomplish thorough testing:

*Page testing*

 "Page testing," as the name implies, tests the presentation and frontend functionality of a page. This can involve both unit and integration testing. We will be using Mocha to achieve this.

*Cross-page testing*

 Cross-page testing involves testing functionality that requires navigation from one page to another. For example, the checkout process in an ecommerce site usually spans multiple pages. Since this kind of testing inherently involves more than one component, it is generally considered integration testing. We will be using Zombie.js for this.

*Logic testing*

 Logic testing will execute unit and integration tests against our logic domain. It will be testing *only* JavaScript, disconnected from any presentation functionality.

*Linting*

 Linting isn't about finding errors, but *potential* errors. The general concept of linting is that it identifies areas that could represent possible errors, or fragile constructs that could lead to errors in the future. We will be using JSHint for linting.

*Link checking*

 Link checking (making sure there are no broken links on your site) falls into the category of "low-hanging fruit." It may seem overkill on a simple project, but simple projects have a way of becoming complicated projects, and broken links *will* happen. Better to work link checking into your QA routine early. Link checking falls under the category of unit testing (a link is either valid or invalid). We will be using Link-Checker for this.

## Running Your Server

All of the techniques in this chapter assume your website is running. So far, we've been running our website manually, with the command node meadowlark.js. This technique has the advantage of simplicity, and I usually have a dedicated window on the desktop for that purpose. That's not your only option, however. If you find yourself forgetting to restart your website when you make JavaScript changes, you might want to look into a monitor utility that will automatically restart your server when it detects changes in JavaScript. nodemon (*https://npmjs.org/package/nodemon*) is very popular, and there's also a Grunt plugin (*https://npmjs.org/package/grunt-nodemon*). You will be learning more about Grunt at the end of this chapter. For now, I recommend just having your app always running in a different window.

# Page Testing

My recommendation for page testing is that you actually embed tests in the page itself. The advantage of this is that while you're working on a page, you can immediately spot any errors as you load it in a browser. Doing this will require a little setup, so let's get started.

The first thing we'll need is a test framework. We'll be using Mocha. First, we add the package to the project:

```
npm install --save-dev mocha
```

Note that we used `--save-dev` instead of `--save`; this tells npm to list this package in the development dependencies instead of the runtime dependencies. This will reduce the number of dependencies the project has when we deploy live instances of the website.

Since we'll be running Mocha in the browser, we need to put the Mocha resources in the public folder so it will be served to the client. We'll put these in a subdirectory, *public/ vendor*:

```
mkdir public/vendor
cp node_modules/mocha/mocha.js public/vendor
cp node_modules/mocha/mocha.css public/vendor
```

It's a good idea to put third-party libraries that you are using in a special directory, like *vendor*. This makes it easier to separate what code you're responsible for testing and modifying, and what code should be hands off.

Tests usually require a function called `assert` (or `expect`). This is available in the Node framework, but not inherently in a browser, so we'll be using the Chai assertion library:

```
npm install --save-dev chai
cp node_modules/chai/chai.js public/vendor
```

Now that we have the necessary files, we can modify the Meadowlark Travel website to allow running tests. The catch is, we don't want the tests to always be there: not only will it slow down your website, but your users don't want to see the results of tests! Tests should be disabled by default, but it should be very easy to enable them. To meet both of these goals, we're going to use a URL parameter to turn on tests. When we're done, going to *http://localhost:3000* will load the home page, and *http://localhost:3000?* *test=1* will load the home page complete with tests.

First, we're going to use some middleware to detect `test=1` in the querystring. It must appear *before* we define any routes in which we wish to use it:

```
app.use(function(req, res, next){
        res.locals.showTests = app.get('env') !== 'production' &&
                req.query.test === '1';
        next();
});

// routes go here....
```

The specifics about this bit of code will become clear in later chapters; what you need to know for right now is that if `test=1` appears in the querystring for any page (and we're not running on a production server), the property `res.locals.showTests` will be `true`. The `res.locals` object is part of the *context* that will be passed to views (this will be explained in more detail in Chapter 7).

Now we can modify *views/layouts/main.handlebars* to conditionally include the test framework. Modify the `<head>` section:

```
<head>
        <title>Meadowlark Travel</title>
        {{#if showTests}}
                <link rel="stylesheet" href="/vendor/mocha.css">
        {{/if}}
        <script src="//code.jquery.com/jquery-2.0.2.min.js"></script>
</head>
```

We're linking in jQuery here because, in addition to using it as our primary DOM manipulation library for the site, we can use it to make test assertions. You're free to use whatever library you like (or none at all), but I recommend jQuery. You'll often hear that JavaScript libraries should be loaded last, right before the closing `</body>` tag. There is good reason for this, and we will learn some techniques to make this possible, but for now, we're going to include jQuery early.[1]

Then, right before the closing `</body>` tag:

```
{{#if showTests}}
        <div id="mocha"></div>
        <script src="/vendor/mocha.js"></script>
        <script src="/vendor/chai.js"></script>
        <script>
                mocha.ui('tdd');
                var assert = chai.assert;
        </script>
```

---

1. Remember the first principle of performance tuning: profile first, then optimize.

```
            <script src="/qa/tests-global.js"></script>
            {{#if pageTestScript}}
                  <script src="{{pageTestScript}}"></script>
            {{/if}}
            <script>mocha.run();</script>
      {{/if}}
</body>
```

Note that Mocha and Chai get included, as well as a script called */qa/global-tests.js*. As the name implies, these are tests that will be run on every page. A little farther down, we optionally link in page-specific tests, so that you can have different tests for different pages. We'll start with the global tests, and then add page-specific tests. Let's start with a single, simple test: making sure the page has a valid title. Create the directory *public/qa* and create a file *tests-global.js* in it:

```
suite('Global Tests', function(){
      test('page has a valid title', function(){
            assert(document.title && document.title.match(/\S/) &&
                        document.title.toUpperCase() !== 'TODO');
      });
});
```

 Mocha supports multiple "interfaces," which control the style of your tests. The default interface, behavior-driven development (BDD), is tailored to make you think in a behavioral sense. In BDD, you describe components and their behaviors, and the tests then verify those behaviors. However, I find that very often, there are tests that don't fit this model, and then the BDD language just looks strange. Test-driven development (TDD) is more matter-of-fact: you describe suites of tests and tests within the suite. There's nothing to stop you from using both interfaces in your tests, but then it becomes a configuration hassle. For that reason, I've opted to stick with TDD in this book. If you prefer BDD, or mixing BDD and TDD, by all means do so.

Go ahead and run the site now. Visit the home page and examine the source: you'll see no evidence of test code. Now, add `test=1` to the querystring (*http://localhost:3000/?test=1*), and you'll see the tests run on the page. Any time you want to test the site, all you have to do is add `test=1` to the querystring!

Now let's add a page-specific test. Let's say that we want to ensure that a link to the yet-to-be-created Contact page always exists on the About page. We'll create a file called *public/qa/tests-about.js*:

```
suite('"About" Page Tests', function(){
      test('page should contain link to contact page', function(){
            assert($('a[href="/contact"]').length);
```

```
        });
    });
```

We have one last thing to do: specify in the route which page test file the view should be using. Modify the About page route in *meadowlark.js*:

```
app.get('/about', function(req, res) {
    res.render('about', {
        fortune: fortune.getFortune(),
        pageTestScript: '/qa/tests-about.js'
    } );
});
```

Load the About page with `test=1` in the querystring: you'll see two suites and one failure! Now add a link to the nonexistent Contact page, and you'll see the test become successful when you reload.

Depending on the nature of your site, you may want this to be more automatic. For example, if your route was */foo*, you could automatically set the page-specific tests to be */foo/tests-foo.js*. The downside of this approach is that you lose flexibility. For example, if you have multiple routes that point to the same view, or even very similar content, you might want to use the same test file.

Let's resist the temptation to add more tests now: those will come as we progress through the book. For now, we have the basic framework necessary to add global and page-specific tests.

# Cross-Page Testing

Cross-page testing is a little more challenging, because you need to be able to control and observe the browser itself. Let's look at an example of a cross-page testing scenario. Let's say your website has a Request Group Rate page that contains a contact form. The marketing department wants to know what page the customer was last on before following a link to Request Group Rate—they want to know whether the customer was viewing the Hood River tour or Oregon Coast retreat. Hooking this up will require some hidden form fields and JavaScript, and testing is going to involve going to a page, then clicking Request Group Rate and verifying that the hidden field is populated appropriately.

Let's set up this scenario, and then see how we can test it. First, we'll create a tour page, *views/tours/hood-river.handlebars*:

```
<h1>Hood River Tour</h1>
<a class="requestGroupRate"
        href="/tours/request-group-rate">Request Group Rate.</a>
```

And a quote page, *views/tours/request-group-rate.handlebars*:

```
<h1>Request Group Rate</h1>
<form>
        <input type="hidden" name="referrer">
        Name: <input type="text" id="fieldName" name="name"><br>
        Group size: <input type="text" name="groupSize"><br>
        Email: <input type="email" name="email"><br>
        <input type="submit" value="Submit">
</form>
{{#section 'jquery'}}
        <script>
                $(document).ready(function(){
                        $('input[name="referrer"]').val(document.referrer);
                });
        </script>
{{/section}}
```

Then we'll create routes for these pages in *meadowlark.js*:

```
app.get('/tours/hood-river', function(req, res){
        res.render('tours/hood-river');
});
app.get('/tours/request-group-rate', function(req, res){
        res.render('tours/request-group-rate');
});
```

Now that we have something to test, we need some way to test it, and this is where things get complicated. To test this functionality, we really need a browser or something a lot like a browser. Obviously, we can do it by hand by going to the */tours/hood-river* page in a browser, then clicking on the Request Group Rate link, then inspecting the hidden form element to see that it's correctly populated with the referring page, but that's a lot of work—we want a way to automate that.

What we're looking for is often called a *headless* browser: meaning that the browser doesn't actually need to display something on the screen, necessarily, it just has to behave like a browser. Currently, there are three popular solutions for this problem: Selenium, PhantomJS, and Zombie. Selenium is incredibly robust, with extensive testing support, but configuring it is beyond the scope of this book. PhantomJS is a great project and actually provides a headless WebKit browser (the same engine used in Chrome and Safari) so, like Selenium, it represents a very high level of realism. However, it doesn't yet provide the simple test assertions that we're looking for, which leaves us with Zombie.

Zombie doesn't use an existing browser engine, so it isn't suitable for testing browser features, but it's great for testing basic functionality, which is what we're looking for. Unfortunately, Zombie doesn't currently support a Windows installation (it used to be possible through Cygwin). People have gotten it to work, however, and there's information on the Zombie home page (*http://zombie.labnotes.org*). I have made an effort to make this book platform-agnostic, but there currently isn't a Windows solution for simple headless browser tests. If you're a Windows developer, I encourage you to check out Selenium or PhantomJS: it will be a steeper learning curve, but these projects have a lot to offer.

First, install Zombie (we specify version 3.1.1 for compatability; this book will be updated to reflect Zombie 4 in the future):

```
npm install --save-dev zombie@3.1.1
```

Now we'll create a new directory called simply *qa* (distinct from *public/qa*). In that directory, we'll create a file, *qa/tests-crosspage.js*:

```javascript
var Browser = require('zombie'),
    assert = require('chai').assert;

var browser;

suite('Cross-Page Tests', function(){

    setup(function(){
        browser = new Browser();
    });

    test('requesting a group rate quote     from the hood river tour page' +
        'should populate the referrer field', function(done){
        var referrer = 'http://localhost:3000/tours/hood-river';
        browser.visit(referrer, function(){
            browser.clickLink('.requestGroupRate', function(){
                assert(browser.field('referrer').value
                    === referrer);
                done();
            });
        });
    });

    test('requesting a group rate from the oregon coast tour page should ' +
            'populate the referrer field', function(done){
        var referrer = 'http://localhost:3000/tours/oregon-coast';
        browser.visit(referrer, function(){
            browser.clickLink('.requestGroupRate', function(){
                assert(browser.field('referrer').value
                    === referrer);
                done();
            });
        });
    });

    test('visiting the "request group rate" page directly should result ' +
            'in an empty referrer field', function(done){
        browser.visit('http://localhost:3000/tours/request-group-rate',
            function(){
                assert(browser.field('referrer').value === '');
                done();
            });
```

```
        });

    });
```

`setup` takes a function that will get executed by the test framework before each test is run: this is where we create a new browser instance for each test. Then we have three tests. The first two check that the referrer is populated correctly if you're coming from a product page. The `browser.visit` method will actually load a page; when the page has been loaded, the callback function is invoked. Then the `browser.clickLink` method looks for a link with the `requestGroupRate` class and follows it. When the linked page loads, the callback function is invoked, and now we're on the Request Group Rate page. All that remains to be done is to assert that the hidden "referrer" field correctly matches the original page we visited. The `browser.field` method returns a DOM `Element` object, which has a `value` property. The last test simply ensures that the referrer is blank if the Request Group Rate page is visited directly.

Before we run the tests, you'll have to start the server (`node meadowlark.js`). You'll want to do that in a different window so you can see any console errors. Then run the test and see how we did (make sure you have Mocha installed globally: `npm install -g mocha`):

```
mocha -u tdd -R spec qa/tests-crosspage.js 2>/dev/null
```

We'll see that one of our tests is failing...it failed for the Oregon Coast Tour page, which should be no surprise, since we haven't added that page yet. But the other two tests are passing! So our test is working; go ahead and add an Oregon Coast Tour page, and all of the tests will pass. Note that in the previous command, I specified that our interface is TDD (it defaults to BDD) and to use a reporter called spec. The spec reporter provides a bit more information than the default reporter. (Once you have hundreds of tests, you might want to switch back to the default reporter.) Finally, you'll note that we're dumping the error output (`2>/dev/null`). Mocha reports all of the stack traces for failed tests. It can be useful information, but usually you just want to see what tests are passing and what tests are failing. If you need more information, leave the `2>/dev/null` off and you will see the error detail.

 One advantage of writing your tests before you implement features is that (if your tests are correct), they will all start out failing. Not only does this give you satisfaction as you see your tests start to pass, but it's additional assurance that the test is correct. If your test starts out passing before you even implement a feature, the test is probably broken. This is sometimes called "red light, green light" testing.

# Logic Testing

We'll also be using Mocha for logic testing. For now, we have only one tiny bit of functionality (the fortune generator), so setting this up will be pretty easy. Also, since we only have one component, we don't have enough for integration tests, so we'll just be adding unit tests. Create the file *qa/tests-unit.js*:

```
var fortune = require('../lib/fortune.js');
var expect = require('chai').expect;

suite('Fortune cookie tests', function(){

    test('getFortune() should return a fortune', function(){
        expect(typeof fortune.getFortune() === 'string');
    });

});
```

Now we can just run Mocha against this new test suite:

```
mocha -u tdd -R spec qa/tests-unit.js
```

Not very exciting! But it provides the template that we will be using throughout the rest of this book.

 Testing *entropic* functionality (functionality that is random) comes with its own challenges. Another test we could add for our fortune cookie generator would be a test to make sure that it returns a *random* fortune cookie. But how do you know if something is random? One approach is to get a large number of fortunes—a thousand, for example—and then measure the distribution of the responses. If the function is properly random, no one response will stand out. The downside of this approach is that it's nondeterministic: it's possible (but unlikely) to get one fortune 10 times more frequently than any other fortune. If that happened, the test could fail (depending on how aggressive you set the threshold of what is "random"), but that might not actually indicate that the system being tested is failing; it's just a consequence of testing entropic systems. In the case of our fortune generator, it would be reasonable to generate 50 fortunes, and expect at least three different ones. On the other hand, if we were developing a random source for a scientific simulation or security component, we would probably want to have much more detailed tests. The point is that testing entropic functionality is difficult and requires more thought.

# Linting

A good linter is like having a second set of eyes: it will spot things that will slide right past our human brains. The original JavaScript linter is Douglas Crockford's JSLint. In 2011, Anton Kovalyov forked JSLint, and JSHint was born. Kovalyov found that JSLint was becoming too opinionated, and he wanted to create a more customizable, community-developed JavaScript linter. While I agree with almost all of Crockford's linting suggestions, I prefer the ability to tailor my linter, and for that reason, I recommend JSHint.[2]

JSHint is very easy to get via npm:

```
npm install -g jshint
```

To run it, simply invoke it with the name of a source file:

```
jshint meadowlark.js
```

If you've been following along, JSHint shouldn't have any complaints about *meadowlark.js*. To see the kind of thing that JSHint will save you from, put the following line in *meadowlark.js*, and run JSHint on it:

```
if( app.thing == null ) console.log( 'bleat!' );
```

(JSHint will complain about using == instead of ===, whereas JSLint would additionally complain about the lack of curly brackets.)

Consistent use of a linter will make you a better programmer: I promise that. Given that, wouldn't it be nice if your linter integrated into your editor and you were informed of potential errors as soon as you made them? Well, you're in luck. JSHint (*http://www.jshint.com/install*) integrates into many popular editors.

# Link Checking

Checking for dead links doesn't seem very glamorous, but it can have a huge impact on how your website is ranked by search engines. It's an easy enough thing to integrate into your workflow, so it's foolish not to.

I recommend LinkChecker (*http://wummel.github.io/linkchecker*); it's cross-platform, and it offers a command-line as well as a graphical interface. Just install it and point it at your home page:

```
linkchecker http://localhost:3000
```

Our site doesn't have very many pages yet, so LinkChecker should whip right through it.

---

2. Nicholas Zakas's *ESLint* (*http://eslint.org*) is also an excellent choice.

# Automating with Grunt

The QA tools we're using—test suites, linting, link checkers—provide value only if they're actually *used*, and this is where many a QA plan withers and dies. If you have to remember all the components in your QA toolchain and all the commands to run them, the chances that you (or other developers you work with) will reliably use them go down considerably. If you're going to invest the time required to come up with a comprehensive QA toolchain, isn't it worth spending a little time automating the process so that the toolchain will actually be used?

Fortunately, a tool called Grunt makes automating these tasks quite easy. We'll be rolling up our logic tests, cross-page tests, linting, and link checking into a single command with Grunt. Why not page tests? This is possible using a headless browser like PhantomJS or Zombie, but the configuration is complicated and beyond the scope of this book. Furthermore, browser tests are usually designed to be run as you work on an individual page, so there isn't quite as much value in rolling them together with the rest of your tests.

First, you'll need to install the Grunt command line, and Grunt itself:

```
sudo npm install -g grunt-cli
npm install --save-dev grunt
```

Grunt relies on *plugins* to get the job done (see the Grunt plugins list (*http://gruntjs.com/plugins*) for all available plugins). We'll need plugins for Mocha, JSHint, and Link-Checker. As I write this, there's no plugin for LinkChecker, so we'll have to use a generic plugin that executes arbitrary shell commands. So first we install all the necessary plugins:

```
npm install --save-dev grunt-cafe-mocha
npm install --save-dev grunt-contrib-jshint
npm install --save-dev grunt-exec
```

Now that all the plugins have been installed, create a file in your project directory called *Gruntfile.js*:

```
module.exports = function(grunt){

    // load plugins
    [
        'grunt-cafe-mocha',
        'grunt-contrib-jshint',
        'grunt-exec',
    ].forEach(function(task){
        grunt.loadNpmTasks(task);
    });

    // configure plugins
    grunt.initConfig({
        cafemocha: {
```

```
                        all: { src: 'qa/tests-*.js', options: { ui: 'tdd' }, }
                },
                jshint: {
                        app: ['meadowlark.js', 'public/js/**/*.js',
                                'lib/**/*.js'],
                        qa: ['Gruntfile.js', 'public/qa/**/*.js', 'qa/**/*.js'],
                },
                exec: {
                        linkchecker :
                                { cmd: 'linkchecker http://localhost:3000' }
                },
        });

        // register tasks
        grunt.registerTask('default', ['cafemocha','jshint','exec']);
};
```

In the section "load plugins," we're specifying which plugins we'll be using, which are the same plugins we installed via npm. Because I don't like to have to type loadNpm Tasks over and over again (and once you start relying on Grunt more, believe me, you will be adding more plugins!), I choose to put them all in an array and loop over them with forEach.

In the "configure plugins" section, we have to do a little work to get each plugin to work properly. For the cafemocha plugin (which will run our logic and cross-browser tests), we have to tell it where our tests are. We've put all of our tests in the *qa* subdirectory, and named them with a *tests-* prefix. Note that we have to specify the tdd interface. If you were mixing TDD and BDD, you would have to have some way to separate them. For example, you could use prefixes *tests-tdd-* and *tests-bdd-*.

For JSHint, we have to specify what JavaScript files should be linted. Be careful here! Very often, dependencies won't pass JSHint cleanly, or they will be using different JSHint settings, and you'll be inundated with JSHint errors for code that you didn't write. In particular, you want to make sure the *node_modules* directory isn't included, as well as any *vendor* directories. Currently, grunt-contrib-jshint doesn't allow you to *exclude* files, only include them. So we have to specify all the files we want to include. I generally break the files I want to include into two lists: the JavaScript that actually makes up our application or website and the QA JavaScript. It all gets linted, but breaking it up like this makes it a little easier to manage. Note that the wildcard /**/ means "all files in all subdirectories." Even though we don't have a *public/js* directory yet, we will. Implicitly excluded are the *node_modules* and *public/vendor* directories.

Lastly, we configure the `grunt-exec` plugin to run LinkChecker. Note that we've hard-coded this plugin to use port 3000; this might be a good thing to parameterize, which I'll leave as an exercise for the reader.[3]

Finally, we "register" the tasks: this puts individual plugins into named groups. A specially named task, default, will be the task that gets run by default, if you just type `grunt`.

Now all you have to do is make sure a server is running (in the background or in a different window), and run Grunt:

```
grunt
```

All of your tests will run (minus the page tests), all your code gets linted, and all your links are checked! If any component fails, Grunt will terminate with an error message; otherwise, it will report "Done, without errors." There's nothing quite so satisfying as seeing that message, so get in the habit of running Grunt before you commit!

# Continuous Integration (CI)

I'll leave you with another extremely useful QA concept: continuous integration. It's especially important if you're working on a team, but even if you're working on your own, it can provide some discipline that you might otherwise lack.

Basically, CI runs some or all of your tests every time you contribute code to a shared server. If all of the tests pass, nothing usually happens (you may get an email saying "good job," depending on how your CI is configured).

If, on the other hand, there are failures, the consequences are usually more...public. Again, it depends on how you configure your CI, but usually the entire team gets an email saying that you "broke the build." If your integration master is really sadistic, sometimes your boss is also on that email list! I've even known teams that set up lights and sirens when someone breaks the build, and in one particularly creative office, a tiny robotic foam missile launcher fired soft projectiles at the offending developer! It's a powerful incentive to run your QA toolchain before committing.

It's beyond the scope of this book to cover installing and configuring a CI server, but a chapter on QA wouldn't be complete without mentioning it.

---

3. See the `grunt.option` documentation (*http://gruntjs.com/api/grunt.option*) to get started.

---

Currently, the most popular CI server for Node projects is Travis CI (*http://about.travis-ci.org/docs/user/getting-started*). Travis CI is a hosted solution, which can be very appealing (it saves you from having to set up your own CI server). If you're using GitHub, it offers excellent integration support. Jenkins, a well-established CI server, now has a Node plugin (*https://wiki.jenkins-ci.org/display/JENKINS/NodeJS+Plugin*). JetBrains's excellent TeamCity (*http://www.jetbrains.com/teamcity*) now offers Node plugins.

If you're working on a project on your own, you may not get much benefit from a CI server, but if you're working on a team or an open source project, I highly recommend looking into setting up CI for your project.

# CHAPTER 6

# The Request and Response Objects

When you're building a web server with Express, most of what you'll be doing starts with a request object and ends with a response object. These two objects originate in Node and are extended by Express. Before we delve into what these objects offer us, let's establish a little background on how a client (a browser, usually) requests a page from a server, and how that page is returned.

## The Parts of a URL

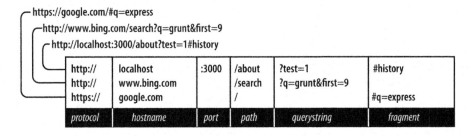

*Protocol*
: The protocol determines how the request will be transmitted. We will be dealing exclusively with *http* and *https*. Other common protocols include *file* and *ftp*.

*Host*
: The host identifies the server. Servers on your computer (localhost) or a local network may simply be one word, or it may be a numeric IP address. On the Internet, the host will end in a top-level domain (TLD) like *.com* or *.net*. Additionally, there may be *subdomains*, which prefix the hostname. *www* is a very common subdomain, though it can be anything. Subdomains are optional.

*Port*

Each server has a collection of numbered ports. Some port numbers are "special," like 80 and 443. If you omit the port, port 80 is assumed for HTTP and 443 for HTTPS. In general, if you aren't using port 80 or 443, you should use a port number greater than 1023.[1] It's very common to use easy-to-remember port numbers like 3000, 8080, and 8088.

*Path*

The path is generally the first part of the URL that your app cares about (it is possible to make decisions based on protocol, host, and port, but it's not good practice). The path should be used to uniquely identify pages or other resources in your app.

*Querystring*

The querystring is an optional collection of name/value pairs. The querystring starts with a question mark (?), and name/value pairs are separated by ampersands (&). Both names and values should be *URL encoded*. JavaScript provides a built-in function to do that: `encodeURIComponent`. For example, spaces will be replaced with plus signs (+). Other special characters will be replaced with numeric character references.

*Fragment*

The *fragment* (or *hash*) is not passed to the server at all: it is strictly for use by the browser. It is becoming increasingly common for single-page applications or AJAX-heavy applications to use the fragment to control the application. Originally, the fragment's sole purpose was to cause the browser to display a specific part of the document, marked by an anchor tag (`<a id="chapter06">`).

# HTTP Request Methods

The HTTP protocol defines a collection of *request methods* (often referred to as *HTTP verbs*) that a client uses to communicate with a server. Far and away, the most common methods are `GET` and `POST`.

When you type a URL into a browser (or click a link), the browser issues an HTTP `GET` request to the server. The important information passed to the server is the URL path and querystring. The combination of method, path, and querystring is what your app uses to determine how to respond.

For a website, most of your pages will respond to `GET` requests. `POST` requests are usually reserved for sending information back to the server (form processing, for example). It's quite common for `POST` requests to respond with the same HTML as the corresponding `GET` request after the server has processed any information included in the request (like

---

1. Ports 0-1023 are "well-known ports." (*http://en.wikipedia.org/wiki/List_of_TCP_and_UDP_port_numbers*)

a form). Browsers will exclusively use the GET and POST methods when communicating with your server (if they're not using AJAX).

Web services, on the other hand, often get more creative with the HTTP methods used. For example, there's an HTTP method called DELETE that is useful for, well, an API call that deletes things.

With Node and Express, you are fully in charge of what methods you respond to (though some of the more esoteric ones are not very well supported). In Express, you'll usually be writing handlers for specific methods.

# Request Headers

The URL isn't the only thing that's passed to the server when you navigate to a page. Your browser is sending a lot of "invisible" information every time you visit a website. I'm not talking about spooky personal information (though if your browser is infected by malware, that can happen). The browser will tell the server what language it prefers to receive the page in (for example, if you download Chrome in Spain, it will request the Spanish version of pages you visit, if they exist). It will also send information about the "user agent" (the browser, operating system, and hardware) and other bits of information. All this information is sent as a request header, which is made available to you through the request object's headers property. If you're curious to see the information your browser is sending, you can create a very simple Express route to display that information:

```
app.get('/headers', function(req,res){
    res.set('Content-Type','text/plain');
    var s = '';
    for(var name in req.headers) s += name + ': ' + req.headers[name] + '\n';
    res.send(s);
});
```

# Response Headers

Just as your browser sends hidden information to the server in the form of request headers, when the server responds, it also sends information back that is not necessarily rendered or displayed by the browser. The information typically included in response headers is metadata and server information. We've already seen the Content-Type header, which tells the browser what kind of content is being transmitted (HTML, an image, CSS, JavaScript, etc.). Note that the browser will respect the Content-Type header regardless of what the URL path is. So you could serve HTML from a path of /image.jpg or an image from a path of /text.html. (There's no legitimate reason to do this; it's just important to understand that paths are abstract, and the browser uses Content-Type to determine how to render content.) In addition to Content-Type, headers can indicate whether the response is compressed and what kind of encoding it's using. Response headers can also contain hints for the browser about how long it can cache the resource. This is an important consideration for optimizing your website, and we'll be discussing that in detail in Chapter 16. It is also common for response headers to contain some information about the server, indicating what type of server it is, and sometimes even details about the operating system. The downside about returning server information is that it gives hackers a starting point to compromise your site. Extremely security-conscious servers often omit this information, or even provide false information. Disabling Express's default X-Powered-By header is easy:

```
app.disable('x-powered-by');
```

If you want to see the response headers, they can be found in your browser's developer tools. To see the response headers in Chrome, for example:

1. Open the JavaScript console.
2. Click the Network tab.
3. Reload the page.
4. Pick the HTML from the list of requests (it will be the first one).
5. Click the Headers tab; you will see all response headers.

## Internet Media Types

The Content-Type header is critically important: without it, the client would have to painfully guess how to render the content. The format of the Content-Type header is an *Internet media type*, which consists of a type, subtype, and optional parameters. For example, text/html; charset=UTF-8 specifies a type of "text," a subtype of "html," and a character encoding of UTF-8. The Internet Assigned Numbers Authority maintains an official list of Internet media types (*http://www.iana.org/assignments/media-types/media-types.xhtml*). Often, you will hear "content type," "Internet media type," and "MIME type" used interchangeably. MIME (Multipurpose Internet Mail Extensions) was a precursor of Internet media types and, for the most part, is equivalent.

## Request Body

In addition to the request headers, a request can have a *body* (just like the body of a response is the actual content that's being returned). Normal GET requests don't have bodies, but POST requests usually do. The most common media type for POST bodies is application/x-www-form-urlencoded, which is simply encoded name/value pairs separated by ampersands (essentially the same format as a querystring). If the POST needs to support file uploads, the media type is multipart/form-data, which is a more complicated format. Lastly, AJAX requests can use application/json for the body.

# Parameters

The word "parameters" can mean a lot of things, and is often a source of confusion. For any request, parameters can come from the querystring, the session (requiring cookies; see Chapter 9), the request body, or the named routing parameters (which we'll learn more about in Chapter 14). In Node applications, the `param` method of the request object munges all of these parameters together. For this reason, I encourage you to avoid it. This commonly causes problems when a parameter is set to one thing in the querystring and another one in the `POST` body or the session: which value wins? It can produce maddening bugs. PHP is largely to blame for this confusion: in an effort to be "convenient," it munged all of these parameters into a variable called `$_REQUEST`, and for some reason, people have thought it was a good idea ever since. We will learn about dedicated properties that hold the various types of parameters, and I feel that that is a much less confusing approach.

# The Request Object

The request object (which is normally passed to a callback, meaning you can name it whatever you want: it is common to name it `req` or `request`) starts its life as an instance of `http.IncomingMessage`, a core Node object. Express adds additional functionality. Let's look at the most useful properties and methods of the request object (all of these methods are added by Express, except for `req.headers` and `req.url`, which originate in Node):

`req.params`
:   An array containing the *named route parameters*. We'll learn more about this in Chapter 14.

`req.param(name)`
:   Returns the named route parameter, or `GET` or `POST` parameters. I recommend avoiding this method.

`req.query`
:   An object containing querystring parameters (sometimes called `GET` parameters) as name/value pairs.

`req.body`
:   An object containing `POST` parameters. It is so named because `POST` parameters are passed in the body of the `REQUEST`, not in the URL like querystring parameters. To make `req.body` available, you'll need middleware that can parse the body content type, which we will learn about in Chapter 10.

`req.route`

Information about the currently matched route. Primarily useful for route debugging.

`req.cookies/req.signedCookies`

Objects containing containing cookie values passed from the client. See Chapter 9.

`req.headers`

The request headers received from the client.

`req.accepts([types])`

A convenience method to determine whether the client accepts a given type or types (optional `types` can be a single MIME type, such as `application/json`, a comma-delimited list, or an array). This method is of primary interest to those writing public APIs; it is assumed that browsers will always accept HTML by default.

`req.ip`

The IP address of the client.

`req.path`

The request path (without protocol, host, port, or querystring).

`req.host`

A convenience method that returns the hostname reported by the client. This information can be spoofed and should not be used for security purposes.

`req.xhr`

A convenience property that returns `true` if the request originated from an AJAX call.

`req.protocol`

The protocol used in making this request (for our purposes, it will either be `http` or `https`).

`req.secure`

A convenience property that returns `true` if the connection is secure. Equivalent to `req.protocol==='https'`.

`req.url/req.originalUrl`

A bit of a misnomer, these properties return the path and querystring (they do not include protocol, host, or port). `req.url` can be rewritten for internal routing purposes, but `req.originalUrl` is designed to remain the original request and querystring.

`req.acceptedLanguages`

A convenience method that returns an array of the (human) languages the client prefers, in order. This information is parsed from the request header.

# The Response Object

The response object (which is normally passed to a callback, meaning you can name it whatever you want: it is common to name it `res`, `resp`, or `response`) starts its life as an instance of `http.ServerResponse`, a core Node object. Express adds additional functionality. Let's look at the most useful properties and methods of the response object (all of these are added by Express):

`res.status(code)`
> Sets the HTTP status code. Express defaults to 200 (OK), so you will have to use this method to return a status of 404 (Not Found) or 500 (Server Error), or any other status code you wish to use. For redirects (status codes 301, 302, 303, and 307), there is a method `redirect`, which is preferable.

`res.set(name, value)`
> Sets a response header. This is not something you will normally be doing manually.

`res.cookie(name, value, [options])`, `res.clearCookie(name, [options])`
> Sets or clears cookies that will be stored on the client. This requires some middleware support; see Chapter 9.

`res.redirect([status], url)`
> Redirects the browser. The default redirect code is 302 (Found). In general, you should minimize redirection unless you are permanently moving a page, in which case you should use the code 301 (Moved Permanently).

`res.send(body)`, `res.send(status, body)`
> Sends a response to the client, with an optional status code. Express defaults to a content type of `text/html`, so if you want to change it to `text/plain` (for example), you'll have to call `res.set('Content-Type', 'text/plain')` before calling `res.send`. If body is an object or an array, the response is sent as JSON instead (with the content type being set appropriately), though if you want to send JSON, I recommend doing so explicitly by calling `res.json` instead.

`res.json(json)`, `res.json(status, json)`
> Sends JSON to the client with an optional status code.

`res.jsonp(json)`, `res.jsonp(status, json)`
> Sends JSONP to the client with an optional status code.

`res.type(type)`
> A convenience method to set the `Content-Type` header. Essentially equivalent to `res.set('Content-Type', type)`, except that it will also attempt to map file extensions to an Internet media type if you provide a string without a slash in it. For example, `res.type('txt')` will result in a `Content-Type` of `text/plain`. There are areas where this functionality could be useful (for example, automatically serving

disparate multimedia files), but in general, you should avoid it in favor of explicitly setting the correct Internet media type.

res.format(object)

This method allows you to send different content depending on the Accept request header. This is of primary use in APIs, and we will discuss this more in Chapter 15. Here's a very simple example: res.format({'text/plain': 'hi there', 'text/html': 'hi there'}).

res.attachment([filename]), res.download(path, [filename], [callback])

Both of these methods set a response header called Content-Disposition to at tachment; this will prompt the browser to download the content instead of displaying it in a browser. You may specify filename as a hint to the browser. With res.download, you can specify the file to download, whereas res.attachment just sets the header; you still have to send content to the client.

res.sendFile(path, [options], [callback])

This method will read a file specified by path and send its contents to the client. There should be little need for this method; it's easier to use the static middleware, and put files you want available to the client in the *public* directory. However, if you want to have a different resource served from the same URL depending on some condition, this method could come in handy.

res.links(links)

Sets the Links response header. This is a specialized header that has little use in most applications.

res.locals, res.render(view, [locals], callback)

res.locals is an object containing *default* context for rendering views. res.ren der will render a view using the configured templating engine (the locals parameter to res.render shouldn't be confused with res.locals: it will override the context in res.locals, but context not overridden will still be available). Note that res.render will default to a response code of 200; use res.status to specify a different response code. Rendering views will be covered in depth in Chapter 7.

# Getting More Information

Because of JavaScript's prototypal inheritance, knowing exactly what you're dealing with can be challenging sometimes. Node provides you with objects that Express extends, and packages that you add may also extend those. Figuring out exactly what's available to you can be challenging sometimes. In general, I would recommend working backward: if you're looking for some functionality, first check the Express API documentation (*http://expressjs.com/api.html*). The Express API is pretty complete, and chances are, you'll find what you're looking for there.

If you need information that isn't documented, sometimes you have to dive into the Express source (*https://github.com/visionmedia/express/tree/master*). I encourage you to do this! You'll probably find that it's a lot less intimidating than you might think. Here's a quick roadmap to where you'll find things in the Express source:

*lib/application.js*
> The main Express interface. If you want to understand how middleware is linked in, or how views are rendered, this is the place to look.

*lib/express.js*
> This is a relatively short shell that extends Connect with the functionality in *lib/application.js*, and returns a function that can be used with `http.createServer` to actually run an Express app.

*lib/request.js*
> Extends Node's `http.IncomingMessage` object to provide a robust request object. For information about all the request object properties and methods, this is where to look.

*lib/response.js*
> Extends Node's `http.ServerResponse` object to provide the response object. For information about response object properties and methods, this is where to look.

*lib/router/route.js*
> Provides basic routing support. While routing is central to your app, this file is less than 200 lines long; you'll find that it's quite simple and elegant.

As you dig into the Express source code, you'll probably want to refer to the Node documentation (*http://nodejs.org/api/http.html*), especially the section on the `HTTP` module.

# Boiling It Down

This chapter has tried to provide an overview of the request and response objects, which are the meat and potatoes of an Express application. However, the chances are that you will be using a small subset of this functionality most of the time. So let's break it down by functionality you'll be using most frequently.

## Rendering Content

When you're rendering content, you'll be using `res.render` most often, which renders views within layouts, providing maximum value. Occasionally, you may wish to write a quick test page, so you might use `res.send` if you just want a test page. You may use `req.query` to get querystring values, `req.session` to get session values, or `req.cook` ie/req.signedCookies to get cookies. Examples 6-1 to 6-8 demonstrate common content rendering tasks:

*Example 6-1. Basic usage*

```
// basic usage
app.get('/about', function(req, res){
        res.render('about');
});
```

*Example 6-2. Response codes other than 200*

```
app.get('/error', function(req, res){
        res.status(500);
        res.render('error');
});
// or on one line...
app.get('/error', function(req, res){
        res.status(500).render('error');
});
```

*Example 6-3. Passing a context to a view, including querystring, cookie, and session values*

```
app.get('/greeting', function(req, res){
        res.render('about', {
                message: 'welcome',
                style: req.query.style,
                userid: req.cookie.userid,
                username: req.session.username,
        });
});
```

*Example 6-4. Rendering a view without a layout*

```
// the following layout doesn't have a layout file, so views/no-layout.handlebars
// must include all necessary HTML
app.get('/no-layout', function(req, res){
        res.render('no-layout', { layout: null });
});
```

*Example 6-5. Rendering a view with a custom layout*

```
// the layout file views/layouts/custom.handlebars will be used
app.get('/custom-layout', function(req, res){
        res.render('custom-layout', { layout: 'custom' });
});
```

*Example 6-6. Rendering plaintext output*

```
app.get('/test', function(req, res){
        res.type('text/plain');
        res.send('this is a test');
});
```

*Example 6-7. Adding an error handler*

```
// this should appear AFTER all of your routes
// note that even if you don't need the "next"
// function, it must be included for Express
// to recognize this as an error handler
app.use(function(err, req, res, next){
        console.error(err.stack);
        res.status(500).render('error');
});
```

*Example 6-8. Adding a 404 handler*

```
// this should appear AFTER all of your routes
app.use(function(req, res){
        res.status(404).render('not-found');
});
```

## Processing Forms

When you're processing forms, the information from the forms will usually be in req.body (or occasionally in req.query). You may use req.xhr to determine if the request was an AJAX request or a browser request (this will be covered in depth in Chapter 8). See Examples 6-9 and 6-10.

*Example 6-9. Basic form processing*

```
// body-parser middleware must be linked in
app.post('/process-contact', function(req, res){
        console.log('Received contact from ' + req.body.name +
                ' <' + req.body.email + '>');
        // save to database....
        res.redirect(303, '/thank-you');
});
```

*Example 6-10. More robust form processing*

```
// body-parser middleware must be linked in
app.post('/process-contact', function(req, res){
        console.log('Received contact from ' + req.body.name +
                ' <' + req.body.email + '>');
        try {
                // save to database....

                return res.xhr ?
```

```
                        res.render({ success: true }) :
                        res.redirect(303, '/thank-you');
    } catch(ex) {
            return res.xhr ?
                        res.json({ error: 'Database error.' }) :
                        res.redirect(303, '/database-error');
    }
});
```

## Providing an API

When you're providing an API, much like processing forms, the parameters will usually
be in req.query, though you can also use req.body. What's different about APIs is that
you'll usually be returning JSON, XML, or even plaintext, instead of HTML, and you'll
often be using less common HTTP methods like PUT, POST, and DELETE. Providing an
API will be covered in Chapter 15. Examples 6-11 and 6-12 use the following "products"
array (which would normally be retrieved from a database):

```
var tours = [
        { id: 0, name: 'Hood River', price: 99.99 },
        { id: 1, name: 'Oregon Coast', price: 149.95 },
];
```

 The term "endpoint" is often used to describe a single function in an
API.

*Example 6-11. Simple GET endpoint returning only JSON*

```
app.get('/api/tours', function(req, res){
        res.json(tours);
});
```

Example 6-12 uses the res.format method in Express to respond according to the
preferences of the client.

*Example 6-12. GET endpoint that returns JSON, XML, or text*

```
app.get('/api/tours', function(req, res){
        var toursXml = '<?xml version="1.0"?><tours>' +
                products.map(function(p){
                        return '<tour price="' + p.price +
                                '" id="' + p.id + '">' + p.name + '</tour>';
                }).join('') + '</tours>';
        var toursText = tours.map(function(p){
                        return p.id + ': ' + p.name + ' (' + p.price + ')';
                }).join('\n');
        res.format({
```

```
                'application/json': function(){
                        res.json(tours);
                },
                'application/xml': function(){
                        res.type('application/xml');
                        res.send(toursXml);
                },
                'text/xml': function(){
                        res.type('text/xml');
                        res.send(toursXml);
                }
                'text/plain': function(){
                        res.type('text/plain');
                        res.send(toursXml);
                }
        });
});
```

In Example 6-13, the PUT endpoint updates a product and returns JSON. Parameters are passed in the querystring (the ":id" in the route string tells Express to add an id property to req.params).

*Example 6-13. PUT endpoint for updating*

```
// API that updates a tour and returns JSON; params are passed using querystring
app.put('/api/tour/:id', function(req, res){
        var p = tours.filter(function(p){ return p.id === req.params.id })[0];
        if( p ) {
                if( req.query.name ) p.name = req.query.name;
                if( req.query.price ) p.price = req.query.price;
                res.json({success: true});
        } else {
                res.json({error: 'No such tour exists.'});
        }
});
```

Finally, Example 6-14 shows a DEL endpoint.

*Example 6-14. DEL endpoint for deleting*

```
// API that deletes a product
api.del('/api/tour/:id', function(req, res){
        var i;
        for( var i=tours.length-1; i>=0; i-- )
                if( tours[i].id == req.params.id ) break;
        if( i>=0 ) {
                tours.splice(i, 1);
                res.json({success: true});
        } else {
                res.json({error: 'No such tour exists.'});
        }
});
```

CHAPTER 7

# Templating with Handlebars

If you aren't using templating—or if you don't know what templating is—it's the single most important thing you're going to get out of this book. If you're coming from a PHP background, you may wonder what the fuss is all about: PHP is one of the first languages that could really be called a templating language. Almost all major languages that have been adapted for the Web have included some kind of templating support. What is different today is that the "templating engine" is being decoupled from the language. Case in point is *Mustache*: an extremely popular language-agnostic templating engine.

So what is templating? Let's start with what templating *isn't* by considering the most obvious and straightforward way to generate one language from another (specifically, we'll generate some HTML with JavaScript):

```
document.write('<h1>Please Don\'t Do This</h1>');
document.write('<p><span class="code">document.write</span> is naughty,\n');
document.write('and should be avoided at all costs.</p>');
document.write('<p>Today\'s date is ' + new Date() + '.</p>');
```

Perhaps the only reason this seems "obvious" is that it's the way programming has always been taught:

```
10 PRINT "Hello world!"
```

In imperative languages, we're used to saying, "Do this, then do that, then do something else." For some things, this approach works fine. If you have 500 lines of JavaScript to perform a complicated calculation that results in a single number, and every step is dependent on the previous step, there's no harm in it. What if it's the other way around, though? You have 500 lines of HTML and 3 lines of JavaScript. Does it make sense to write document.write 500 times? Not at all.

Really, the problem boils down to this: switching context is problematic. If you're writing lots of JavaScript, it's inconvenient and confusing to be mixing in HTML. The other way isn't so bad: we're quite used to writing JavaScript in <script> blocks, but hopefully you see the difference: there's still a context switch, and you're either writing HTML or you're in a `<script>` block writing JavaScript. Having JavaScript emit HTML is fraught with problems:

- You have to constantly worry about what characters need to be escaped, and how to do that.
- Using JavaScript to generate HTML that itself includes JavaScript quickly leads to madness.
- You usually lose the nice syntax highlighting and other handy language-specific features your editor has.
- It can be much harder to spot malformed HTML.
- It's hard to visually parse.
- It can make it harder for other people to understand your code.

Templating solves the problem by allowing you to write in the target language, while at the same time providing the ability to insert dynamic data. Consider the previous example rewritten as a Mustache template:

```
<h1>Much Better</h1>
<p>No <span class="code">document.write</span> here!</p>
<p>Today's date is {{today}}.</p>
```

Now all we have to do is provide a value for {{today}}, and that's at the heart of templating languages.

# There Are No Absolute Rules Except This One[1]

I'm not suggesting that you should *never* write HTML in JavaScript: only that you should avoid it whenever possible. In particular, it's slightly more palatable in frontend code, thanks to libraries like jQuery. For example, this would pass with little comment from me:

```
$('#error').html('Something <b>very bad</b> happened!');
```

However, if that eventually mutated into this:

```
$('#error').html('<div class="error"><h3>Error</h3>' +
    '<p>Something <b><a href="/error-detail/' + errorNumber
    +'">very bad</a></b> ' +
    'happened.  <a href="/try-again">Try again<a>, or ' +
    '<a href="/contact">contact support</a>.</p></div>');
```

1. To paraphrase my friend and mentor, Paul Inman.

I might suggest it's time to employ a template. The point is, I suggest you use your best judgment when deciding where to draw the line between HTML in strings and using templates. I would err on the side of templates, however, and avoid generating HTML with JavaScript except for the simplest cases.

# Choosing a Template Engine

In the Node world, you have many templating engines to choose from, so how to pick? It's a complicated question, and very much depends on your needs. Here are some criteria to consider, though:

*Performance*
Clearly, you want your templating engine to be as fast as possible. It's not something you want slowing down your website.

*Client, server, or both?*
Most, but not all, templating engines are available on both the server and client sides. If you need to use templates in both realms (and you will), I recommend you pick something that is equally capable in either capacity.

*Abstraction*
Do you want something familiar (like normal HTML with curly brackets thrown in, for example), or do you secretly hate HTML and would love something that saves you from all those angle brackets? Templating (especially server-side templating) gives you some choices here.

These are just some of the more prominent criteria in selecting a templating language. If you want a more detailed discussion on this topic, I highly recommend Veena Basavaraj's blog post about her selection criteria when choosing a templating language for LinkedIn (*http://bit.ly/templating_selection_criteria*).

LinkedIn's choice was *Dust* (*http://akdubya.github.io/dustjs*), but *Handlebars* (*http://handlebarsjs.com*) was also in the winner's circle, which is my preferred template engine, and the one we'll be using in this book.

Express allows you to use any templating engine you wish, so if Handlebars is not to your liking, you'll find it's very easy to switch it out. If you want to explore your options, you can use this fun and useful Template-Engine-Chooser (*http://garann.github.io/template-chooser*).

# Jade: A Different Approach

Where most templating engines take a very HTML-centric approach, Jade stands out by abstracting the details of HTML away from you. It is also worth noting that Jade is the brainchild of TJ Holowaychuk, the same person who brought us Express. It should come as no surprise, then, that Jade integration with Express is very good. The approach that Jade takes is very noble: at its core is the assertion that HTML is a fussy and tedious language to write by hand. Let's take a look at what a Jade template looks like, along with the HTML it will output (taken from the Jade home page (*http://jade-lang.com*), and modified slightly to fit the book format):

```
doctype html
html(lang="en")
  head
    title= pageTitle
    script.
      if (foo) {
        bar(1 + 5)
      }
  body

    h1 Jade
    #container
      if youAreUsingJade
        p You are amazing
      else
        p Get on it!
      p.
        Jade is a terse and
        simple templating
        language with a
        strong focus on
        performance and
        powerful features.
```

```
<!DOCTYPE html>
<html lang="en">
<head>
<title>Jade Demo</title>
<script>
    if (foo) {
        bar(1 + 5)
    }
</script>
<body>
<h1>Jade</h1>
<div id="container">

<p>You are amazing</p>


<p>
  Jade is a terse and
  simple templating
  language with a
  strong focus on
  performance and
  powerful features.
</p>
</body>
</html>
```

Jade certainly represents a lot less typing: no more angle brackets or closing tags. Instead it relies on indentation and some common-sense rules, making it easier to say what you mean. Jade has an additional advantage: theoretically, when HTML itself changes, you can simply get Jade to retarget the newest version of HTML, allowing you to "future proof" your content.

As much as I admire the Jade philosophy and the elegance of its execution, I've found that I don't want the details of HTML abstracted away from me. As a web developer, HTML is at the heart of everything I do, and if the price is wearing out the angle bracket keys on my keyboard, then so be it. A lot of frontend developers I talk to feel the same, so maybe the world just isn't ready for Jade....

Here's where we'll part ways with Jade; you won't be seeing it in this book. However, if the abstraction appeals to you, you will certainly have no problems using Jade with Express, and there are plenty of resources to help you do so.

# Handlebars Basics

Handlebars is an extension of Mustache, another popular templating engine. I recommend Handlebars for its easy JavaScript integration (both frontend and backend) and familiar syntax. For me, it strikes all the right balances and is what we'll be focusing on in this book. The concepts we're discussing are broadly applicable to other templating engines, though, so you will be well prepared to try different templating engines if Handlebars doesn't strike your fancy.

The key to understanding templating is understanding the concept of *context*. When you render a template, you pass the templating engine an object called the *context object*, and this is what allows replacements to work.

For example, if my context object is { name: 'Buttercup' }, and my template is `<p>Hello, {{name}}!</p>`, {{name}} will be replaced with Buttercup. What if you want to pass HTML to the template? For example, if our context was instead { name: 'Buttercup' }, using the previous template will result in `<p>Hello, &lt;b&gt;Buttercup&lt;b&gt;</p>`, which is probably not what you're looking for. To solve this problem, simply use three curly brackets instead of two: {{{name}}}.

> While we've already established that we should avoid writing HTML in JavaScript, the ability to turn off HTML escaping with triple curly brackets has some important uses. For example, if you were building a CMS with WYSIWYG editors, you would probably want to be able to pass HTML to your views. Also, the ability to render properties from the context without HTML escaping is important for *layouts* and *sections*, which we'll learn about shortly.

In Figure 7-1, we see how the Handlebars engine uses the context (represented by an oval) combined with the template to render HTML.

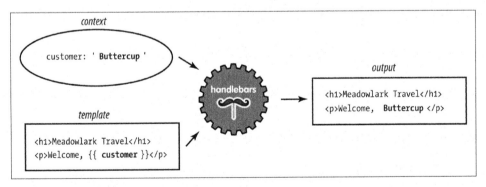

*Figure 7-1. Rendering HTML with Handlebars*

## Comments

Comments in Handlebars look like {{! comment goes here }}. It's important to understand the distinction between Handlebars comments and HTML comments. Consider the following template:

```
{{! super-secret comment }}
<!-- not-so-secret comment -->
```

Assuming this is a server-side template, the super-secret comment will never be sent to the browser, whereas the not-so-secret comment will be visible if the user inspects the HTML source. You should prefer Handlebars comments for anything that exposes implementation details, or anything else you don't want exposed.

## Blocks

Things start to get more complicated when you consider *blocks*. Blocks provide flow control, conditional execution, and extensibility. Consider the following context object:

```
{
        currency: {
                name: 'United States dollars',
                abbrev: 'USD',
        },
        tours: [
                { name: 'Hood River', price: '$99.95' },
                { name: 'Oregon Coast', price, '$159.95' },
        ],
        specialsUrl: '/january-specials',
        currencies: [ 'USD', 'GBP', 'BTC' ],
}
```

Now let's examine a template we can pass that context to:

```
<ul>
        {{#each tours}}
                {{! I'm in a new block...and the context has changed }}
                <li>
                        {{name}} - {{price}}
                        {{#if ../currencies}}
                                ({{../../currency.abbrev}})
                        {{/if}}
                </li>
        {{/each}}
</ul>
{{#unless currencies}}
        <p>All prices in {{currency.name}}.</p>
{{/unless}}
{{#if specialsUrl}}
        {{! I'm in a new block...but the context hasn't changed (sortof) }}
        <p>Check out our <a href="{{specialsUrl}}">specials!</p>
{{else}}
```

```
            <p>Please check back often for specials.</p>
{{/if}}
<p>
        {{#each currencies}}
                <a href="#" class="currency">{{.}}</a>
        {{else}}
                Unfortunately, we currently only accept {{currency.name}}.
        {{/each}}
</p>
```

There's a lot going on in this template, so let's break it down. It starts off with the each helper, which allows us to iterate over an array. What's important to understand is that between {{#each tours}} and {{/each tours}}, the context changes. On the first pass, it changes to { name: 'Hood River', price: '$99.95' }, and on the second pass, the context is { name: 'Oregon Coast', price: '$159.95' }. So within that block, we can refer to {{name}} and {{price}}. However, if we want to access the currency object, we have to use ../ to access the *parent* context.

If a property of the context is itself an object, we can access its properties as normal with a period, such as {{currency.name}}.

The if helper is special, and slightly confusing. In Handlebars, *any* block will change the context, so within an if block, there is a new context...which happens to be a duplicate of the parent context. In other words, inside an if or else block, the context is the same as the parent context. This is normally a completely transparent implementation detail, but it becomes necessary to understand when you're using if blocks inside an each loop. In the loop {{#each tours}}, we can access the parent context with ../. However, in our {{#if ../currencies}} block, we have entered a new context...so to get at the currency object, we have to use ../../. The first ../ gets to the product context, and the second one gets back to the outermost context. This produces a lot of confusion, and one simple expedient is to avoid using if blocks within each blocks.

Both if and each have an optional else block (with each, if there are no elements in the array, the else block will execute). We've also used the unless helper, which is essentially the opposite of the if helper: it executes only if the argument is false.

The last thing to note about this template is the use of {{.}} in the {{#each currencies}} block. {{.}} simply refers to the current context; in this case, the current context is simply a string in an array that we want to print out.

 Accessing the current context with a lone period has another use: it can distinguish helpers (which we'll learn about soon) from properties of the current context. For example, if you have a helper called foo and a property in the current context called foo, {{foo}} refers to the helper, and {{./foo}} refers to the property.

## Server-Side Templates

Server-side templates allow you to render HTML *before* it's sent to the client. Unlike client-side templating, where the templates are available for the curious user who knows how to view HTML source, your users will never see your server-side template, or the context objects used to generate the final HTML.

Server-side templates, in addition to hiding your implementation details, support template *caching*, which is important for performance. The templating engine will cache compiled templates (only recompiling and recaching when the template itself changes), which will improve the performance of templated views. By default, view caching is disabled in development mode and enabled in production mode. If you want to explicitly enable view caching, you can do so thusly: `app.set('view cache', true);`.

Out of the box, Express supports Jade, EJS, and JSHTML. We've already discussed Jade, and I find little to recommend EJS or JSHTML (neither go far enough, syntactically, for my taste). So we'll need to add a node package that provides Handlebars support for Express:

```
npm install --save express-handlebars
```

Then we'll link it into Express:

```
var handlebars = require('express-handlebars')
        .create({ defaultLayout: 'main' });
app.engine('handlebars', handlebars.engine);
app.set('view engine', 'handlebars');
```

 express-handlebars expects Handlebars templates to have the *.handlebars* extension. I've grown used to this, but if it's too wordy for you, you can change the extension to the also common *.hbs* when you create the express-handlebars instance: `require('express-handlebars').create({ extname: '.hbs' })`.

## Views and Layouts

A *view* usually represents an individual page on your website (though it could represent an AJAX-loaded portion of a page, or an email, or anything else for that matter). By default, Express looks for views in the *views* subdirectory. A *layout* is a special kind of view—essentially, a template for templates. Layouts are essential because most (if not all) of the pages on your site will have an almost identical layout. For example, they must have an `<html>` element and a `<title>` element, they usually all load the same CSS files, and so on. You don't want to have to duplicate that code for every single page, which is where layouts come in. Let's look at a bare-bones layout file:

```
<!doctype>
<html>
<head>
        <title>Meadowlark Travel</title>
        <link rel="stylesheet" href="/css/main.css">
</head>
<body>
        {{{body}}}
</body>
</html>
```

Notice the text inside the <body> tag: {{{body}}}. That's so the view engine knows where to render the content of your view. It's important to use three curly brackets instead of two: our view is most likely to contain HTML, and we don't want Handlebars trying to escape it. Note that there's no restriction on where you place the {{{body}}} field. For example, if you were building a responsive layout in Bootstrap 3, you would probably want to put your view inside a container <div>. Also, common page elements like headers and footers usually live in the layout, not the view. Here's an example:

```
<!-- ... -->
<body>
        <div class="container">
                <header><h1>Meadowlark Travel</h1></header>
                {{{body}}}
                <footer>&copy; {{copyrightYear}} Meadowlark Travel</footer>
        </div>
</body>
```

In Figure 7-2, we see how the template engine combines the view, layout, and context. The important thing that this diagram makes clear is the order of operations. The *view is rendered first*, before the layout. At first, this may seem counterintuitive: the view is being rendered *inside* the layout, so shouldn't the layout be rendered first? While it could technically be done this way, there are advantages to doing it in reverse. Particularly, it allows the view itself to further customize the layout, which will come in handy when we discuss *sections*.

 Because of the order of operations, you can pass a property called body into the view, and it will render correctly in the view. However, when the layout is rendered, the value of body will be overwritten by the rendered view.

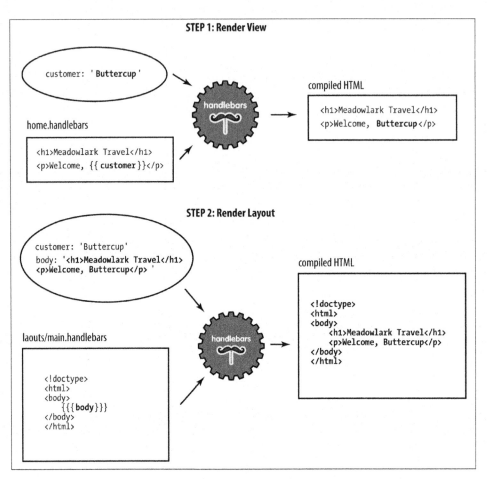

*Figure 7-2. Rendering a view with a layout*

## Using Layouts (or Not) in Express

Chances are, most (if not all) of your pages will use the same layout, so it doesn't make sense to keep specifying the layout every time we render a view. You'll notice that when we created the view engine, we specified the name of the default layout:

```
var handlebars = require('express-handlebars')
        .create({ defaultLayout: 'main' });
```

By default, Express looks for views in the *views* subdirectory and layouts in *views/layouts*. So if you have a view *views/foo.handlebars*, you can render it this way:

```
app.get('/foo', function(req, res){
        res.render('foo');
});
```

It will use *views/layouts/main.handlebars* as the layout. If you don't want to use a layout at all (meaning you'll have to have all of the boilerplate in the view), you can specify `layout: null` in the context object:

```
app.get('/foo', function(req, res){
        res.render('foo', { layout: null });
});
```

Or, if we want to use a different template, we can specify the template name:

```
app.get('/foo', function(req, res){
        res.render('foo', { layout: 'microsite' });
});
```

This will render the view with layout *views/layouts/microsite.handlebars*.

Keep in mind that the more templates you have, the more basic HTML layout you have to maintain. On the other hand, if you have pages that are substantially different in layout, it may be worth it: you have to find a balance that works for your projects.

## Partials

Very often, you'll have components that you want to reuse on different pages (often called "widgets" in frontend circles). One way to achieve that with templates is to use *partials* (so named because they don't render a whole view or a whole page). Let's imagine we want a Current Weather component that displays the current weather conditions in Portland, Bend, and Manzanita. We want this component to be reusable so we can easily put it on whatever page we want, so we'll use a partial. First, we create a partial file, *views/partials/weather.handlebars*:

```
<div class="weatherWidget">
        {{#each partials.weatherContext.locations}}
                <div class="location">
                        <h3>{{name}}</h3>
                        <a href="{{forecastUrl}}">
                                <img src="{{iconUrl}}" alt="{{weather}}">
                                {{weather}}, {{temp}}
                        </a>
                </div>
        {{/each}}
        <small>Source: <a href="http://www.wunderground.com">Weather
                Underground</a></small>
</div>
```

Note that we namespace our context by starting with `partials.weatherContext`: since we want to be able to use the partial on any page, it's not practical to pass the context in for every view, so instead we use `res.locals` (which is available to every view). But because we don't want to interfere with the context specified by individual views, we put all partial context in the `partials` object.

express-handlebars allows you to pass in partial templates as part of the context. For example, if you add partials.foo = "Tem plate!" to your context, you can render this partial with {{> foo}}. This usage will override any *.handlebars* view files, which is why we used partials.weatherContext above, instead of partials.weath er, which would override *views/partials/weather.handlebars*.

In Chapter 19, we'll see how to get current weather information from the free Weather Underground API. For now, we're just going to use dummy data. In our application file, we'll create a function to get current weather data:

```
function getWeatherData(){
    return {
        locations: [
            {
                name: 'Portland',
                forecastUrl: 'http://www.wunderground.com/US/OR/Portland.html',
                iconUrl: 'http://icons-ak.wxug.com/i/c/k/cloudy.gif',
                weather: 'Overcast',
                temp: '54.1 F (12.3 C)',
            },
            {
                name: 'Bend',
                forecastUrl: 'http://www.wunderground.com/US/OR/Bend.html',
                iconUrl: 'http://icons-ak.wxug.com/i/c/k/partlycloudy.gif',
                weather: 'Partly Cloudy',
                temp: '55.0 F (12.8 C)',
            },
            {
                name: 'Manzanita',
                forecastUrl: 'http://www.wunderground.com/US/OR/Manzanita.html',
                iconUrl: 'http://icons-ak.wxug.com/i/c/k/rain.gif',
                weather: 'Light Rain',
                temp: '55.0 F (12.8 C)',
            },
        ],
    };
}
```

Now we'll create a middleware to inject this data into the res.locals.partials object (we'll learn more about middleware in Chapter 10):

```
app.use(function(req, res, next){
        if(!res.locals.partials) res.locals.partials = {};
        res.locals.partials.weatherContext = getWeatherData();
        next();
});
```

Now that everything's set up, all we have to do is use the partial in a view. For example, to put our widget on the home page, edit *views/home.handlebars*:

```
<h2>Welcome to Meadowlark Travel!</h2>
{{> weather}}
```

The `{{> partial_name}}` syntax is how you include a partial in a view: `express-handlebars` will know to look in *views/partials* for a view called *partial_name.handlebars* (or *weather.handlebars*, in our example).

 `express-handlebars` supports subdirectories, so if you have a lot of partials, you can organize them. For example, if you have some social media partials, you could put them in the *views/partials/social* directory and include them using `{{> social/facebook}}`, `{{> social/twitter}}`, etc.

## Sections

One technique I'm borrowing from Microsoft's excellent *Razor* template engine is the idea of *sections*. Layouts work well if all of your view fits neatly within a single element in your layout, but what happens when your view needs to inject itself into different parts of your layout? A common example of this is a view needing to add something to the `<head>` element, or to insert a `<script>` that uses jQuery (meaning it needs to come after jQuery is referenced, which is sometimes the very last thing in the layout, for performance reasons).

Neither Handlebars nor `express-handlebars` has a built-in way to do this. Fortunately, Handlebars helpers make this really easy. When we instantiate the Handlebars object, we'll add a helper called `section`:

```
var handlebars = require('express-handlebars').create({
    defaultLayout:'main',
    helpers: {
        section: function(name, options){
            if(!this._sections) this._sections = {};
            this._sections[name] = options.fn(this);
            return null;
        }
    }
});
```

Now we can use the `section` helper in a view. Let's add a view (*views/jquery-test.handlebars*) to add something to the `<head>` and a script that uses jQuery:

```
{{#section 'head'}}
        <!-- we want Google to ignore this page -->
        <meta name="robots" content="noindex">
{{/section}}

<h1>Test Page</h1>
<p>We're testing some jQuery stuff.</p>
```

```
{{#section 'jquery'}}
    <script>
            $('document').ready(function(){
                    $('h1').html('jQuery Works');
            });
    </script>
{{/section}}
```

Now in our layout, we can place the sections just as we place {{{body}}}:

```
<!doctype html>
<html>
<head>
    <title>Meadowlark Travel</title>
    {{{_sections.head}}}
</head>
<body>
    {{{body}}}
    <script src="http://code.jquery.com/jquery-2.0.2.min.js"></script>
    {{{_sections.jquery}}}
</body>
</html>
```

# Perfecting Your Templates

Your templates are at the heart of your website. A good template structure will save you development time, promote consistency across your website, and reduce the number of places that layout quirks can hide. To achieve these benefits, though, you must spend some time crafting your templates carefully. Deciding how many templates you should have is an art: generally, fewer is better, but there is a point of diminishing returns, depending on the uniformity of your pages. Your templates are also your first line of defense against cross-browser compatibility issues and valid HTML. They should be lovingly crafted and maintained by someone who is well versed in frontend development. A great place to start—especially if you're new—is HTML5 Boilerplate (*http:// html5boilerplate.com*). In the previous examples, we've been using a minimal HTML5 template to fit the book format, but for our actual project, we'll be using HTML5 Boilerplate.

Another popular place to start with your template are third-party themes. Sites like Themeforest (*http://themeforest.net/category/site-templates*) and WrapBootstrap (*https://wrapbootstrap.com*) have hundreds of ready-to-use HTML5 themes that you can use as a starting place for your template. Using a third-party theme starts with taking the primary file (usually *index.html*) and renaming it to *main.handlebars* (or whatever you choose to call your layout file), and placing any resources (CSS, JavaScript, images) in the *public* directory you use for static files. Then you'll have to edit the template file and figure out where you want to put the {{{body}}} expression. Depending on the elements of your template, you may want to move some of them into partials. A great example is a "hero" (a tall banner designed to grab the user's attention. If the hero appears on every page (probably a poor choice), you would leave the hero in the template file. If it appears on only one page (usually the home page), then it would go only in that view. If it appears on several—but not all—pages, then you might consider putting it in a partial. The choice is yours, and herein lies the artistry of making a unique, captivating website.

## Client-Side Handlebars

Client-side templating with handlebars is useful whenever you want to have dynamic content. Of course our AJAX calls can return HTML fragments that we can just insert into the DOM as-is, but client-side Handlebars allows us to receive the results of AJAX calls as JSON data, and format it to fit our site. For that reason, it's especially useful for communicating with third-party APIs, which are going to return JSON, not HTML formatted to fit your site.

Before we use Handlebars on the client side, we need to load Handlebars. We can either do that by putting Handlebars in with our static content or using an already available CDN. We'll be using the latter approach in *views/nursery-rhyme.handlebars*:

```
{{#section 'head'}}
        <script src="//cdnjs.cloudflare.com/ajax/libs/handlebars.js/1.3.0/↵
handlebars.min.js"></script>
{{/section}}
```

Now we'll need somewhere to put our templates. One way is to use an existing element in our HTML, preferably a hidden one. You can accomplish this by putting your HTML in <script> elements in the <head>. It seems odd at first, but it works quite well:

```
{{#section 'head'}}
        <script src="//cdnjs.cloudflare.com/ajax/libs/handlebars.js/1.3.0/↵
handlebars.min.js"></script>

        <script id="nurseryRhymeTemplate" type="text/x-handlebars-template">
                Marry had a little <b>\{{animal}}</b>, its <b>\{{bodyPart}}</b>
                was <b>\{{adjective}}</b> as <b>\{{noun}}</b>.
        </script>
{{/section}}
```

Note that we have to escape at least one of the curly brackets; otherwise, server-side view processing would attempt to make the replacements instead.

Before we use the template, we have to compile it:

```
{{#section 'jquery'}}
        $(document).ready(function(){
                var nurseryRhymeTemplate = Handlebars.compile(
                        $('#nurseryRhymeTemplate').html());
        });
{{/section}}
```

And we'll need a place to put the rendered template. For testing purposes, we'll add a couple of buttons, one to render directly from our JavaScript, the other to render from an AJAX call:

```
<div id="nurseryRhyme">Click a button....</div>
<hr>
<button id="btnNurseryRhyme">Generate nursery rhyme</button>
<button id="btnNurseryRhymeAjax">Generate nursery rhyme from AJAX</button>
```

And finally the code to render the template:

```
{{#section 'jquery'}}
    <script>
        $(document).ready(function(){

            var nurseryRhymeTemplate = Handlebars.compile(
                $('#nurseryRhymeTemplate').html());

            var $nurseryRhyme = $('#nurseryRhyme');

            $('#btnNurseryRhyme').on('click', function(evt){
                evt.preventDefault();
                $nurseryRhyme.html(nurseryRhymeTemplate({
                    animal: 'basilisk',
                    bodyPart: 'tail',
                    adjective: 'sharp',
                    noun: 'a needle'
                }));
            });

            $('#btnNurseryRhymeAjax').on('click', function(evt){
                evt.preventDefault();
                $.ajax('/data/nursery-rhyme', {
                    success: function(data){
                        $nurseryRhyme.html(
                            nurseryRhymeTemplate(data))
                    }
                });
            });

        });
    </script>
{{/section}}
```

And route handlers for our nursery rhyme page and our AJAX call:

```
app.get('/nursery-rhyme', function(req, res){
    res.render('nursery-rhyme');
});
app.get('/data/nursery-rhyme', function(req, res){
    res.json({
        animal: 'squirrel',
        bodyPart: 'tail',
```

```
                adjective: 'bushy',
                noun: 'heck',
            });
        });
```

Essentially, `Handlebars.compile` takes in a template, and returns a function. That function accepts a context object and returns a rendered string. So once we've compiled our templates, we have reusable template renderers that we just call like functions.

## Conclusion

We've seen how templating can make your code easier to write, read, and maintain. Thanks to templates, we don't have to painfully cobble together HTML from JavaScript strings: we can write HTML in our favorite editor and use a compact and easy-to-read templating language to make it dynamic.

# CHAPTER 8

# Form Handling

The usual way you collect information from your users is to use HTML *forms*. Whether you let the browser submit the form normally, use AJAX, or employ fancy frontend controls, the underlying mechanism is generally still an HTML form. In this chapter, we'll discuss the different methods for handling forms, form validation, and file uploads.

## Sending Client Data to the Server

Broadly speaking, your two options for sending client data to the server are the querystring and the request body. Normally, if you're using the querystring, you're making a GET request, and if you're using the request body, you're using a POST request (the HTTP protocol doesn't prevent you from doing it the other way around, but there's no point to it: best to stick to standard practice here).

It is a common misperception that POST is secure and GET is not: in reality, both are secure if you use HTTPS, and neither is secure if you don't. If you're not using HTTPS, an intruder can look at the body data for a POST just as easily as the querystring of a GET request. However, if you're using GET requests, your users will see all of their input (including hidden fields) in the querystring, which is ugly and messy. Also, browsers often place limits on querystring length (there is no such restriction for body length). For these reasons, I generally recommend using POST for form submission.

## HTML Forms

This book is focusing on the server side, but it's important to understand some basics about constructing HTML forms. Here's a simple example:

```
<form action="/process" method="POST">
    <input type="hidden" name="hush" val="hidden, but not secret!">
    <div>
        <label for="fieldColor">Your favorite color: </label>
```

```
            <input type="text" id="fieldColor" name="color">
        </div>
        <div>
            <button type="submit">Submit</button>
        </div>
    </form>
```

Notice the method is specified explicitly as POST in the <form> tag; if you don't do this, it defaults to GET. The action attribute specifies the URL that will receive the form when it's posted. If you omit this field, the form will be submitted to the same URL the form was loaded from. I recommend that you always provide a valid action, even if you're using AJAX (this is to prevent you from losing data; see Chapter 22 for more information).

From the server's perspective, the important attribute in the <input> fields are the name attributes: that's how the server identifies the field. It's important to understand that the name attribute is distinct from the id attribute, which should be used for styling and frontend functionality only (it is not passed to the server).

Note the hidden field: this will not render in the user's browser. However, you should not use it for secret or sensitive information: all the user has to do is examine the page source, and the hidden field will be exposed.

HTML does not restrict you from having multiple forms on the same page (this was an unfortunate restriction of some early server frameworks; ASP, I'm looking at you).[1] I recommend keeping your forms logically consistent: a form should contain all the fields you would like submitted (optional/empty fields are okay), and none that you don't. If you have two different actions on a page, use two different forms. An example of this would be to have a form for a site search and a separate form for signing up for an email newsletter. It is possible to use one large form and figure out what action to take based on what button a person clicked, but it is a headache, and often not friendly for people with disabilities (because of the way accessibility browsers render forms).

When the user submits the form, the */process* URL will be invoked, and the field values will be transmitted to the server in the request body.

# Encoding

When the form is submitted (either by the browser or via AJAX), it must be encoded somehow. If you don't explicitly specify an encoding, it defaults to application/x-www-form-urlencoded (this is just a lengthy media type for "URL encoded"). This is a basic, easy-to-use encoding that's supported by Express out of the box.

---

1. Very old browsers can sometimes have issues with multiple forms, so if you're aiming for maximum compatability, you might want to consider using only one form per page.

If you need to upload files, things get more complicated. There's no easy way to send files using URL encoding, so you're forced to use the `multipart/form-data` encoding type, which is and is not handled directly by Express (actually, Express still supports this encoding, but it will be removed in the next version of Express, and its use is not recommended: we will be discussing an alternative shortly).

# Different Approaches to Form Handling

If you're not using AJAX, your only option is to submit the form through the browser, which will reload the page. However, how the page is reloaded is up to you. There are two things to consider when processing forms: what path handles the form (the action), and what response is sent to the browser.

If your form uses `method="POST"` (which is recommended), it is quite common to use the same path for displaying the form and processing the form: these can be distinguished because the former is a GET request, and the latter is a POST request. If you take this approach, you can omit the `action` attribute on the form.

The other option is to use a separate path to process the form. For example, if your contact page uses the path */contact*, you might use the path */process-contact* to process the form (by specifying `action="/process-contact"`). If you use this approach, you have the option of submitting the form via GET (which I do not recommend; it needlessly exposes your form fields on the URL). This approach might be preferred if you have multiple URLs that use the same submission mechanism (for example, you might have an email sign-up box on multiple pages on the site).

Whatever path you use to process the form, you have to decide what response to send back to the browser. Here are your options:

*Direct HTML response*
> After processing the form, you can send HTML directly back to the browser (a view, for example). This approach will produce a warning if the user attempts to reload the page and can interfere with bookmarking and the Back button, and for these reasons, it is not recommended.

*302 redirect*
> While this is a common approach, it is a misuse of the original meaning of the 302 (Found) response code. HTTP 1.1 added the 303 (See Other) response code, which is preferable. Unless you have reason to target browsers made before 1996, you should use 303 instead.

*303 redirect*
> The 303 (See Other) response code was added in HTTP 1.1 to address the misuse of the 302 redirect. The HTTP specification specifically indicates that the browser should use a GET request when following a 303 redirect, regardless of the original

method. This is the recommended method for responding to a form submission request.

Since the recommendation is that you respond to a form submission with a 303 redirect, the next question is "Where does the redirection point to?" The answer to that is up to you. Here are the most common approaches:

*Redirect to dedicated success/failure pages*

This method requires that you dedicate URLs for appropriate success or failure messages. For example, if the user signs up for promotional emails, but there was a database error, you might want to redirect to */error/database*. If a user's email address were invalid, you could redirect to */error/invalid-email*, and if everything was successful, you could redirect to */promo-email/thank-you*. One of the advantages of this method is that it's very analytics friendly: the number of visits to your */promo-email/thank-you* page should roughly correlate to the number of people signing up for your promotional email. It is also very straightforward to implement. It has some downsides, however. It does mean you have to allocate URLs to every possibility, which means pages to design, write copy for, and maintain. Another disadvantage is that the user experience can be suboptimal: users like to be thanked, but then they have to navigate back to where they were or where they want to go next. This is the approach we'll be using for now: we'll switch to using "flash messages" (not to be confused with Adobe Flash) in Chapter 9.

*Redirect to the original location with a flash message*

For small forms that are scattered throughout your site (like an email sign-up, for example), the best user experience is not to interrupt the user's navigation flow. That is, provide a way to submit an email address without leaving the page. One way to do this, of course, is AJAX, but if you don't want to use AJAX (or you want your fallback mechanism to provide a good user experience), you can redirect back to the page the user was originally on. The easiest way to do this is to use a hidden field in the form that's populated with the current URL. Since you want there to be some feedback that the user's submission was received, you can use flash messages.

*Redirect to a new location with a flash message*

Large forms generally have their own page, and it doesn't make sense to stay on that page once you've submitted the form. In this situation, you have to make an intelligent guess about where the user might want to go next and redirect accordingly. For example, if you're building an admin interface, and you have a form to create a new vacation package, you might reasonably expect your user to want to go to the admin page that lists all vacation packages after submitting the form. However, you should still employ a flash message to give the user feedback about the result of the submission.

If you are using AJAX, I recommend a dedicated URL. It's tempting to start AJAX handlers with a prefix (for example, */ajax/enter*), but I discourage this approach: it's attaching implementation details to a URL. Also, as we'll see shortly, your AJAX handler should handle regular browser submissions as a failsafe.

# Form Handling with Express

If you're using GET for your form handling, your fields will be available on the req.query object. For example, if you have an HTML input field with a name attribute of email, its value will be passed to the handler as req.query.email. There's really not much more that needs to be said about this approach: it's just that simple.

If you're using POST (which I recommend), you'll have to link in middleware to parse the URL-encoded body. First, install the body-parser middleware (npm install -- save body-parser), then link it in:

```
app.use(require('body-parser').urlencoded({ extended: true }));
```

 Ocassionally, you will see the use of express.bodyParser discouraged, and for good reason. However, this issue went away with Express 4.0, and the body-parser middleware is safe and recommended.

Once you've linked in body-parser, you'll find that req.body now becomes available for you, and that's where all of your form fields will be made available. Note that req.body doesn't prevent you from using the querystring. Let's go ahead and add a form to Meadowlark Travel that lets the user sign up for a mailing list. For demonstration's sake, we'll use the querystring, a hidden field, and visible fields in /views/newslet ter.handlebars:

```
<h2>Sign up for our newsletter to receive news and specials!</h2>
<form class="form-horizontal" role="form"
      action="/process?form=newsletter" method="POST">
    <input type="hidden" name="_csrf" value="{{csrf}}">
    <div class="form-group">
        <label for="fieldName" class="col-sm-2 control-label">Name</label>
        <div class="col-sm-4">
            <input type="text" class="form-control"
            id="fieldName" name="name">
        </div>
    </div>
    <div class="form-group">
        <label for="fieldEmail" class="col-sm-2 control-label">Email</label>
        <div class="col-sm-4">
            <input type="email" class="form-control" required
                id="fieldEmail" name="email">
        </div>
    </div>
```

```
    <div class="form-group">
        <div class="col-sm-offset-2 col-sm-4">
            <button type="submit" class="btn btn-default">Register</button>
        </div>
    </div>
</form>
```

Note we are using Twitter Bootstrap styles, as we will be throughout the rest of the book. If you are unfamiliar with Bootstrap, you may want to refer to the Twitter Bootstrap documentation (*http://getbootstrap.com*). Then see Example 8-1.

*Example 8-1. Application file*

```
app.use(require('body-parser').urlencoded({ extended: true }));

app.get('/newsletter', function(req, res){
    // we will learn about CSRF later...for now, we just
    // provide a dummy value
    res.render('newsletter', { csrf: 'CSRF token goes here' });
});

app.post('/process', function(req, res){
    console.log('Form (from querystring): ' + req.query.form);
    console.log('CSRF token (from hidden form field): ' + req.body._csrf);
    console.log('Name (from visible form field): ' + req.body.name);
    console.log('Email (from visible form field): ' + req.body.email);
    res.redirect(303, '/thank-you');
});
```

That's all there is to it. Note that in our handler, we're redirecting to a "thank you" view. We could render a view here, but if we did, the URL field in the visitor's browser would remain */process*, which could be confusing: issuing a redirect solves that problem.

 It's very important that you use a 303 (or 302) redirect, not a 301 redirect in this instance. 301 redirects are "permanent," meaning your browser may cache the redirection destination. If you use a 301 redirect and try to submit the form a second time, your browser may bypass the /process handler altogether and go directly to /thank-you since it correctly believes the redirect to be permanent. The 303 redirect, on the other hand, tells your browser "Yes, your request is valid, and you can find your response here," and does not cache the redirect destination.

# Handling AJAX Forms

Handling AJAX forms is very easy in Express; it's even easy to use the same handler for AJAX and regular browser fallbacks. Consider Examples 8-2 and 8-3.

*Example 8-2. HTML (in /views/newsletter.handlebars)*

```
<div class="formContainer">
    <form class="form-horizontal newsletterForm" role="form"
            action="/process?form=newsletter" method="POST">
        <input type="hidden" name="_csrf" value="{{csrf}}">
        <div class="form-group">
            <label for="fieldName" class="col-sm-2 control-label">Name</label>
            <div class="col-sm-4">
                <input type="text" class="form-control"
                id="fieldName" name="name">
            </div>
        </div>
        <div class="form-group">
            <label for="fieldEmail" class="col-sm-2 control-label">Email</label>
            <div class="col-sm-4">
                <input type="email" class="form-control" required
                    id="fieldEmail" name="email">
            </div>
        </div>
        <div class="form-group">
            <div class="col-sm-offset-2 col-sm-4">
                <button type="submit" class="btn btn-default">Register</button>
            </div>
        </div>
    </form>
</div>
{{#section 'jquery'}}
    <script>
        $(document).ready(function(){
            $('.newsletterForm').on('submit', function(evt){
                evt.preventDefault();
                var action = $(this).attr('action');
                var $container = $(this).closest('.formContainer');
                $.ajax({
                    url: action,
                    type: 'POST',
                    data: $(this).serialize(),
                    success: function(data){
                        if(data.success){
                            $container.html('<h2>Thank you!</h2>');
                        } else {
                            $container.html('There was a problem.');
                        }
                    },
                    error: function(){
                        $container.html('There was a problem.');
                    }
                });
            });
        });
    </script>
{{/section}}
```

*Example 8-3. Application file*

```
app.post('/process', function(req, res){
    if(req.xhr || req.accepts('json,html')==='json'){
        // if there were an error, we would send { error: 'error description' }
        res.send({ success: true });
    } else {
        // if there were an error, we would redirect to an error page
        res.redirect(303, '/thank-you');
    }
});
```

Express provides us with a couple of convenience properties, `req.xhr` and `req.ac cepts`. `req.xhr` will be true if the request is an AJAX request (XHR is short for XML HTTP Request, which is what AJAX relies on). `req.accepts` will try to determine the most appropriate response type to return. In our case, `req.accepts('json,html')` is asking if the best format to return is JSON or HTML: this is inferred from the `Ac cepts` HTTP header, which is an ordered list of acceptable response types provided by the browser. If the request is an AJAX request, or if the user agent has specifically requested that JSON is better than HTML, appropriate JSON will be returned; otherwise, a redirect would be returned.

We can do whatever processing we need in this function: usually we would be saving the data to the database. If there are problems, we send back a JSON object with an `err` property (instead of `success`), or redirect to an error page (if it's not an AJAX request).

In this example, we're assuming all AJAX requests are looking for JSON, but there's no requirement that AJAX must use JSON for communication (as a matter of fact, the "X" in AJAX stands for XML). This approach is very jQuery-friendly, as jQuery routinely assumes everything is going to be in JSON. If you're making your AJAX endpoints generally available, or if you know your AJAX requests might be using something other than JSON, you should return an appropriate response *exclusively* based on the `Accepts` header, which we can conveniently access through the `req.accepts` helper method. If you're responding based only on the `Accepts` header, you might want to also look at c (*http://expressjs.com/api.html#res.format*), which is a handy convenience method that makes it easy to respond appropriately depending on what the client expects. If you do that, you'll have to make sure to set the `dataType` or `accepts` properties when making AJAX requests with jQuery.

# File Uploads

We've already mentioned that file uploads bring a raft of complications. Fortunately, there are some great projects that help make file handling a snap.

Currently, file uploads can be handled with Connect's built-in `multipart` middleware; however, that middleware has already been removed from Connect, and as soon as Express updates its dependency on Connect, it will vanish from Express as well, so I strongly recommend that you do not use that middleware.

There are two popular and robust options for multipart form processing: Busboy and Formidable. I find Formidable to be slightly easier, because it has a convenience callback that provides objects containing the fields and the files, whereas with Busboy, you must listen for each field and file event. We'll be using Formidable for this reason.

 While it is possible to use AJAX for file uploads using XMLHttpRequest Level 2's `FormData` interface (*https://developer.mozilla.org/en-US/docs/Web/API/FormData*), it is supported only on modern browsers and requires some massaging to use with jQuery. We'll be discussing an AJAX alternative later on.

Let's create a file upload form for a Meadowlark Travel vacation photo contest (*views/contest/vacation-photo.handlebars*):

```
<form class="form-horizontal" role="form"
        enctype="multipart/form-data" method="POST"
        action="/contest/vacation-photo/{year}/{month}">
    <div class="form-group">
        <label for="fieldName" class="col-sm-2 control-label">Name</label>
        <div class="col-sm-4">
            <input type="text" class="form-control"
            id="fieldName" name="name">
        </div>
    </div>
    <div class="form-group">
        <label for="fieldEmail" class="col-sm-2 control-label">Email</label>
        <div class="col-sm-4">
            <input type="email" class="form-control" required
                id="fieldEmail" name="email">
        </div>
    </div>
    <div class="form-group">
        <label for="fieldPhoto" class="col-sm-2 control-label">Vacation photo
        </label>
        <div class="col-sm-4">
            <input type="file" class="form-control" required accept="image/*"
                id="fieldPhoto" name="photo">
        </div>
</form>
```

```
        </div>
        <div class="form-group">
            <div class="col-sm-offset-2 col-sm-4">
                <button type="submit" class="btn btn-primary">Submit</button>
            </div>
        </div>
    </form>
```

Note that we must specify enctype="multipart/form-data" to enable file uploads. We're also restricting the type of files that can be uploaded by using the accept attribute (which is optional).

Now install Formidable (npm install --save formidable) and create the following route handlers:

```
var formidable = require('formidable');

app.get('/contest/vacation-photo',function(req,res){
    var now = new Date();
    res.render('contest/vacation-photo',{
        year: now.getFullYear(),month: now.getMonth()
    });
});

app.post('/contest/vacation-photo/:year/:month', function(req, res){
    var form = new formidable.IncomingForm();
    form.parse(req, function(err, fields, files){
        if(err) return res.redirect(303, '/error');
        console.log('received fields:');
        console.log(fields);
        console.log('received files:');
        console.log(files);
        res.redirect(303, '/thank-you');
    });
});
```

(Year and month are being specified as *route parameters*, which you'll learn about in Chapter 14.) Go ahead and run this and examine the console log. You'll see that your form fields come across as you would expect: as an object with properties corresponding to your field names. The files object contains more data, but it's relatively straightforward. For each file uploaded, you'll see there are properties for size, the path it was uploaded to (usually a random name in a temporary directory), and the original name of the file that the user uploaded (just the filename, not the whole path, for security and privacy reasons).

What you do with this file is now up to you: you can store it in a database, copy it to a more permanent location, or upload it to a cloud-based file storage system. Remember that if you're relying on local storage for saving files, your application won't scale well, making this a poor choice for cloud-based hosting. We will be revisiting this example in Chapter 13.

# jQuery File Upload

If you want to offer really fancy file uploads to your users—with the ability to drag and drop, see thumbnails of the uploaded files, and see progress bars—then I recommend Sebastian Tschan's jQuery File Upload (*http://blueimp.github.io/jQuery-File-Upload*).

Setting up jQuery File Upload is not a walk in the park. Fortunately, there's an npm package to help you with the server-side intricacies. The frontend scripting is another matter. The jQuery File Upload package uses jQuery UI and Bootstrap, and looks pretty good out of the box. If you want to customize it, though, there's a lot to work through.

To display file thumbnails, `jquery-file-upload-middleware` uses *ImageMagick* (*http://www.imagemagick.org*), a venerable image manipulation library. This does mean your app has a dependency on ImageMagick, which could cause problems depending on your hosting situation. On Ubuntu and Debian systems, you can install ImageMagick with `apt-get install imagemagick`, and on OS X, you can use `brew install imagemagick`. For other operating systems, consult the ImageMagick documentation (*http://www.imagemagick.org/script/binary-releases.php*).

Let's start with the server-side setup. First, install the `jquery-file-upload-middleware` package (`npm install --save jquery-file-upload-middleware`), then add the following to your app file:

```
var jqupload = require('jquery-file-upload-middleware');

app.use('/upload', function(req, res, next){
    var now = Date.now();
    jqupload.fileHandler({
        uploadDir: function(){
            return __dirname + '/public/uploads/' + now;
        },
        uploadUrl: function(){
            return '/uploads/' + now;
        },
    })(req, res, next);
});
```

If you look at the documentation, you'll see something similar under "more sophisticated examples." Unless you are implementing a file upload area that's quite literally shared by all of your visitors, you'll probably want to be able to partition off the file uploads. The example simply creates a timestamped directory to store the file uploads. A more realistic example would be to create a subdirectory that uses the user's ID or some other unique ID. For example, if you were implementing a chat program that supports shared files, you might want to use the ID of the chat room.

Note that we are mounting the jQuery File Upload middleware on the */upload* prefix. You can use whatever you want here, but make sure you don't use that prefix for other routes or middleware, as it will interfere with the operation of your file uploads.

To hook up your views to the file uploader, you can replicate the demo uploader: you can upload the latest bundle on the project's GitHub page (*https://github.com/blueimp/jQuery-File-Upload/releases*). It will inevitably include a lot of things you don't need, like PHP scripts and other implementation examples, which you are free to delete. Most of the files, you'll put in your *public* directory (so they can be served statically), but the HTML files you'll have to copy over to views.

If you just want a minimal example that you can build on, you'll need the following scripts from the bundle: *js/vendor/jquery.ui.widget.js, js/jquery.iframe-transport.js*, and *js/jquery.fileupload.js*. You'll also need jQuery, obviously. I generally prefer to put all of these scripts in *public/vendor/jqfu* for neatness. In this minimal implementation, we wrap the `<input type="file">` element in a `<span>`, and add a `<div>` in which we will list the names of uploaded files:

```
<span class="btn btn-default btn-file">
    Upload
    <input type="file" class="form-control" required accept="image/*"
        id="fieldPhoto" data-url="/upload" multiple name="photo">
</span>
<div id="uploads"></div>
```

Then we attach jQuery File Upload:

```
{{#section 'jquery'}}
    <script src="/vendor/jqfu/js/vendor/jquery.ui.widget.js"></script>
    <script src="/vendor/jqfu/js/jquery.iframe-transport.js"></script>
    <script src="/vendor/jqfu/js/jquery.fileupload.js"></script>
    <script>
        $(document).ready(function(){

            $('#fieldPhoto').fileupload({
                dataType: 'json',
                done: function(e, data){
                    $.each(data.result.files, function(index, file){
                        $('#fileUploads').append($('<div class="upload">' +
                            '<span class="glyphicon glyphicon-ok"></span>' +
                            ' ' + file.originalName + '</div>'));
                    });
                }
            });

        });
    </script>
{{/section}}
```

We have to do some CSS gymnastics to style the upload button:

```
.btn-file {
    position: relative;
    overflow: hidden;
}
```

```
.btn-file input[type=file] {
    position: absolute;
    top: 0;
    right: 0;
    min-width: 100%;
    min-height: 100%;
    font-size: 999px;
    text-align: right;
    filter: alpha(opacity=0);
    opacity: 0;
    outline: none;
    background: white;
    cursor: inherit;
    display: block;
}
```

Note that the `data-url` attribute of the `<input>` tag must match the route prefix you used for the middleware. In this simple example, when a file upload successfully completes, a `<div class="upload">` element is appended to `<div id="uploads">`. This lists only filename and size, and does not offer controls for deletion, progress, or thumbnails. But it's a good place to start. Customizing the jQuery File Upload demo can be daunting, and if your vision is significantly different, it might be easier to start from the minimum and build your way up instead of starting with the demo and customizing. Either way, you will find the resources you need on the jQuery File Upload documentation page (*https://github.com/blueimp/jQuery-File-Upload/wiki*).

For simplicity, the Meadowlark Travel example will not continue to use jQuery File Upload, but if you wish to see this approach in action, refer to the `jquery-file-upload-example` branch in the repository.

# CHAPTER 9

# Cookies and Sessions

HTTP is a *stateless* protocol. That means that when you load a page in your browser, and then you navigate to another page on the same website, neither the server nor the browser has any intrinsic way of knowing that it's the same browser visiting the same site. Another way of saying this is that the way the Web works is that *every HTTP request contains all the information necessary for the server to satisfy the request.*

This is a problem, though: if the story ended there, we could never "log in" to anything. Streaming media wouldn't work. Websites wouldn't be able to remember your preferences from one page to the next. So there needs be a way to build state on top of HTTP, and that's where cookies and sessions enter the picture.

Cookies, unfortunately, have gotten a bad name thanks to the nefarious things that people have done with them. This is unfortunate because cookies are really quite essential to the functioning of the "modern web" (although HTML5 has introduced some new features, like local storage, that could be used for the same purpose).

The idea of a cookie is simple: the server sends a bit of information, and the browser stores it for some configurable period of time. It's really up to the server what the particular bit of information is: often it's just a unique ID number that identifies a specific browser so that the illusion of state can be maintained.

There are some important things you need to know about cookies:

*Cookies are not secret from the user*
All cookies that the server sends to the client are available for the client to look at. There's no reason you can't send something encrypted to protect its contents, but there's seldom any need for this (at least if you're not doing anything nefarious!). *Signed* cookies, which we'll discuss in a bit, can obfuscate the contents of the cookie, but this is in no way cryptographically secure from prying eyes.

*The user can delete or disallow cookies*

Users have full control over cookies, and browsers make it possible to delete cookies in bulk or individually. Unless you're up to no good, there's no real reason for users to do this, but it is useful during testing. Users can also disallow cookies, which is more problematic: only the simplest web applications can make do without cookies.

*Regular cookies can be tampered with*

Whenever a browser makes a request of your server that has an associated cookie, and you blindly trust the contents of that cookie, you are opening yourself up for attack. The height of foolishness, for example, would be to execute code contained in a cookie. To ensure cookies aren't tampered with, use signed cookies.

*Cookies can be used for attacks*

A category of attacks called cross-site scripting attacks (XSS) has sprung up in recent years. One technique of XSS attacks involves malicious JavaScript modifying the contents of cookies. This is additional reason not to trust the contents of cookies that come back to your server. Using signed cookies helps (tampering will be evident in a signed cookie whether the user or malicious JavaScript modified it), and there's also a setting that specifies that cookies are to be modified only by the server. These cookies can be limited in usefulness, but they are certainly safer.

*Users will notice if you abuse cookies*

If you set a lot of cookies on your users' computers, or store a lot of data, it will irritate your users, something you should avoid. Try to keep your use of cookies to a minimum.

*Prefer sessions over cookies*

For the most part, you can use *sessions* to maintain state, and it's generally wise to do so. It's easier, you don't have to worry about abusing your users' storage, and it can be more secure. Sessions rely on cookies, of course, but with sessions, Express will be doing the heavy lifting for you.

 Cookies are not magic: when the server wishes the client to store a cookie, it sends a header called Set-Cookie containing name/value pairs, and when a client sends a request to a server for which it has cookies, it sends multiple Cookie request headers containing the value of the cookies.

# Externalizing Credentials

To make cookies secure, a *cookie secret* is necessary. The cookie secret is a string that's known to the server and used to encrypt secure cookies before they're sent to the client. It's not a password that has to be remembered, so it can just be a random string. I usually use a random password generator inspired by xkcd (*http://bit.ly/xkcd_pw_generator*) to generate the cookie secret.

It's a common practice to externalize third-party credentials, such as the cookie secret, database passwords, and API tokens (Twitter, Facebook, etc.). Not only does this ease maintenance (by making it easy to locate and update credentials), it also allows you to omit the credentials file from your version control system. This is especially critical for open source repositories hosted on GitHub or other public source control repositories.

To that end, we're going to externalize our credentials in a JavaScript file (it's also fine to use JSON or XML, though I find JavaScript to be the easiest appraoch). Create a file called *credentials.js*:

```
module.exports = {
    cookieSecret: 'your cookie secret goes here',
};
```

Now, to make sure we don't accidentally add this file to our repository, add *credentials.js* to your *.gitignore* file. To import your credentials into your application, all you need to do is:

```
var credentials = require('./credentials.js');
```

We'll be using this same file to store other credentials later on, but for now, all we need is our cookie secret.

 If you're following along by using the companion repository, you'll have to create your own *credentials.js* file, as it is not included in the repository.

## Cookies in Express

Before you start setting and accessing cookies in your app, you need to include the `cookie-parser` middleware. First, `npm install --save cookie-parser`, then:

```
app.use(require('cookie-parser')(credentials.cookieSecret));
```

Once you've done this, you can set a cookie or a signed cookie anywhere you have access to a response object:

```
res.cookie('monster', 'nom nom');
res.cookie('signed_monster', 'nom nom', { signed: true });
```

Signed cookies take precedence over unsigned cookies. If you name your signed cookie signed_monster, you cannot have an unsigned cookie with the same name (it will come back as undefined).

To retrieve the value of a cookie (if any) sent from the client, just access the cookie or signedCookie properties of the request object:

```
var monster = req.cookies.monster;
var signedMonster = req.signedCookies.signed_monster;
```

 You can use any string you want for a cookie name. For example, we could have used 'signed monster' instead of 'signed_monster', but then we would have to use the bracket notation to retrieve the cookie: req.signedCookies['signed monster']. For this reason, I recommend using cookie names without special characters.

To delete a cookie, use req.clearCookie:

```
res.clearCookie('monster');
```

When you set a cookie, you can specify the following options:

domain
Controls the domains the cookie is associated with; this allows you to assign cookies to specific subdomains. Note that you cannot set a cookie for a different domain than the server is running on: it will simply do nothing.

path
Controls the path this cookie applies to. Note that paths have an implicit wildcard after them: if you use a path of / (the default), it will apply to all pages on your site. If you use a path of /foo, it will apply to the paths /foo, /foo/bar, etc.

maxAge
Specifies how long the client should keep the cookie before deleting it, in milliseconds. If you omit this, the cookie will be deleted when you close your browser. (You can also specify a date for expiration with the expires option, but the syntax is frustrating. I recommend using maxAge.)

secure
Specifies that this cookie will be sent only over a secure (HTTPS) connection.

httpOnly
Setting this to true specifies the cookie will be modified only by the server. That is, client-side JavaScript cannot modify it. This helps prevent XSS attacks.

`signed`

> Set to true to sign this cookie, making it available in `res.signedCookies` instead of `res.cookies`. Signed cookies that have been tampered with will be rejected by the server, and the cookie value will be reset to its original value.

# Examining Cookies

As part of your testing, you'll probably want a way to examine the cookies on your system. Most browsers have a way to view individual cookies and the values they store. In Chrome, open the developer tools, and select the Resources tab. In the tree on the left, you'll see Cookies. Expand that, and you'll see the site you're currently visiting listed. Click that, and you will see all the cookies associated with this site. You can also right-click the domain to clear all cookies, or right-click an individual cookie to remove it specifically.

# Sessions

Sessions are really just a more convenient way to maintain state. To implement sessions, *something* has to be stored on the client; otherwise, the server wouldn't be able to identify the client from one request to the next. The usual method of doing this is a cookie that contains a unique identifier. The server then uses that identifier to retrieve the appropriate session information. Cookies aren't the only way to accomplish this: during the height of the "cookie scare" (when cookie abuse was rampant), many users were simply turning off cookies, and other ways to maintain state were devised, such as decorating URLs with session information. These techniques were messy, difficult, and inefficient, and best left in the past. HTML5 provides another option for sessions, called local storage, but there's currently no compelling reason to use this technique over tried and true cookies.

Broadly speaking, there are two ways to implement sessions: store everything in the cookie, or store only a unique identifier in the cookie and everything else on the server. The former are called "cookie-based sessions," and merely represent a convenience over using cookies. However, it still means that everything you add to the session will be stored on the client's browser, which is an approach I don't recommend. I would recommend this approach only if you know that you will be storing just a small amount of information, that you don't mind the user having access to the information, and that it won't be growing out of control over time. If you want to take this approach, see the `cookie-session` middleware (*https://www.npmjs.org/package/cookie-session*).

## Memory Stores

If you would rather store session information on the server, which I recommend, you have to have somewhere to store it. The entry-level option is memory sessions. They are very easy to set up, but they have a huge downside: when you restart the server (which you will be doing a lot of over the course of this book!), your session information disappears. Even worse, if you scale out by having multiple servers (see Chapter 12), a different server could service a request every time: session data would sometimes be there, and sometimes not. This is clearly an unacceptable user experience. However, for our development and testing needs, it will suffice. We'll see how to permanently store session information in Chapter 13.

First, install express-session (npm install --save express-session); then, after linking in the cookie parser, link in express-session:

```
app.use(require('cookie-parser')(credentials.cookieSecret));
app.use(require('express-session')({
    resave: false,
    saveUninitialized: false,
    secret: credentials.cookieSecret,
}));
```

The express-session middleware accepts a configuration object with the following options:

resave

Forces the session to be saved back to the store even if the request wasn't modified. Setting this to false is generally preferable; see the express-session documentation for more information.

saveUninitialized

Setting this to true causes new (uninitialized) sessions to be saved to the store, even if they haven't been modified. Setting this to false is generally preferable, and is required when you need to get the user's permission before setting a cookie. See the express-session documentation for more information.

secret

The key (or keys) used to sign the session ID cookie. Can be the same key used for cookie-parser.

key

The name of the cookie that will store the unique session identifier. Defaults to connect.sid.

store

An instance of a session store. Defaults to an instance of MemoryStore, which is fine for our current purposes. We'll see how to use a database store in Chapter 13.

cookie

Cookie settings for the session cookie (path, domain, secure, etc.). Regular cookie defaults apply.

## Using Sessions

Once you've set up sessions, using them couldn't be simpler: just use properties of the request object's `session` variable:

```
req.session.userName = 'Anonymous';
var colorScheme = req.session.colorScheme || 'dark';
```

Note that with sessions, we don't have to use the request object for retrieving the value and the response object for setting the value: it's all performed on the request object. (The response object does not have a `session` property.) To delete a session, you can use JavaScript's `delete` operator:

```
req.session.userName = null;          // this sets 'userName' to null,
                                      // but doesn't remove it

delete req.session.colorScheme;       // this removes 'colorScheme'
```

# Using Sessions to Implement Flash Messages

"Flash" messages (not to be confused with Adobe Flash) are simply a way to provide feedback to users in a way that's not disruptive to their navigation. The easiest way to implement flash messages is to use sessions (you can also use the querystring, but in addition to those having uglier URLs, the flash messages will be included in a bookmark, which is probably not what you want). Let's set up our HTML first. We'll be using Bootstrap's alert messages to display our flash messages, so make sure you have Bootstrap linked in. In your template file, somewhere prominent (usually directly below your site's header), add the following:

```
{{#if flash}}
    <div class="alert alert-dismissible alert-{{flash.type}}">
        <button type="button" class="close"
            data-dismiss="alert" aria-hidden="true">&times;<button>
        <strong>{{flash.intro}}</strong> {{{flash.message}}}
    </div>
{{/if}}
```

Note that we use three curly brackets for `flash.message`: this will allow us to provide some simple HTML in our messages (we might want to emphasize words or include hyperlinks). Now let's add some middleware to add the `flash` object to the context if there's one in the session. Once we've displayed a flash message once, we want to remove it from the session so it isn't displayed on the next request. Add this code before your routes:

```
app.use(function(req, res, next){
        // if there's a flash message, transfer
        // it to the context, then clear it
        res.locals.flash = req.session.flash;
        delete req.session.flash;
```

```
            next();
    });
```

Now let's see how to actually use the flash message. Imagine we're signing up users for a newsletter, and we want to redirect them to the newsletter archive after they sign up. This is what our form handler might look like:

```
// slightly modified version of the official W3C HTML5 email regex:
// https://html.spec.whatwg.org/multipage/forms.html#valid-e-mail-address
var VALID_EMAIL_REGEX = new RegExp('^[a-zA-Z0-9.!#$%&\'*+\/=?^_`{|}~-]+@' +
    '[a-zA-Z0-9](?:[a-zA-Z0-9-]{0,61}[a-zA-Z0-9])?' +
    '(?:\.[a-zA-Z0-9](?:[a-zA-Z0-9-]{0,61}[a-zA-Z0-9])?)+$');

app.post('/newsletter', function(req, res){
    var name = req.body.name || '', email = req.body.email || '';
    // input validation
    if(!email.match(VALID_EMAIL_REGEX)) {
        if(req.xhr) return res.json({ error: 'Invalid name email address.' });
        req.session.flash = {
            type: 'danger',
            intro: 'Validation error!',
            message: 'The email address you entered was  not valid.',
        };
        return res.redirect(303, '/newsletter/archive');
    }
    // NewsletterSignup is an example of an object you might create;
    // since every implementation will vary, it is up to you to write these
    // project-specific interfaces.  This simply shows how a typical Express
    // implementation might look in your project.
    new NewsletterSignup({ name: name, email: email }).save(function(err){
        if(err) {
            if(req.xhr) return res.json({ error: 'Database error.' });
            req.session.flash = {
                type: 'danger',
                intro: 'Database error!',
                message: 'There was a database error; please try again later.',
            }
            return res.redirect(303, '/newsletter/archive');
        }
        if(req.xhr) return res.json({ success: true });
        req.session.flash = {
            type: 'success',
            intro: 'Thank you!',
            message: 'You have now been signed up for the newsletter.',
        };
        return res.redirect(303, '/newsletter/archive');
    });
});
```

Note how the same handler can be used for AJAX submissions (because we check req.xhr), and that we're careful to distinguish between input validation and database errors. Remember that even if we do input validation on the frontend (and you should), you should also perform it on the backend, because malicious users can circumvent frontend validation.

Flash messages are a great mechanism to have available in your website, even if other methods are more appropriate in certain areas (for example, flash messages aren't always appropriate for multiform "wizards" or shopping cart checkout flows). Flash messages are also great during development, because they are an easy way to provide feedback, even if you replace them with a different technique later. Adding support for flash messages is one of the first things I do when setting up a website, and we'll be using this technique throughout the rest of the book.

 Because the flash message is being transferred from the session to res.locals.flash in middleware, you have to perform a redirect for the flash message to be displayed. If you want to display a flash message without redirecting, set res.locals.flash instead of req.session.flash.

# What to Use Sessions For

Sessions are useful whenever you want to save a user preference that applies across pages. Most commonly, sessions are used to provide user authentication information: you log in, and a session is created. After that, you don't have to log in again every time you re-load the page. Sessions can be useful even without user accounts, though. It's quite common for sites to remember how you like things sorted, or what date format you prefer—all without your having to log in.

While I encourage you to prefer sessions over cookies, it's important to understand how cookies work (especially because they enable sessions to work). It will help you with diagnosing issues and understanding the security and privacy considerations of your application.

# CHAPTER 10

# Middleware

By now, we've already had some exposure to middleware: we've used existing middleware (body-parser, cookie-parser, static, and connect-session, to name a few), and we've even written some of our own (when we check for the presence of &test=1 in the querystring, and our 404 handler). But what is middleware, exactly?

Conceptually, middleware is a way to encapsulate functionality: specifically, functionality that operates on an HTTP request to your application. Practically, a middleware is simply a function that takes three arguments: a request object, a response object, and a "next" function, which will be explained shortly. (There is also a form that takes four arguments, for error handling, which will be covered at the end of this chapter.)

Middleware is executed in what's known as a *pipeline*. You can imagine a physical pipe, carrying water. The water gets pumped in at one end, and then there are gauges and valves before the water gets where it's going. The important part about this analogy is that *order matters*: if you put a pressure gauge before a valve, it has a different effect than if you put the pressure gauge after the valve. Similarly, if you have a valve that injects something into the water, everything "downstream" from that valve will contain the added ingredient. In an Express app, you insert middleware into the pipeline by calling app.use.

Prior to Express 4.0, the pipeline was complicated by your having to link the *router* in explicitly. Depending on where you linked in the router, routes could be linked in out of order, making the pipeline sequence less clear when you mixed middleware and route handlers. In Express 4.0, middleware and route handlers are invoked in the order in which they were linked in, making it much clearer what the sequence is.

It's common practice to have the very last middleware in your pipeline be a "catch all" handler for any request that doesn't match any other routes. This middleware usually returns a status code of 404 (Not Found).

So how is a request "terminated" in the pipeline? That's what the next function passed to each middleware does: if you don't call next(), the request terminates with that middleware.

Learning how to think flexibly about middleware and route handlers is key to understanding how Express works. Here are the things you should keep in mind:

- Route handlers (app.get, app.post, etc.—often referred to collectively as app.VERB) can be thought of as middleware that handle only a specific HTTP verb (GET, POST, etc.). Conversely, middleware can be thought of as a route handler that handles all HTTP verbs (this is essentially equivalent to app.all, which handles any HTTP verb; there are some minor differences with exotic verbs such as PURGE, but for the common verbs, the effect is the same).

- Route handlers require a path as their first parameter. If you want that path to match any route, simply use /*. Middleware can also take a path as its first parameter, but it is optional (if it is omitted, it will match any path, as if you had specified /\*).

- Route handlers and middleware take a callback function that takes two, three, or four parameters (technically, you could also have zero or one parameters, but there is no sensible use for these forms). If there are two or three parameters, the first two parameters are the request and response objects, and the third paramater is the next function. If there are four parameters, it becomes an *error-handling* middleware, and the first parameter becomes an error object, followed by the request, response, and next objects.

- If you don't call next(), the pipeline will be terminated, and no more route handlers or middleware will be processed. If you don't call next(), you should send a response to the client (res.send, res.json, res.render, etc.); if you don't, the client will hang and eventually time out.

- If you do call next(), it's generally inadvisable to send a response to the client. If you do, middleware or route handlers further down the pipeline will be executed, but any client responses they send will be ignored.

If you want to see this in action, let's try some really simple middlewares:

```
app.use(function(req, res, next){
        console.log('processing request for "' + req.url + '"....');
        next();
});

app.use(function(req, res, next){
        console.log('terminating request');
        res.send('thanks for playing!');
        // note that we do NOT call next() here...this terminates the request
});

app.use(function(req, res, next){
        console.log('whoops, i\'ll never get called!');
});
```

Here we have three middlewares. The first one simply logs a message to the console before passing on the request to the next middleware in the pipeline by calling next(). Then the next middleware actually handles the request. Note that if we omitted the res.send here, no response would ever be returned to the client. Eventually the client would time out. The last middleware will never execute, because all requests are terminated in the prior middleware.

Now let's consider a more complicated, complete example (file *route-example.js* in the companion repository):

```
var app = require('express')();

app.use(function(req, res, next){
        console.log('\n\nALLWAYS');
        next();
});

app.get('/a', function(req, res){
        console.log('/a: route terminated');
        res.send('a');
});
app.get('/a', function(req, res){
        console.log('/a: never called');
});
app.get('/b', function(req, res, next){
        console.log('/b: route not terminated');
        next();
});
app.use(function(req, res, next){
        console.log('SOMETIMES');
        next();
});
app.get('/b', function(req, res, next){
        console.log('/b (part 2): error thrown' );
        throw new Error('b failed');
```

```
    });
    app.use('/b', function(err, req, res, next){
            console.log('/b error detected and passed on');
            next(err);
    });
    app.get('/c', function(err, req){
            console.log('/c: error thrown');
            throw new Error('c failed');
    });
    app.use('/c', function(err, req, res, next){
            console.log('/c: error detected but not passed on');
            next();
    });

    app.use(function(err, req, res, next){
            console.log('unhandled error detected: ' + err.message);
            res.send('500 - server error');
    });

    app.use(function(req, res){
            console.log('route not handled');
            res.send('404 - not found');
    });

    app.listen(3000, function(){
            console.log('listening on 3000');
    });
```

Before trying this example, try to imagine what the result will be. What are the different routes? What will the client see? What will be printed on the console? If you can correctly answer all of those questions, then you've got the hang of routes in Express! Pay particular attention to the difference between a request to /b and a request to /c; in both instances, there was an error, but one results in a 404 and the other results in a 500.

Note that middleware *must* be a function. Keep in mind that in JavaScript, it's quite easy (and common) to return a function from a function. For example, you'll note that express.static is a function, but we actually invoke it, so it must return another function. Consider:

```
app.use(express.static);        // this will NOT work as expected
console.log(express.static());  // will log "function", indicating
                                // that express.static is a function
                                // that itself returns a function
```

Note also that a module can export a function, which can in turn be used directly as middleware. For example, here's a module called *lib/tourRequiresWaiver.js* (Meadowlark Travel's rock climbing packages require a liability waiver):

```
module.exports = function(req,res,next){
        var cart = req.session.cart;
        if(!cart) return next();
        if(cart.some(function(item){ return item.product.requiresWaiver; })){
```

```
            if(!cart.warnings) cart.warnings = [];
            cart.warnings.push('One or more of your selected tours' +
                    'requires a waiver.');
        }
        next();
    }
```

We could link this middleware in like so:

```
app.use(require('./lib/requiresWaiver.js'));
```

More commonly, though, you would export an object that contains properties that are middleware. For example, let's put all of our shopping cart validation code in *lib/cartValidation.js*:

```
module.exports = {
        checkWaivers: function(req, res, next){
                var cart = req.session.cart;
                if(!cart) return next();
                if(cart.some(function(i){ return i.product.requiresWaiver; })){
                        if(!cart.warnings) cart.warnings = [];
                        cart.warnings.push('One or more of your selected ' +
                                'tours requires a waiver.');
                }
                next();
        },

        checkGuestCounts: function(req, res, next){
                var cart = req.session.cart;
                if(!cart) return next();
                if(cart.some(function(item){ return item.guests >
                                item.product.maximumGuests; })){
                        if(!cart.errors) cart.errors = [];
                        cart.errors.push('One or more of your selected tours ' +
                                'cannot accommodate the number of guests you ' +
                                'have selected.');
                }
                next();
        }
}
```

Then you could link the middleware in like this:

```
var cartValidation = require('./lib/cartValidation.js');

app.use(cartValidation.checkWaivers);
app.use(cartValidation.checkGuestCounts);
```

 In the previous example, we have a middleware aborting early with the statement return next(). Express doesn't expect middleware to return a value (and it doesn't do anything with any return values), so this is just a shortened way of writing next(); return;.

# Common Middleware

Prior to Express 4.0, Express bundled Connect, which is the component that contains most of the most common middleware. Because of the way Express bundled it, it appeared as if the middleware was actually part of Express (for example, you would link in the body parser like so: `app.use(express.bodyParser)`). This osbscured the fact that this middleware was actually part of Connect. With Express 4.0, Connect was removed from Express. Along with this change, some Connect middleware (`body-parser` is an example) has itself moved out of Connect into its own project. The only middleware Express retains is `static`. Removing middleware from Express frees Express from having to manage so many dependencies, and allows the individual projects to progress and mature independent of Express.

Much of the middleware previously bundled with Express is quite fundamental, so it's important to know "where it went" and how to get it. You will almost always want Connect, so it's recommended that you always install it alongside Express (`npm install --save connect`), and have it available in your application (`var connect = require(connect);`).

`basicAuth` *(app.use(connect.basicAuth)();)*

> Provides basic access authorization. Keep in mind that basic auth offers only the most basic security, and you should use basic auth *only* over HTTPS (otherwise, usernames and passwords are transmitted in the clear). You should use basic auth only when you need something very quick and easy *and* you're using HTTPS.

`body-parser` *(npm install --save body-parser, app.use(require(body-parser).urlencoded({ extended: true }));)*

> Convenience middleware that simply links in `json` and `urlencoded`. This middleware is also still available in Connect, but will be removed in 3.0, so it's recommended that you start using this package instead. Unless you have a specific reason to use `json` or `urlencoded` individually, I recommend using this package.

`json` *(see body-parser)*

> Parses JSON-encoded request bodies. You'll need this middleware if you're writing an API that's expecting a JSON-encoded body. This is not currently very common (most APIs still use `application/x-www-form-urlencoded`, which can be parsed by the `urlencoded` middleware), but it does make your application robust and future-proof.

`urlencoded` *(see body-parser)*

> Parses request bodies with Internet media type `application/x-www-form-urlencoded`. This is the most common way to handle forms and AJAX requests.

`multipart` *(DEPRECATED)*

Parses request bodies with Internet media type `multipart/form-data`. This middleware is deprecated and will be removed in Connect 3.0. You should be using Busboy or Formidable instead (see Chapter 8).

`compress (app.use(connect.compress);)`

Compresses response data with gzip. This is a good thing, and your users will thank you, especially those on slow or mobile connections. It should be linked in early, before any middleware that might send a response. The only thing that I recommend linking in before `compress` is debugging or logging middleware (which do not send responses).

`cookie-parser (npm install --save cookie-parser, app.use(require(cookie-parser)(your secret goes here);`

Provides cookie support. See Chapter 9.

`cookie-session (npm install --save cookie-session, app.use(require(cookie-session)());)`

Provides cookie-storage session support. I do not generally recommend this approach to sessions. Must be linked in after `cookie-parser`. See Chapter 9.

`express-session (npm install --save express-session, app.use(require(express-session)());)`

Provides session ID (stored in a cookie) session support. Defaults to a memory store, which is not suitable for production, and can be configured to use a database store. See Chapters 9 and 13.

`csurf (npm install --save csurf, app.use(require(csurf)());`

Provides protection against cross-site request forgery (CSRF) attacks. Uses sessions, so must be linked in after `express-session` middleware. Currently, this is identical to the `connect.csrf` middleware. Unfortunately, simply linking this middleware in does not magically protect against CSRF attacks; see Chapter 18 for more information.

`directory (app.use(connect.directory());)`

Provides directory listing support for static files. There is no need to include this middleware unless you specifically need directory listing.

`errorhandler (npm install --save errorhandler, app.use(require(errorhandler)());`

Provides stack traces and error messages to the client. I do not recommend linking this in on a production server, as it exposes implementation details, which can have security or privacy consequences. See Chapter 20 for more information.

`static-favicon` (npm install --save static-favicon,
`app.use(require(`*`static-favicon`*`)(`*`path_to_favicon`*`));`
> Serves the "favicon" (the icon that appears in the title bar of your browser). This is not strictly necessary: you can simply put a *favicon.ico* in the root of your static directory, but this middleware can improve performance. If you use it, it should be linked in very high in the middleware stack. It also allows you to designate a filename other than *favicon.ico*.

`morgan` (*previously* `logger`, npm install --save morgan, `app.use(require(`*`mor gan`*`)());`
> Provides automated logging support: all requests will be logged. See Chapter 20 for more information.

`method-override` (npm install --save method-override,
`app.use(require(`*`method-override`*`)());`
> Provides support for the `x-http-method-override` request header, which allows browsers to "fake" using HTTP methods other than `GET` and `POST`. This can be useful for debugging. Only needed if you're writing APIs.

`query`
> Parses the querystring and makes it available as the `query` property on the request object. This middleware is linked in implicitly by Express, so do not link it in yourself.

`response-time` (npm install --save response-time,
`app.use(require(`*`response-time`*`)());`
> Adds the `X-Response-Time` header to the response, providing the response time in milliseconds. You usually don't need this middleware unless you are doing performance tuning.

`static` (`app.use(express.static(`*`path_to_static_files`*`)());`
> Provides support for serving static (public) files. You can link this middleware in multiple times, specifying different directories. See Chapter 16 for more details.

`vhost` (npm install --save vhost, `var vhost = require(`*`vhost`*`);`
> Virtual hosts (vhosts), a term borrowed from Apache, makes subdomains easier to manage in Express. See Chapter 14 for more information.

# Third-Party Middleware

Currently, there is no "store" or index for third-party middleware. Almost all Express middleware, however, will be available on npm, so if you search npm for "Express," "Connect," and "Middleware," you'll get a pretty good list.

# CHAPTER 11

# Sending Email

One of the primary ways your website can communicate with the world is email. From user registration to password reset instructions to promotional emails to problem notification, the ability to send email is an important feature.

Neither Node or Express has any built-in way of sending email, so we have to use a third-party module. The package I recommend is Andris Reinman's excellent *Node-mailer* (*https://npmjs.org/package/nodemailer*). Before we dive into configuring Node-mailer, let's get some email basics out of the way.

## SMTP, MSAs, and MTAs

The lingua franca for sending email is the Simple Mail Transfer Protocol (SMTP). While it is possible to use SMTP to send an email directly to the recipient's mail server, this is generally a very bad idea: unless you are a "trusted sender" like Google or Yahoo!, chances are your email will be be tossed directly into the spam bin. Better to use a Mail Submission Agent (MSA), which will deliver the email through trusted channels, reducing the chance that your email will be marked as spam. In addition to ensuring that your email arrives, MSAs handle nuisances like temporary outages and bounced emails. The final piece of the equation is the Mail Transfer Agent (MTA), which is the service that actually sends the email to its final destination. For the purposes of this book, MSA, MTA, and "SMTP server" are essentially equivalent.

So you'll need access to an MSA. The easiest way to get started is to use a free email service, such as Gmail, Hotmail, iCloud, SendGrid, or Yahoo!. This is a short-term solution: in addition to having limits (Gmail, for example, allows only 500 emails in any 24-hour period, and no more than 100 recipients per email), it will expose your personal email. While you can specify how the sender should appear, such as *joe@meadowlark-travel.com*, a cursory glance at the email headers will reveal that it was delivered by *joe@gmail.com*; hardly professional. Once you're ready to go to production, you can switch to a professional MSA such as Sendgrid or Amazon Simple Email Service (SES).

If you're working for an organization, the organization itself may have an MSA; you can contact your IT department and ask them if there's an SMTP relay available for sending automated emails.

## Receiving Email

Most websites only need the ability to *send* email, like password reset instructions and promotional emails. However, some applications need to receive email as well. A good example is an issue tracking system that sends out an email when someone updates an issue: if you reply to that email, the issue is automatically updated with your response.

Unfortunately, receiving email is much more involved and will not be covered in this book. If this is functionality you need, you should look into Andris Reinman's SimpleSMTP (*http://bit.ly/simplesmtp*) or Haraka (*http://haraka.github.com*).

## Email Headers

An email message consists of two parts: the header and the body (very much like an HTTP request). The header contains information about the email: who it's from, who it's addressed to, the date it was received, the subject, and more. Those are the headers that are normally displayed to the user in an email application, but there are many more headers. Most email clients allow you to look at the headers; if you've never done so, I recommend you take a look. The headers give you all the information about how the email got to you; every server and MTA that the email passed through will be listed in the header.

It often comes as a surprise to people that some headers, like the "from" address, can be set arbitrarily by the sender. When you specify a "from" address other than the account from which you're sending, it's often referred to as "spoofing." There is nothing preventing you from sending an email with the from address Bill Gates *<billg@micro-soft.com>*. I'm not recommending that you try this, just driving home the point that you can set certain headers to be whatever you want. Sometimes there are legitimate reasons to do this, but you should never abuse it.

An email you send *must* have a "from" address, however. This can sometimes cause problems when sending automated email, which is why you often see email with a return addresses like DO NOT REPLY *<do-not-reply@meadowlarktravel.com>*. Whether you want to take this approach, or have automated emails come from an address like Meadowlark Travel *<info@meadowlarktravel.com>* is up to you; if you take the latter approach, though, you should be prepared to respond to emails that come to *info@meadowlarktravel.com*.

# Email Formats

When the Internet was new, all email was simply ASCII text. The world has changed a lot since then, and people want to send email in different languages, and do crazy things like include formatted text, images, and attachments. This is where things start to get ugly: email formats and encoding are a horrible jumble of techniques and standards. Fortunately, we won't really have to address these complexities: Nodemailer will handle that for us.

What's important for you to know is that your email can either be plaintext (Unicode) or HTML.

Almost all modern email applications support HTML email, so it's generally pretty safe to format your emails in HTML. Still, there are "text purists" out there who eschew HTML email, so I recommend always including both text and HTML email. If you don't want to have to write text and HTML email, Nodemailer supports a shortcut that will automatically generate the plaintext version from the HTML.

# HTML Email

HTML email is a topic that could fill an entire book. Unfortunately, it's not as simple as just writing HTML like you would for your site: most mail clients support only a small subset of HTML. Mostly, you have to write HTML like it was still 1996; it's not much fun. In particular, you have to go back to using tables for layout (cue sad music).

If you have experience with browser compatibility issues with HTML, you know what a headache it can be. Email compatibility issues are much worse. Fortunately, there are some things that can help.

First, I encourage you to read MailChimp's excellent article about writing HTML email (*http://bit.ly/writing_html_email*). It does a good job covering the basics and explaining the things you need to keep in mind when writing HTML email.

The next is a real time saver: HTML Email Boilerplate (*http://htmlemailboiler plate.com*). It's essentially a very well-written, rigorously tested template for HTML email.

Finally, there's testing…. You've read up on how to write HTML email, and you're using HTML Email Boilerplate, but testing is the only way to know for sure your email is not going to explode on Lotus Notes 7 (yes, people still use it). Feel like installing 30 different mail clients to test one email? I didn't think so. Fortunately, there's a great service that does it for you: Litmus (*https://litmus.com/email-testing*). It's not an inexpensive service: plans start at about $80 a month. But if you send a lot of promotional emails, it's hard to beat.

On the other hand, if your formatting is modest, there's no need for an expensive testing service like Litmus. If you're sticking to things like headers, bold/italic text, horizontal rules, and some image links, you're pretty safe.

# Nodemailer

First, we need to install the Nodemailer package:

```
npm install --save nodemailer
```

Then, require the `nodemailer` package and create a Nodemailer instance (a "transport" in Nodemailer parlance):

```
var nodemailer = require('nodemailer');

var mailTransport = nodemailer.createTransport('SMTP',{
        service: 'Gmail',
        auth: {
                user: credentials.gmail.user,
                pass: credentials.gmail.password,
        }
});
```

Notice we're using the credentials module we set up in Chapter 9. You'll need to update your *credentials.js* file accordingly:

```
module.exports = {
        cookieSecret: 'your cookie secret goes here',
        gmail: {
                user: 'your gmail username',
                password: 'your gmail password',
        }
};
```

Nodemailer offers shortcuts for most popular email services: Gmail, Hotmail, iCloud, Yahoo!, and many more. If your MSA isn't on this list, or you need to connect to an SMTP server directly, that is supported:

```
var mailTransport = nodemailer.createTransport('SMTP',{
        host: 'smtp.meadowlarktravel.com',
        secureConnection: true,        // use SSL
        port: 465,
        auth: {
                user: credentials.meadowlarkSmtp.user,
                pass: credentials.meadowlarkSmtp.password,
        }
});
```

## Sending Mail

Now that we have our mail transport instance, we can send mail. We'll start with a very simple example that sends text mail to only one recipient:

```
mailTransport.sendMail({
        from: '"Meadowlark Travel" <info@meadowlarktravel.com>',
        to: 'joecustomer@gmail.com',
        subject: 'Your Meadowlark Travel Tour',
        text: 'Thank you for booking your trip with Meadowlark Travel.  ' +
                'We look forward to your visit!',
}, function(err){
        if(err) console.error( 'Unable to send email: ' + error );
});
```

You'll notice that we're handling errors here, but it's important to understand that no errors doesn't necessarily mean your email was delivered successfully to the *recipient*: the callback's error parameter will be set only if there was a problem communicating with the MSA (such as a network or authentication error). If the MSA was unable to deliver the email (for example, due to an invalid email address or an unknown user), you will get a failure email delivered to the MSA account (for example, if you're using your personal Gmail as an MSA, you will get a failure message in your Gmail inbox).

If you need your system to automatically determine if the email was delivered successfully, you have a couple of options. One is to use an MSA that supports error reporting. Amazon's Simple Email Service (SES) is one such service, and email bounce notices are delivered through their Simple Notification Service (SNS), which you can configure to call a web service running on your website. The other option is to use direct delivery, bypassing the MSA. I do not recommend direct delivery, as it is a complex solution, and your email is likely to be flagged as spam. Neither of these options is simple, and thus they are beyond the scope of this book.

## Sending Mail to Multiple Recipients

Nodemail supports sending mail to multiple recipients simply by separating recipients with commas:

```
mailTransport.sendMail({
        from: '"Meadowlark Travel" <info@meadowlarktravel.com>',
        to: 'joe@gmail.com, "Jane Customer" <jane@yahoo.com>, ' +
                'fred@hotmail.com',
        subject: 'Your Meadowlark Travel Tour',
        text: 'Thank you for booking your trip with Meadowlark Travel.  ' +
                'We look forward to your visit!',
}, function(err){
        if(err) console.error( 'Unable to send email: ' + error );
});
```

Note that, in this example, we mixed plain email addresses (*joe@gmail.com*) with email addresses specifying the recipient's name ("Jane Customer" *<jane@yahoo.com>*). This is allowed syntax.

When sending email to multiple recipients, you must be careful to observe the limits of your MSA. Gmail, for example, limits the number of recipients to 100 per email. Even more robust services, like SendGrid, recommend limiting the number of recipients (SendGrid recommends no more than a thousand in one email). If you're sending bulk email, you probably want to deliver multiple messages, each with multiple recipients:

```
// largeRecipientList is an array of email addresses
var recipientLimit = 100;
for(var i=0; i<largeRecipientList.length/recipientLimit; i++){
        mailTransport.sendMail({
                from: '"Meadowlark Travel" <info@meadowlarktravel.com>',
                to: largeRecipientList
                        .slice(i*recipientLimit, i*(recipientLimit+1)).join(','),
                subject: 'Special price on Hood River travel package!',
                text: 'Book your trip to scenic Hood River now!',
        }, function(err){
                if(err) console.error( 'Unable to send email: ' + error );
        });
}
```

# Better Options for Bulk Email

While you can certainly send bulk email with Nodemailer and an appropriate MSA, you should think carefully before going this route. A responsible email campaign must provide a way for people to unsubscribe from your promotional emails, and that is not a trivial task. Multiply that by every subscription list you maintain (perhaps you have a weekly newsletter and a special announcements campaign, for example). This is an area in which it's best not to reinvent the wheel. Services like MailChimp (*http://mail chimp.com*) and Campaign Monitor (*http://www.campaignmonitor.com*) offer everything you need, including great tools for monitoring the success of your email campaigns. They're very affordable, and I highly recommend using them for promotional emails, newsletters, etc.

# Sending HTML Email

So far, we've just been sending plaintext email, but most people these days expect something a little prettier. Nodemailer allows you to send both HTML and plaintext versions in the same email, allowing the email client to choose which version is displayed (usually HTML):

```
mailTransport.sendMail({
        from: '"Meadowlark Travel" <info@meadowlarktravel.com>',
        to: 'joecustomer@gmail.com, "Jane Customer" ' +
```

```
                       '<janecustomer@gyahoo.com>, frecsutomer@hotmail.com',
              subject: 'Your Meadowlark Travel Tour',
              html: '<h1>Meadowlark Travel</h1>\n<p>Thanks for book your trip with ' +
                       'Meadowlark Travel.  <b>We look forward to your visit!</b>',
              text: 'Thank you for booking your trip with Meadowlark Travel.  ' +
                       'We look forward to your visit!',
       }, function(err){
              if(err) console.error( 'Unable to send email: ' + error );
       });
```

This is a lot of work, and I don't recommend this approach. Fortunately, Nodemailer will automatically translate your HTML into plaintext if you ask it to:

```
mailTransport.sendMail({
       from: '"Meadowlark Travel" <info@meadowlarktravel.com>',
       to: 'joecustomer@gmail.com, "Jane Customer" ' +
              '<janecustomer@gyahoo.com>, frecsutomer@hotmail.com',
       subject: 'Your Meadowlark Travel Tour',
       html: '<h1>Meadowlark Travel</h1>\n<p>Thanks for book your trip with ' +
              'Meadowlark Travel.  <b>We look forward to your visit!</b>',
       generateTextFromHtml: true,
}, function(err){
       if(err) console.error( 'Unable to send email: ' + error );
});
```

## Images in HTML Email

While it is possible to embed images in HTML email, I strongly discourage it: they bloat your email messages, and it isn't generally considered good practice. Instead, you should make images you want to use in email available on your web server, and link appropriately from the email.

It is best to have a dedicated location in your static assets folder for email images. You should even keep assets that you use both on your site and in emails (like your log) separate: it reduces the chance of negatively affecting the layout of your emails.

Let's add some email resources in our Meadowlark Travel project. In your *public* directory, create a subdirectory called *email*. You can place your *logo.png* in there, and any other images you want to use in your email. Then, in your email, you can use those images directly:

```
<img src="//meadowlarktravel.com/email/logo.png" alt="Meadowlark Travel">
```

It should be obvious that you do not want to use *localhost* when sending out email to other people; they probably won't even have a server running, much less on port 3000! Depending on your mail client, you might be able to use *localhost* in your email for testing purposes, but it won't work outside of your computer. In Chapter 16, we'll discuss some techniques to smooth the transition from development to production.

## Using Views to Send HTML Email

So far, we've been putting our HTML in strings in JavaScript, a practice you should try to avoid. So far, our HTML has been simple enough, but take a look at HTML Email Boilerplate (*http://htmlemailboilerplate.com*): do you want to put all that boilerplate in a string? Absolutely not.

Fortunately, we can leverage views to handle this. Let's consider our "Thank you for booking your trip with Meadowlark Travel" email example, which we'll expand a little bit. Let's imagine that we have a shopping cart object that contains our order information. That shopping cart object will be stored in the session. Let's say the last step in our ordering process is a form that's processed by */cart/chckout*, which sends a confirmation email. Let's start by creating a view for the "thank you" page, *views/cart-thank-you.handlebars*:

```
<p>Thank you for booking your trip with Meadowlark Travel, {{cart.billing.name}}!</p>
<p>Your reservation number is {{cart.number}}, and an email has been
sent to {{cart.billing.email}} for your records.</p>
```

Then we'll create an email template for the email. Download HTML Email Boilerplate, and put in *views/email/cart-thank-you.handlebars*. Edit the file, and modify the body:

```
<body>
<table cellpadding="0" cellspacing="0" border="0" id="backgroundTable">
    <tr>
        <td valign="top">
            <table cellpadding="0" cellspacing="0" border="0" align="center">
                <tr>
                    <td width="200" valign="top"><img class="image_fix"
                        src="http://meadowlarktravel.com/email/logo.png"
                        alt="Meadowlark Travel" title="Meadowlark Travel"
                        width="180" height="220" /></td>
                </tr>
                <tr>
                    <td width="200" valign="top"><p>
                        Thank you for booking your trip with Meadowlark Travel,
                        {{cart.billing.name}}.</p><p>Your reservation number
                        is {{cart.number}}.</p></td>
                </tr>
                <tr>
                    <td width="200" valign="top">Problems with your reservation?
```

```
            Contact Meadowlark Travel at
            <span class="mobile_link">555-555-0123</span>.</td>
        </tr>
      </table>
    </td>
  </tr>
</table>
</body>
```

 Because you can't use *localhost* addresses in email, if your site isn't live yet, you can use a placeholder service for any graphics. For example, *http://placehold.it/100x100* dynamically serves a 100-pixel-square graphic you can use. This technique is used quite often for for-placement-only (FPO) images and layout purposes.

Now we can create a route for our cart "Thank you" page:

```
app.post('/cart/checkout', function(req, res){
    var cart = req.session.cart;
    if(!cart) next(new Error('Cart does not exist.'));
    var name = req.body.name || '', email = req.body.email || '';
    // input validation
    if(!email.match(VALID_EMAIL_REGEX))
        return res.next(new Error('Invalid email address.'));
    // assign a random cart ID; normally we would use a database ID here
    cart.number = Math.random().toString().replace(/^0\.0*/, '');
    cart.billing = {
        name: name,
        email: email,
    };
    res.render('email/cart-thank-you',
        { layout: null, cart: cart }, function(err,html){
            if( err ) console.log('error in email template');
            mailTransport.sendMail({
                from: '"Meadowlark Travel": info@meadowlarktravel.com',
                to: cart.billing.email,
                subject: 'Thank You for Book your Trip with Meadowlark',
                html: html,
                generateTextFromHtml: true
            }, function(err){
                if(err) console.error('Unable to send confirmation: '
                        + err.stack);
            });
        }
    );
    res.render('cart-thank-you', { cart: cart });
});
```

Note that we're calling res.render twice. Normally, you call it only once (calling it twice will display only the results of the first call). However, in this instance, we're circumventing the normal rendering process the first time we call it: notice that we provide a callback. Doing that prevents the results of the view from being rendered to the browser. Instead, the callback receives the rendered view in the parameter html: all we have to do is take that rendered HTML and send the email! We specify layout: null to prevent our layout file from being used, because it's all in the email template (an alternate approach would be to create a separate layout file for emails and use that instead). Lastly, we call res.render again. This time, the results will be rendered to the HTML response as normal.

## Encapsulating Email Functionality

If you're using email a lot throughout your site, you may want to encapsulate the email functionality. Let's assume you always want your site to send email from the same sender ("Meadowlark Travel" <info@meadowlarktravel.com>) and you always want the email to be sent in HTML with automatically generated text. Create a module called *lib/email.js*:

```
var nodemailer = require('nodemailer');

module.exports = function(credentials){

        var mailTransport = nodemailer.createTransport('SMTP',{
                service: 'Gmail',
                auth: {
                        user: credentials.gmail.user,
                        pass: credentials.gmail.password,
                }
        });

        var from = '"Meadowlark Travel" <info@meadowlarktravel.com>';
        var errorRecipient = 'youremail@gmail.com';

        return {
                send: function(to, subj, body){
                        mailTransport.sendMail({
                                from: from,
                                to: to,
                                subject: subj,
                                html: body,
                                generateTextFromHtml: true
                        }, function(err){
                                if(err) console.error('Unable to send email: ' + err);
                        });
                }),

                emailError: function(message, filename, exception){
                        var body = '<h1>Meadowlark Travel Site Error</h1>' +
                                'message:<br><pre>' + message + '</pre><br>';
                        if(exception) body += 'exception:<br><pre>' + exception
```

```
                                  + '</pre><br>';
                  if(filename) body += 'filename:<br><pre>' + filename
                                  + '</pre><br>';
              mailTransport.sendMail({
                  from: from,
                  to: errorRecipient,
                  subject: 'Meadowlark Travel Site Error',
                  html: body,
                  generateTextFromHtml: true
              }, function(err){
                  if(err) console.error('Unable to send email: ' + err);
              });
          },
      }
```

Now all we have to do to send an email is:

```
var emailService = require('./lib/email.js')(credentials);

emailService.send('joecustomer@gmail.com', 'Hood River tours on sale today!',
        'Get \'em while they\'re hot!');
```

You'll notice we also added a method emailError, which we'll discuss in the next section.

# Email as a Site Monitoring Tool

If something goes wrong with your site, wouldn't you rather know about it before your client does? Or before your boss does? One great way to accomplish that is to have your site email you distress messages when something goes wrong. In the previous example, we added just such a method, so that when there's an error in your site, you can do the following:

```
if(err){
        email.sendError('the widget broke down!', __filename);
        // ... display error message to user
}

// or

try {
        // do something iffy here....
} catch(ex) {
        email.sendError('the widget broke down!', __filename, ex);
        // ... display error message to user
}
```

This is not a substitute for logging, and in Chapter 12, we will consider a more robust logging and notification mechanism.

# CHAPTER 12

# Production Concerns

While it may feel premature to start discussing production concerns at this point, you can save yourself a lot of time and suffering down the line if you start thinking about production early on: launch day will be here before you know it.

In this chapter, we'll learn about Express's support for different execution environments, methods to scale your website, and how to monitor your website's health. We'll see how you can simulate a production environment for testing and development, and also how to perform stress testing so you can identify production problems before they happen.

## Execution Environments

Express supports the concept of *execution environments*: a way to run your application in production, development, or test mode. You could actually have as many different environments as you want. For example, you could have a staging environment, or a training environment. However, keep in mind that development, production, and test are "standard" environments: Express, Connect, and third-party middleware may make decisions based on those environments. In other words, if you have a "staging" environment, there's no way to make it automatically inherit the properties of a production environment. For this reason, I recommend you stick with the standards of production, development, and test.

While it is possible to specify the execution environment by calling `app.set('env', 'production')`, it is inadvisable to do so: it means your app will always run in that environment, no matter what the situation. Worse, it may start running in one environment and then switch to another.

It's preferable to specify the execution environment by using the environment variable `NODE_ENV`. Let's modify our app to report on the mode it's running in by calling `app.get('env')`:

```
app.listen(app.get('port'), function() {
    console.log( 'Express started in ' + app.get('env') +
        ' mode on http://localhost:' + app.get('port') +
        '; press Ctrl-C to terminate.' );
});
```

If you start your server now, you'll see you're running in development mode: it's the default if you don't specify otherwise. Let's try putting it in production mode:

```
$ export NODE_ENV=production
$ node meadowlark.js
```

If you're using a Unix/BSD system or Cygwin, there's a handy syntax that allows you to modify the environment only for the duration of that command:

```
$ NODE_ENV=production node meadowlark.js
```

This will run the server in production mode, but once the server terminates, the NODE_ENV environment variable won't be modified.

> If you start Express in production mode, you may notice warnings about components that are not suitable for use in production mode. If you've been following along with the examples in this book, you'll see that connect.session is using a memory store, which is not suitable for a production environment. Once we switch to a database store in Chapter 13, this warning will disappear.

## Environment-Specific Configuration

Just changing the execution environment won't do much, though Express will log more warnings to the console in production mode (for example, informing you of modules that are deprecated and will be removed in the future). Also, in production mode, view caching is enabled by default (see Chapter 7).

Mainly, the execution environment is a tool for you to leverage, allowing you to easily make decisions about how your application should behave in the different environments. As a word of caution, you should try to minimize the differences between your development, test, and production environments. That is, you should use this feature sparingly. If your development or test environments differ wildly from production, you are increasing your chances of different behavior in production, which is a recipe for more defects (or harder-to-find ones). Some differences are inevitable: for example, if your app is highly database driven, you probably don't want to be messing with the production database during development, and that would be a good candidate for environment-specific configuration. Another low-impact area is more verbose logging. There are a lot of things you might want to log in development that are unnecessary to record in production.

Let's add some logging to our application. For development, we'll use *Morgan* (npm install --save morgan), which uses colorized output that's easy on the eyes. For production, we'll use *express-logger* (npm install --save express-logger), which supports log rotation (every 24 hours, the log is copied, and a new one starts, to prevent logfiles from growing unwieldy). Let's add logging support to our application file:

```
switch(app.get('env')){
    case 'development':
        // compact, colorful dev logging
        app.use(require('morgan')('dev'));
        break;
    case 'production':
        // module 'express-logger' supports daily log rotation
        app.use(require('express-logger')({
            path: __dirname + '/log/requests.log'
        }));
        break;
}
```

If you want to test the logger, you can run your application in production mode (NODE_ENV=production node meadowlark.js). If you would like to see the rotation feature in action, you can edit *node_modules/express-logger/logger.js* and change the variable defaultInterval to something like 10 seconds instead of 24 hours (remember that modifying packages in *node_modules* is only for experimentation or learning).

 In the previous example, we're using __dirname to store the request log in a subdirectory of the project itself. If you take this approach, you will want to add log to your *.gitignore* file. Alternatively, you could take a more Unix-like approach, and save the logs in a subdirectory of */var/log*, like Apache does by default.

I will stress again that you should use your best judgment when making environment-specific configuration choices. Always keep in mind that when your site is live, your production instances will be running in production mode (or they should be). Whenever you're tempted to make a development-specific modification, you should always think first about how that might have QA consequences in production. We'll see a more robust example of environment-specific configuration in Chapter 13.

# Scaling Your Website

These days, scaling usually means one of two things: scaling up or scaling out. Scaling up refers to making servers more powerful: faster CPUs, better architecture, more cores, more memory, etc. Scaling out, on the other hand, simply means more servers. With the increased popularity of cloud computing and the ubiquity of virtualization, server computational power is becoming less relevant, and scaling out is the most cost-effective method for scaling websites according to their needs.

When developing websites for Node, you should always consider the possibility of scaling out. Even if your application is tiny (maybe it's even an intranet application that will always have a very limited audience) and will never conceivably need to be scaled out, it's a good habit to get into. After all, maybe your next Node project will be the next Twitter, and scaling out will be essential. Fortunately, Node's support for scaling out is very good, and writing your application with this in mind is painless.

The most important thing to remember when building a website designed to be scaled out is persistence. If you're used to relying on file-based storage for persistence, *stop right there*. That way lies madness. My first experience with this problem was nearly disastrous. One of our clients was running a web-based contest, and the web application was designed to inform the first 50 winners that they would receive a prize. With that particular client, we were unable to easily use a database due to some corporate IT restrictions, so most persistence was achieved by writing flat files. I proceeded just as I always had, saving each entry to a file. Once the file had recorded 50 winners, no more people would be notified that they had won. The problem is that the server was load-balanced: half the requests were served by one server, and the other half by another. One server notified 50 people that they had won…and so did the other server. Fortunately, the prizes were small (fleece blankets) and not iPads, and the client took their lumps and handed out 100 prizes instead of 50 (I offered to pay for the extra 50 blankets out-of-pocket for my mistake, but they generously refused to take me up on my offer). The moral of this story is that unless you have a filesystem that's accessible to *all* of your servers, you should not rely on the local filesystem for persistence. The exceptions are read-only data, like logging, and backups. For example, I have commonly backed up form submission data to a local flat file in case the database connection failed. In the case of a database outage, it is a hassle to go to each server and collect the files, but at least no damage has been done.

## Scaling Out with App Clusters

Node itself supports *app clusters*, a simple, single-server form of scaling out. With app clusters, you can create an independent server for each core (CPU) on the system (having more servers than the number of cores will not improve the performance of your app). App clusters are good for two reasons: first, they can help maximize the performance of a given server (the hardware, or virtual machine), and second, it's a low-overhead way to test your app under parallel conditions.

Let's go ahead and add cluster support to our website. While it's quite common to do all of this work in your main application file, we are going to create a second application file that will run the app in a cluster, using the nonclustered application file we've been using all along. To enable that, we have to make a slight modification to *meadow-lark.js* first:

```
function startServer() {
    app.listen(app.get('port'), function() {
        console.log( 'Express started in ' + app.get('env') +
          ' mode on http://localhost:' + app.get('port') +
          '; press Ctrl-C to terminate.' );
    });
}

if(require.main === module){
    // application run directly; start app server
    startServer();
} else {
    // application imported as a module via "require": export function
    // to create server
    module.exports = startServer;
}
```

This modification allows *meadowlark.js* to either be run directly (node meadow lark.js) or included as a module via a require statement.

 When a script is run directly, require.main === module will be true; if it is false, it means your script has been loaded from another script using require.

Then, we create a new script, *meadowlark_cluster.js*:

```
var cluster = require('cluster');

function startWorker() {
    var worker = cluster.fork();
    console.log('CLUSTER: Worker %d started', worker.id);
}

if(cluster.isMaster){

    require('os').cpus().forEach(function(){
            startWorker();
    });

    // log any workers that disconnect; if a worker disconnects, it
    // should then exit, so we'll wait for the exit event to spawn
    // a new worker to replace it
    cluster.on('disconnect', function(worker){
        console.log('CLUSTER: Worker %d disconnected from the cluster.',
            worker.id);
    });
```

```
    // when a worker dies (exits), create a worker to replace it
    cluster.on('exit', function(worker, code, signal){
        console.log('CLUSTER: Worker %d died with exit code %d (%s)',
            worker.id, code, signal);
        startWorker();
    });

} else {

    // start our app on worker; see meadowlark.js
    require('./meadowlark.js')();

}
```

When this JavaScript is executed, it will either be in the context of master (when it is run directly, with `node meadowlark_cluster.js`), or in the context of a worker, when Node's cluster system executes it. The properties `cluster.isMaster` and `cluster.is Worker` determine which context you're running in. When we run this script, it's executing in master mode, and we start a worker using `cluster.fork` for each CPU in the system. Also, we respawn any dead workers by listening for `exit` events from workers.

Finally, in the `else` clause, we handle the worker case. Since we configured *meadowlark.js* to be used as a module, we simply import it and immediately invoke it (remember, we exported it as a function that starts the server).

Now start up your new clustered server:

```
node meadowlark_cluster.js
```

 If you are using virtualization (like Oracle's VirtualBox), you may have to configure your VM to have multiple CPUs. By default, virtual machines often have a single CPU.

Assuming you're on a multicore system, you should see some number of workers started. If you want to see evidence of different workers handling different requests, add the following middleware before your routes:

```
app.use(function(req,res,next){
    var cluster = require('cluster');
    if(cluster.isWorker) console.log('Worker %d received request',
        cluster.worker.id);
});
```

Now you can connect to your application with a browser. Reload a few times, and see how you can get a different worker out of the pool on each request.

## Handling Uncaught Exceptions

In the asynchronous world of Node, uncaught exceptions are of particular concern. Let's start with a simple example that doesn't cause too much trouble (I encourage you to follow along with these examples):

```
app.get('/fail', function(req, res){
    throw new Error('Nope!');
});
```

When Express executes route handlers, it wraps them in a try/catch block, so this isn't actually an uncaught exception. This won't cause too much problem: Express will log the exception on the server side, and the visitor will get an ugly stack dump. However, your server is stable, and other requests will continue to be served correctly. If we want to provide a "nice" error page, create a file *views/500.handlebars* and add an error handler after all of your routes:

```
app.use(function(err, req, res, next){
    console.error(err.stack);
    app.status(500).render('500');
});
```

It's always a good practice to provide a custom error page: not only does it look more professional to your users when errors do occur, but it allows you to take action when errors occur. For example, this error handler would be a good place to send an email to your dev team letting them know that an error occurred. Unfortunately, this helps only for exceptions that Express can catch. Let's try something worse:

```
app.get('/epic-fail', function(req, res){
    process.nextTick(function(){
        throw new Error('Kaboom!');
    });
});
```

Go ahead and try it. The result is considerably more catastrophic: it brought your whole server down! In addition to not displaying a friendly error message to your user, now your server is down, and *no* requests are being served. This is because setTimeout is executing *asynchronously*; execution of the function with the exception is being deferred until Node is idle. The problem is, when Node is idle and gets around to executing the function, it no longer has context about the request it was being served from, so it has no resource but to unceremoniously shut down the whole server, because now it's in an undefined state (Node can't know the purpose of the function, or its caller, so it can no longer assume that any further functions will work correctly).

process.nextTick is very similar to calling setTimeout with an argument of zero, but it's more efficient. We're using it here for demonstration purposes: it's not something you would generally use in server-side code. However, in coming chapters, we will be dealing with many things that execute asynchronously: database access, filesystem access, and network access, to name a few, and they are all subject to this problem.

There is action that we can take to handle uncaught exceptions, but *if Node can't determine the stability of your application, neither can you.* In other words, if there is an uncaught exception, the only recourse is to shut down the server. The best we can do in this circumstance is to shut down as gracefully as possible and have a failover mechanism. The easiest failover mechanism is to use a cluster (as mentioned previously). If your application is operating in clustered mode and one worker dies, the master will spawn another worker to take its place. (You don't even have to have multiple workers: a cluster with one worker will suffice, though the failover may be slightly slower.)

So with that in mind, how can we shut down as gracefully as possible when confronted with an unhandled exception? Node has two mechanisms to deal with this: the uncaugh tException event and *domains*.

Using domains is the more recent and recommended approach (uncaughtException may even be removed in future versions of Node). A *domain* is basically an execution context that will catch errors that occur inside it. Domains allow you to be more flexible in your error handling: instead of having one global uncaught exception handler, you can have as many domains as you want, allowing you to create a new domain when working with error-prone code.

A good practice is to process every request in a domain, allowing you to trap any uncaught errors in that request and respond appropriately (by gracefully shutting down the server). We can accomplish this very easily by adding a middleware. This middleware should go above any other routes or middleware:

```
app.use(function(req, res, next){
    // create a domain for this request
    var domain = require('domain').create();
    // handle errors on this domain
    domain.on('error', function(err){
        console.error('DOMAIN ERROR CAUGHT\n', err.stack);
        try {
            // failsafe shutdown in 5 seconds
            setTimeout(function(){
                console.error('Failsafe shutdown.');
                process.exit(1);
            }, 5000);

            // disconnect from the cluster
```

```
        var worker = require('cluster').worker;
        if(worker) worker.disconnect();

        // stop taking new requests
        server.close();

        try {
            // attempt to use Express error route
            next(err);
        } catch(err){
            // if Express error route failed, try
            // plain Node response
            console.error('Express error mechanism failed.\n', err.stack);
            res.statusCode = 500;
            res.setHeader('content-type', 'text/plain');
            res.end('Server error.');
        }
    } catch(err){
        console.error('Unable to send 500 response.\n', err.stack);
    }
  });

  // add the request and response objects to the domain
  domain.add(req);
  domain.add(res);

  // execute the rest of the request chain in the domain
  domain.run(next);
});

// other middleware and routes go here

var server = app.listen(app.get('port'), function() {
    console.log('Listening on port %d.', app.get('port'));
});
```

The first thing we do is create a domain, and then attach an error handler to it. This function will be invoked any time an uncaught error occurs in the domain. Our approach here is to attempt to respond appropriately to any in-progress requests, and then shut down this server. Depending on the nature of the error, it may not be possible to respond to in-progress requests, so the first thing we do is establish a deadline for shutting down. In this case, we're allowing the server five seconds to respond to any in-progress requests (if it can). The number you choose will be dependent on your application: if it's common for your application to have long-running requests, you should allow more time. Once we establish the deadline, we disconnect from the cluster (if we're in a cluster), which should prevent the cluster from assigning us any more requests. Then we explicitly tell the server that we're no longer accepting new connections. Finally, we attempt to respond to the request that generated the error by passing on to the error-handling route (next(err)). If that throws an exception, we fall back to trying to respond with the plain

Node API. If all else fails, we log the error (the client will receive no response, and eventually time out).

Once we've set up the unhandled exception handler, we add the request and response objects to the domain (allowing any methods on those objects that throw an error to be handled by the domain), and finally, we run the next middleware in the pipeline in the context of the domain. Note that this effectively runs *all* middleware in the pipeline in the domain, since calls to next() are chained.

If you search npm, you will find several middleware that essentially offer this functionality. However, it's very important to understand how domain error handling works, and also the importance of shutting down your server when there are uncaught exceptions. Lastly, what "shutting down gracefully" means is going to vary depending on your deployment configuration. For example, if you were limited to one worker, you may want to shut down immediately, at the expense of any sessions in progress, whereas if you had multiple workers, you would have more leeway in letting the dying worker serve the remaining requests before shutting down.

I highly recommend reading William Bert's excellent article, The 4 Keys to 100% Uptime with Node.js (*http://bit.ly/100_percent_uptime*). William's real-world experience running Fluencia and SpanishDict on Node make him an authority on the subject, and he considers using domains to be essential to Node uptime. It is also worth going through the official Node documentation (*http://nodejs.org/api/domain.html*) on domains.

## Scaling Out with Multiple Servers

Where scaling out using clustering can maximize the performance of an individual server, what happens when you need more than one server? That's where things get a little more complicated. To achieve this kind of parallelism, you need a *proxy* server. (It's often called a *reverse proxy* or *forward-facing proxy* to distinguish it from proxies commonly used to access external networks, but I find this language to be confusing and unnecessary, so I will simply refer to it as a proxy).

The two rising stars in the proxy sphere are Nginx (pronounced "engine X") and HAProxy. Nginx servers in particular are springing up like weeds: I recently did a competitive analysis for my company and found upward of 80% of our competitors were using Nginx. Nginx and HAproxy are both robust, high-performance proxy servers, and are capable of the most demanding applications (if you need proof, consider that Netflix, which accounts for as much as 30% of *all Internet traffic*, uses Nginx).

There are also some smaller Node-based proxy servers, such as proxy (*https://npmjs.org/package/proxy*) and node-http-proxy (*https://npmjs.org/package/http-proxy*). These are great options if your needs are modest, or for development. For production, I would recommend using Nginx or HAProxy (both are free, though they offer support for a fee).

Installing and configuring a proxy is beyond the scope of this book, but it is not as hard as you might think (especially if you use proxy or node-http-proxy). For now, using clusters gives us some assurance that our website is ready for scaling out.

If you do configure a proxy server, make sure you tell Express that you are using a proxy and that it should be trusted:

```
app.enable('trust proxy');
```

Doing this will ensure that `req.ip`, `req.protocol`, and `req.secure` will reflect the details about the connection between the *client and the proxy*, not between the client and your app. Also, `req.ips` will be an array that indicates the original client IP, and the names or IP addresses of any intermediate proxies.

# Monitoring Your Website

Monitoring your website is one of the most important—and most often overlooked—QA measures you can take. The only thing worse than being up at three in the morning fixing a broken website is being woken up at three by your boss because the website is down (or, worse still, coming in in the morning to realize that your client just lost ten thousand dollars in sales because the website had been down all night and no one noticed).

There's nothing you can do about failures: they are as inevitable as death and taxes. However, if there is one thing you can do to convince your boss and your clients that you are great at your job, it's to *always* know about failures before they do.

## Third-Party Uptime Monitors

Having an uptime monitor running on your website's server is as effective as having a smoke alarm in a house that nobody lives in. It might be able to catch errors if a certain page goes down, but if the whole *server* goes down, it may go down without even sending out an SOS. That's why your first line of defense should be third-party uptime monitors. UptimeRobot (*http://uptimerobot.com*) is free for up to 50 monitors and is simple to configure. Alerts can go to email, SMS (text message), Twitter, or an iPhone app. You can monitor for the return code from a single page (anything other than a 200 is considered an error), or to check for the presence or absence of a keyword on the page. Keep in mind that if you use a keyword monitor, it may affect your analytics (you can exclude traffic from uptime monitors in most analytics services).

If your needs are more sophisticated, there are other, more expensive services out there such as Pingdom (*http://pingdom.com*) and Site24x7 (*http://www.site24x7.com*).

## Application Failures

Uptime monitors are great for detecting massive failures. And they can even be used to detect application failures if you use keyword monitors. For example, if you religiously include they keyword "server failure" when your website reports an error, keyword monitoring may meet your needs. However, often there are failures that you want to handle gracefully. Your user gets a nice "We're sorry, but this service is currently not functioning" message, and you get an email or text message letting you know about the failure. Commonly, this is the approach you would take when you rely on third-party components, such as databases or other web servers.

One easy way to handle application failures is to have errors emailed to yourself. In Chapter 11, we showed how you can create an error-handling mechanism that notifies you of errors.

If your notification needs are sophisticated (for example, if you have a large IT staff, some of whom are "on call" on a rotating basis), you might consider looking into a notification service, like Amazon's Simple Notification Service (SNS).

You can also look into dedicated error-monitoring services, such as Sentry (*https://getsentry.com*) or Airbrake (*https://airbrake.io*), which can provide a more friendly experience than getting error emails.

# Stress Testing

Stress testing (or load testing) is designed to give you some confidence that your server will function under the load of hundreds or thousands of simultaneous requests. This is another deep area that could be the subject for a whole book: stress testing can be arbitrarily sophisticated, and how complicated you want to get depends largely on the nature of your project. If you have reason to believe that your site could be massively popular, you might want to invest more time in stress testing.

For now, let's add a simple test to make sure your application can serve the home page fifty times in under a second. For the stress testing, we'll use a Node module called *loadtest*:

```
npm install --save loadtest
```

Now let's add a test suite, called *qa/tests-stress.js*:

```
var loadtest = require('loadtest');
var expect = require('chai').expect;

suite('Stress tests', function(){
```

```
test('Homepage should handle 50 requests in a second', function(done){
    var options = {
        url: 'http://localhost:3000',
        concurrency: 4,
        maxRequests: 50,
    };
    loadtest.loadTest(options, function(err,result){
      expect(!err);
      expect(result.totalTimeSeconds < 1);
      done();
    });
});

});
```

We've already got our Mocha task configured in Grunt, so we should just be able to run grunt, and see our new test passing (don't forget to start your server in a separate window first).

# CHAPTER 13

# Persistence

All but the simplest websites and web applications are going to require *persistence* of some kind; that is, some way to store data that's more permanent than volatile memory, so that your data will survive server crashes, power outages, upgrades, and relocations. In this chapter, we'll be discussing the options available for persistence, with a focus on document databases.

## Filesystem Persistence

One way to achieve persistence is to simply save data to so-called "flat files" ("flat" because there's no inherent structure in a file: it's just a sequence of bytes). Node makes filesystem persistence possible through the fs (filesystem) module.

Filesystem persistence has some drawbacks. In particular, it doesn't scale well: the minute you need more than one server to meet traffic demands, you will run into problems with filesystem persistence, unless all of your servers have access to a shared filesystem. Also, because flat files have no inherent structure, the burden of locating, sorting, and filtering data will be on your application. For these reasons, you should favor databases over filesystems for storing data. The one exception is storing binary files, such as images, audio files, or videos. While many databases can handle this type of data, they rarely do so more efficiently than a filesystem (though information *about* the binary files is usually stored in a database to enable searching, sorting, and filtering).

If you do need to store binary data, keep in mind that filesystem storage still has the problem of not scaling well. If your hosting doesn't have access to a shared filesystem (which is usually the case), you should consider storing binary files in a database (which usually requires some configuration so the database doesn't grind to a stop), or a cloud-based storage service, like Amazon S3 or Microsoft Azure Storage.

Now that we've got the caveats out of the way, let's look at Node's filesystem support. We'll revisit the vacation photo contest from Chapter 8. In our application file, let's fill in the handler that processes that form (make sure you have `var fs = require(fs)` before this code):

```
// make sure data directory exists
var dataDir = __dirname + '/data';
var vacationPhotoDir = dataDir + '/vacation-photo';
fs.existsSync(dataDir) || fs.mkdirSync(dataDir);
fs.existsSync(vacationPhotoDir) || fs.mkdirSync(vacationPhotoDir);

function saveContestEntry(contestName, email, year, month, photoPath){
    // TODO...this will come later
}

app.post('/contest/vacation-photo/:year/:month', function(req, res){
    var form = new formidable.IncomingForm();
    form.parse(req, function(err, fields, files){
        if(err) {
            res.session.flash = {
                type: 'danger',
                intro: 'Oops!',
                message: 'There was an error processing your submission. ' +
                    'Please try again.',
            };
            return res.redirect(303, '/contest/vacation-photo');
        }
        var photo = files.photo;
        var dir = vacationPhotoDir + '/' + Date.now();
        var path = dir + '/' + photo.name;
        fs.mkdirSync(dir);
        fs.renameSync(photo.path, dir + '/' + photo.name);
        saveContestEntry('vacation-photo', fields.email,
            req.params.year, req.params.month, path);
        req.session.flash = {
            type: 'success',
            intro: 'Good luck!',
            message: 'You have been entered into the contest.',
        };
        return res.redirect(303, '/contest/vacation-photo/entries');
    });
});
```

There's a lot going on there, so let's break it down. We first create a directory to store the uploaded files (if it doesn't already exist). You'll probably want to add the *data* directory to your *.gitignore* file so you don't accidentally commit uploaded files. We then create a new instance of Formidable's `IncomingForm` and call its `parse` method, passing in the req object. The callback provides all the fields and the files that were uploaded. Since we called the upload field `photo`, there will be a `files.photo` object containing information about the uploaded files. Since we want to prevent collisions, we can't just use the filename (in case two users both upload *portland.jpg*). To avoid this problem, we create a unique directory based on the timestamp: it's pretty unlikely that two users will both upload *portland.jpg* in the same millisecond! Then we rename (move) the uploaded file (Formidable will have given it a temporary name, which we can get from the `path` property) to our constructed name.

Finally, we need some way to associate the files that users upload with their email addresses (and the month and year of the submission). We could encode this information into the file or directory names, but we are going to prefer storing this information in a database. Since we haven't learned how to do that yet, we're going to encapsulate that functionality in the `vacationPhotoContest` function and complete that function later in this chapter.

 In general, you should never trust anything that the user uploads: it's a possible vector for your website to be attacked. For example, a malicious user could easily take a harmful executable, rename it with a *.jpg* extension, and upload it as the first step in an attack (hoping to find some way to execute it at a later point). Likewise, we are taking a little risk here by naming the file using the `name` property provided by the browser: someone could also abuse this by inserting special characters into the filename. To make this code completely safe, we would give the file a random name, taking only the extension (making sure it consists only of alphanumeric characters).

## Cloud Persistence

Cloud storage is becoming increasingly popular, and I highly recommend you take advantage of one of these inexpensive, easy-to-use services. Here's an example of how easy it is to save a file to an Amazon S3 account:

```
var filename = 'customerUpload.jpg';

aws.putObject({
    ACL: 'private',
    Bucket: 'uploads',
    Key: filename,
    Body: fs.readFileSync(__dirname + '/tmp/ + filename)
});
```

See the AWS SDK documentation (*http://aws.amazon.com/sdkfornodejs*) for more information.

And an example of how to do the same thing with Microsoft Azure:

```
var filename = 'customerUpload.jpg';

var blobService = azure.createBlobService();
blobService.putBlockBlobFromFile('uploads', filename, __dirname +
    '/tmp/' + filename);
```

See the Microsoft Azure documentation (*http://bit.ly/azure_documentation*) for more information.

# Database Persistence

All except the simplest websites and web applications require a database. Even if the bulk of your data is binary, and you're using a shared filesystem or cloud storage, the chances are you'll want a database to help catalog that binary data.

Traditionally, the word "database" is shorthand for "relational database management system" (RDBMS). Relational databases, such as Oracle, MySQL, PostgreSQL, or SQL Server are based on decades of research and formal database theory. It is a technology that is quite mature at this point, and the power of these databases is unquestionable. However, unless you are Amazon or Facebook, you have the luxury of expanding your ideas of what constitutes a database. "NoSQL" databases have come into vogue in recent years, and they're challenging the status quo of Internet data storage.

It would be foolish to claim that NoSQL databases are somehow better than relational databases, but they do have certain advantages (and vice versa). While it is quite easy to integrate a relational database with Node apps, there are NoSQL databases that seem almost to have been designed for Node.

The two most popular types of NoSQL databases are *document databases* and *key-value* databases. Document databases excel at storing objects, which makes them a natural fit for Node and JavaScript. Key-value databases, as the name implies, are extremely simple, and are a great choice for applications with data schemas that are easily mapped into key-value pairs.

I feel that document databases represent the optimal compromise between the constraints of relational databases and the simplicity of key-value databases, and for that reason, we will be using a document database for our examples. MongoDB is the leading document database, and is very robust and established at this point.

## A Note on Performance

The simplicity of NoSQL databases is a double-edged sword. Carefully planning a relational database can be a very involved task, but the benefit of that careful planning is databases that offer excellent performance. Don't be fooled into thinking that because NoSQL databases are generally more simple, that there isn't an art and a science to tuning them for maximum performance.

Relational databases have traditionally relied on their rigid data structures and decades of optimization research to achieve high performance. NoSQL databases, on the other hand, have embraced the distributed nature of the Internet and, like Node, have instead focused on concurrency to scale performance (relational databases also support concurrency, but this is usually reserved for the most demanding applications).

Planning for database performance and scalability is a large, complex topic that is beyond the scope of this book. If your application requires a high level of database performance, I recommend starting with Kristina Chodorow's *MongoDB: The Definitive Guide* (O'Reilly).

## Setting Up MongoDB

The difficulty involved in setting up a MongoDB instance varies with your operating system. For this reason, we'll be avoiding the problem altogether by using an excellent free MongoDB hosting service, MongoLab.

MongoLab is not the only MongoDB service available. MongoHQ (*https://www.mongohq.com*), among others, offer free development/sandbox accounts. These accounts are not recommended for production purposes, though. Both MongoLab and MongoHQ offer production-ready accounts, so you should look into their pricing before making a choice: it will be less hassle to stay with the same hosting service when you make the switch to production.

Getting started with MongoLab is simple. Just go to *http://mongolab.com* and click Sign Up. Fill out the registration form and log in, and you'll be at your home screen. Under Databases, you'll see "no databases at this time." Click "Create new," and you will be taken to a page with some options for your new database. The first thing you'll select is a cloud provider. For a free (sandbox) account, the choice is largely irrelevant, though you should look for a data center near you (not every data center will offer sandbox accounts, however). Select "Single-node (development)," and Sandbox. You can select the version of MongoDB you want to use: the examples in this book use version 2.4. Finally, choose a database name, and click "Create new MongoDB deployment."

## Mongoose

While there's a low-level driver available for MongoDB (*https://npmjs.org/package/mongodb*), you'll probably want to use an "object document mapper" (ODM). The officially supported ODM for MongoDB is *Mongoose*.

One of the advantages of JavaScript is that its object model is extremely flexible: if you want to add a property or method to an object, you just do it, and you don't need to worry about modifying a class. Unfortunately, that kind of free-wheeling flexibility can have a negative impact on your databases: they can become fragmented and hard to optimize. Mongoose attempts to strike a balance: it introduces *schemas* and *models* (combined, schemas and models are similar to classes in traditional object-oriented programming). The schemas are flexible but still provide some necessary structure for your database.

Before we get started, we'll need to install the Mongoose module:

```
npm install --save mongoose@3.8
```

Then we'll add our database credentials to the *credentials.js* file:

```
mongo: {
    development: {
        connectionString: 'your_dev_connection_string',
    },
    production: {
        connectionString: 'your_production_connection_string',
    },
},
```

You'll find your connection string on the database page in MongoLab: from your home screen, click the appropriate database. You'll see a box with your MongoDB connection URI (it starts with *mongodb://*). You'll also need a user for your database. To create one, click Users, then "Add database user."

Notice that we store two sets of credentials: one for development and one for production. You can go ahead and set up two databases now, or just point both to the same database (when it's time to go live, you can switch to using two separate databases).

## Database Connections with Mongoose

We'll start by creating a connection to our database:

```
var mongoose = require('mongoose');
var opts = {
    server: {
        socketOptions: { keepAlive: 1 }
    }
};
switch(app.get('env')){
    case 'development':
        mongoose.connect(credentials.mongo.development.connectionString, opts);
        break;
    case 'production':
        mongoose.connect(credentials.mongo.production.connectionString, opts);
        break;
    default:
        throw new Error('Unknown execution environment: ' + app.get('env'));
}
```

The options object is optional, but we want to specify the keepAlive option, which will prevent database connection errors for long-running applications (like a website).

# Creating Schemas and Models

Let's create a vacation package database for Meadowlark Travel. We start by defining a schema and creating a model from it. Create the file *models/vacation.js*:

```
var mongoose = require('mongoose');

var vacationSchema = mongoose.Schema({
    name: String,
    slug: String,
    category: String,
    sku: String,
    description: String,
    priceInCents: Number,
    tags: [String],
    inSeason: Boolean,
    available: Boolean,
    requiresWaiver: Boolean,
    maximumGuests: Number,
    notes: String,
    packagesSold: Number,
});
vacationSchema.methods.getDisplayPrice = function(){
    return '$' + (this.priceInCents / 100).toFixed(2);
};
var Vacation = mongoose.model('Vacation', vacationSchema);
module.exports = Vacation;
```

This code declares the properties that make up our vacation model, and the types of those properties. You'll see there are several string properties, two numeric properties, two Boolean properties, and an array of strings (denoted by [String]). At this point, we can also define methods on our schema. We're storing product prices in cents instead of dollars to help prevent any floating-point rounding trouble, but obviously we want to display our products in US dollars (until it's time to internationalize, of course!). So we add a method called getDisplayPrice to get a price suitable for display. Each product has a "stock keeping unit" (SKU); even though we don't think about vacations being "stock items," the concept of an SKU is pretty standard for accounting, even when tangible goods aren't being sold.

Once we have the schema, we create a model using mongoose.model: at this point, Vacation is very much like a class in traditional object-oriented programming. Note that we have to define our methods before we create our model.

 Due to the nature of floating-point numbers, you should always be careful with financial computations in JavaScript. Storing prices in cents helps, but it doesn't eliminate the problems. A decimal type suitable for financial calculations will be available in the next version of JavaScript (ES6).

We are exporting the `Vacation` model object created by Mongoose. To use this model in our application, we can import it like this:

```
var Vacation = require('./models/vacation.js');
```

## Seeding Initial Data

We don't yet have any vacation packages in our database, so we'll add some to get us started. Eventually, you may want to create a way to manage products, but for the purposes of this book, we're just going to do it in code:

```
Vacation.find(function(err, vacations){
    if(err) return cosole.error(err);
    if(vacations.length) return;

    new Vacation({
        name: 'Hood River Day Trip',
        slug: 'hood-river-day-trip',
        category: 'Day Trip',
        sku: 'HR199',
        description: 'Spend a day sailing on the Columbia and ' +
            'enjoying craft beers in Hood River!',
        priceInCents: 9995,
        tags: ['day trip', 'hood river', 'sailing', 'windsurfing', 'breweries'],
        inSeason: true,
        maximumGuests: 16,
        available: true,
        packagesSold: 0,
    }).save();

    new Vacation({
        name: 'Oregon Coast Getaway',
        slug: 'oregon-coast-getaway',
        category: 'Weekend Getaway',
        sku: 'OC39',
        description: 'Enjoy the ocean air and quaint coastal towns!',
        priceInCents: 269995,
        tags: ['weekend getaway', 'oregon coast', 'beachcombing'],
        inSeason: false,
        maximumGuests: 8,
        available: true,
        packagesSold: 0,
    }).save();

    new Vacation({
        name: 'Rock Climbing in Bend',
        slug: 'rock-climbing-in-bend',
        category: 'Adventure',
        sku: 'B99',
        description: 'Experience the thrill of climbing in the high desert.',
        priceInCents: 289995,
        tags: ['weekend getaway', 'bend', 'high desert', 'rock climbing'],
```

```
        inSeason: true,
        requiresWaiver: true,
        maximumGuests: 4,
        available: false,
        packagesSold: 0,
        notes: 'The tour guide is currently recovering from a skiing accident.',
    }).save();
});
```

There are two Mongoose methods being used here. The first, find, does just what it says. In this case, it's finding all instances of Vacation in the database and invoking the callback with that list. We're doing that because we don't want to keep readding our seed vacations: if there are already vacations in the database, it's been seeded, and we can go on our merry way. The first time this executes, though, find will return an empty list, so we proceed to create two vacations, and then call the save method on them, which saves these new objects to the database.

## Retrieving Data

We've already seen the find method, which is what we'll use to display a list of vacations. However, this time we're going to pass an option to find that will filter the data. Specifically, we want to display only vacations that are currently available.

Create a view for the products page, *views/vacations.handlebars*:

```
<h1>Vacations</h1>
{{#each vacations}}
    <div class="vacation">
        <h3>{{name}}</h3>
        <p>{{description}}</p>
        {{#if inSeason}}
            <span class="price">{{price}}</span>
            <a href="/cart/add?sku={{sku}}" class="btn btn-default">Buy Now!</a>
        {{else}}
            <span class="outOfSeason">We're sorry, this vacation is currently
            not in season.
            {{! The "notify me when this vacation is in season"
                page will be our next task. }}
            <a href="/notify-me-when-in-season?sku={{sku}}">Notify me when
            this vacation is in season.</a>
        {{/if}}
    </div>
{{/each}}
```

Now we can create route handlers that hook it all up:

```
// see companion repository for /cart/add route....

app.get('/vacations', function(req, res){
    Vacation.find({ available: true }, function(err, vacations){
        var context = {
```

```
            vacations: vacations.map(function(vacation){
                return {
                    sku: vacation.sku,
                    name: vacation.name,
                    description: vacation.description,
                    price: vacation.getDisplayPrice(),
                    inSeason: vacation.inSeason,
                }
            })
        };
        res.render('vacations', context);
    });
});
```

Most of this should be looking pretty familiar, but there might be some things that surprise you. For instance, how we're handling the view context for the vacation listing might seem odd. Why did we map the products returned from the database to a nearly identical object? One reason is that there's no built-in way for a Handlebars view to use the output of a function in an expression. So to display the price in a neatly formatted way, we have to convert it to a simple string property. We could have done this:

```
var context = {
    vacations: products.map(function(vacations){
        vacation.price = vacation.getDisplayPrice();
        return vacation;
    });
};
```

That would certainly save us a few lines of code, but in my experience, there are good reasons not to pass unmapped database objects directly to views. The view gets a bunch of properties it may not need, possibly in formats that are incompatible with it. Our example is pretty simple so far, but once it starts to get more complicated, you'll probably want to do even more customization of the data that's passed to a view. It also makes it easy to accidentally expose confidential information, or information that could compromise the security of your website. For these reasons, I recommend mapping the data that's returned from the database and passing only what's needed onto the view (transforming as necessary, as we did with price).

In some variations of the MVC architecture, a third component called a "view model" is introduced. A view model essentially distills and transforms a model (or models) so that it's more appropriate for display in a view. What we're doing above is essentially creating a view model on the fly.

# Adding Data

We've already seen how we can add data (we added data when we seeded the vacation collection) and how we can update data (we update the count of packages sold when we book a vacation), but let's take a look at a slightly more involved scenario that highlights the flexibility of document databases.

When a vacation is out of season, we display a link that invites the customer to be notified when the vacation is in season again. Let's hook up that functionality. First, we create the schema and model (*models/vacationInSeasonListener.js*):

```
var mongoose = require('mongoose');

var vacationInSeasonListenerSchema = mongoose.Schema({
    email: String,
    skus: [String],
});
var VacationInSeasonListener = mongoose.model('VacationInSeasonListener',
    vacationInSeasonListenerSchema);

module.exports = VacationInSeasonListener;
```

Then we'll create our view, *views/notify-me-when-in-season.handlebars*:

```
<div class="formContainer">
    <form class="form-horizontal newsletterForm" role="form"
            action="/notify-me-when-in-season" method="POST">
        <input type="hidden" name="sku" value="{{sku}}">
        <div class="form-group">
            <label for="fieldEmail" class="col-sm-2 control-label">Email</label>
            <div class="col-sm-4">
                <input type="email" class="form-control" required
                    id="fieldEmail" name="email">
            </div>
        </div>
        <div class="form-group">
            <div class="col-sm-offset-2 col-sm-4">
                <button type="submit" class="btn btn-default">Submit</button>
            </div>
        </div>
    </form>
</div>
```

And finally, the route handlers:

```
var VacationInSeasonListener = require('./models/vacationInSeasonListener.js');

app.get('/notify-me-when-in-season', function(req, res){
    res.render('notify-me-when-in-season', { sku: req.query.sku });
});

app.post('/notify-me-when-in-season', function(req, res){
    VacationInSeasonListener.update(
        { email: req.body.email },
        { $push: { skus: req.body.sku } },
        { upsert: true },
        function(err){
```

```
                    if(err) {
                        console.error(err.stack);
                        req.session.flash = {
                            type: 'danger',
                            intro: 'Ooops!',
                            message: 'There was an error processing your request.',
                        };
                        return res.redirect(303, '/vacations');
                    }
                    req.session.flash = {
                        type: 'success',
                        intro: 'Thank you!',
                        message: 'You will be notified when this vacation is in season.',
                    };
                    return res.redirect(303, '/vacations');
                }
            );
    });
```

What magic is this? How can we "update" a record in the `VacationInSeasonListen`
`er` collection before it even exists? The answer lies in a Mongoose convenience called
an *upsert* (a portmanteau of "update" and "insert"). Basically, if a record with the given
email address doesn't exist, it will be created. If a record does exist, it will be updated.
Then we use the magic variable `$push` to indicate that we want to add a value to an array.
Hopefully this will give you a taste of what Mongoose provides for you, and why you
may want to use it instead of the low-level MongoDB driver.

 This code doesn't prevent multiple SKUs from being added to the
record if the user fills out the form multiple times. When a vacation
comes into season, and we find all the customers who want to be
notified, we will have to be careful not to notify them multiple times.

## Using MongoDB for Session Storage

As we discussed in Chapter 9, using a memory store for session data is unsuitable in a
production environment. Fortunately, it's very easy to set up MongoDB to use as a
session store.

We'll be using a package called `session-mongoose` to provide MongoDB session storage. Once you've installed it (`npm install --save session-mongoose`), we can set it
up in our main application file:

```
var MongoSessionStore = require('session-mongoose')(require('connect'));
var sessionStore = new MongoSessionStore({ url:
    credentials.mongo[app.get('env')].connectionString });

app.use(require('cookie-parser')(credentials.cookieSecret));
app.use(require('express-session')({
```

```
        resave: false,
        saveUninitialized: false,
        secret: credentials.cookieSecret,
        store: sessionStore,
}));
```

Let's use our newly minted session store for something useful. Imagine we want to be able to display vacation prices in different currencies. Furthermore, we want the site to remember the user's currency preference.

We'll start by adding a currency picker at the bottom of our vacations page:

```
<hr>
<p>Currency:
    <a href="/set-currency/USD" class="currency {{currencyUSD}}">USD</a> |
    <a href="/set-currency/GBP" class="currency {{currencyGBP}}">GBP</a> |
    <a href="/set-currency/BTC" class="currency {{currencyBTC}}">BTC</a>
</p>
```

Now a little CSS:

```
a.currency {
    text-decoration: none;
}
.currency.selected {
    font-weight: bold;
    font-size: 150%;
}
```

Lastly, we'll add a route handler to set the currency, and modify our route handler for *vacations* to display prices in the current currency:

```
app.get('/set-currency/:currency', function(req,res){
    req.session.currency = req.params.currency;
    return res.redirect(303, '/vacations');
});

function convertFromUSD(value, currency){
    switch(currency){
        case 'USD': return value * 1;
        case 'GBP': return value * 0.6;
        case 'BTC': return value * 0.0023707918444761;
        default: return NaN;
    }
}

app.get('/vacations', function(req, res){
    Vacation.find({ available: true }, function(err, vacations){
        var currency = req.session.currency || 'USD';
        var context = {
            currency: currency,
            vacations: vacations.map(function(vacation){
                return {
                    sku: vacation.sku,
```

```
                name: vacation.name,
                description: vacation.description,
                inSeason: vacation.inSeason,
                price: convertFromUSD(vacation.priceInCents/100, currency),
                qty: vacation.qty,
            }
        })
    };
    switch(currency){
        case 'USD': context.currencyUSD = 'selected'; break;
        case 'GBP': context.currencyGBP = 'selected'; break;
        case 'BTC': context.currencyBTC = 'selected'; break;
    }
    res.render('vacations', context);
    });
});
```

This isn't a great way to perform currency conversion, of course: we would want to utilize a third-party currency conversion API to make sure our rates are up-to-date. But this will suffice for demonstration purposes. You can now switch between the various currencies and—go ahead and try it—stop and restart your server…you'll find it re-members your currency preference! If you clear your cookies, the currency preference will be forgotten. You'll notice that now we've lost our pretty currency formatting: it's now more complicated, and I will leave that as an exercise for the reader.

If you look in your database, you'll find there's a new collection called "sessions": if you explore that collection, you'll find a document with your session ID (property sid) and your currency preference.

 MongoDB is not necessarily the best choice for session storage: it is overkill for that purpose. Another popular and easy-to-use alternative for session persistence is Redis (*http://redis.io*). See the connect-redis package (*https://www.npmjs.org/package/connect-redis*) for instructions on setting up a session store with Redis.

CHAPTER 14

# Routing

Routing is one of the most important aspects of your website or web service; fortunately, routing in Express is simple, flexible, and robust. *Routing* is the mechanism by which requests (as specified by a URL and HTTP method) are routed to the code that handles them. As we've already noted, routing used to be file based and very simple: if you put the file *foo/about.html* on your website, you would access it from the browser with the path */foo/about.html*. Simple, but inflexible. And, in case you hadn't noticed, having "HTML" in your URL is extremely passé these days.

Before we dive into the technical aspects of routing with Express, we should discuss the concept of *information architecture* (IA). IA refers to the conceptual organization of your content. Having an extensible (but not overcomplicated) IA before you begin thinking about routing will pay huge dividends down the line.

One of the most intelligent and timeless essays on IA is by Tim Berners-Lee, who practically *invented the Internet*. You can (and should) read it now: *http://www.w3.org/Provider/Style/URI.html*. It was written in 1998. Let that sink in for a minute: there's not much that was written on Internet technology in 1998 that is just as true today as it was then.

From that essay, here is the lofty responsibility we are being asked to take on:

> It is the duty of a Webmaster to allocate URIs which you will be able to stand by in 2 years, in 20 years, in 200 years. This needs thought, and organization, and commitment.
>
> — Tim Berners-Lee

I like to think that if web design ever required professional licensing, like other kinds of engineering, that we would take an oath to that effect. (The astute reader of that article will find humor in the fact that the URL to that article ends with *.html*.)

To make an analogy (that may sadly be lost on the younger audience), imagine that every two years, your favorite library completely reordered the Dewey Decimal System.

You would walk into the library one day, and you wouldn't be able to find anything. That's exactly what happens when you redesign your URL structure.

Put some serious thought into your URLs: will they still make sense in 20 years? (200 years may be a bit of a stretch: who knows if we'll even be using URLs by then. Still, I admire the dedication of thinking that far into the future.) Carefully consider the breakdown of your content. Categorize things logically, and try not to paint yourself into a corner. It's a science, but it's also an art.

Perhaps most important, work with others to design your URLs. Even if you are the best information architect for miles around, you might be surprised at how people look at the same content with a different perspective. I'm not saying that you should try for an IA that makes sense from *everyone's* perspective (because that is usually quite impossible), but being able to see the problem from multiple perspectives will give you better ideas and expose the flaws in your own IA.

Here are some suggestions to help you achieve a lasting IA:

*Never expose technical details in your URLs*
> Have you ever been to a website, noticed that the URL ended in *.asp*, and thought that the website was hopelessly out-of-date? Remember that, once upon a time, ASP was cutting-edge. Though it pains me to say it, so too shall fall JavaScript and JSON and Node and Express. Hopefully not for many, many productive years, but time is not often kind to technology.

*Avoid meaningless information in your URLs*
> Think carefully about every word in your URL. If it doesn't mean anything, leave it out. For example, it always makes me cringe when websites use the word *home* in URLs. Your root URL *is* your home page. You don't need to additionally have URLs like */home/directions* and */home/contact*.

*Avoid needlessly long URLs*
> All things being equal, a short URL is better than a longer URL. However, you should not try to make URLs short at the expense of clarity, or SEO. Abbreviations are tempting, but think carefully about them: they should be very common and ubiquitous before you immortalize them in a URL.

*Be consistent with word separators*
> It's quite common to separate words with hyphens, and a little less common to do so with underscores. Hyphens are generally considered more aesthetically pleasing than underscores, and most SEO experts recommend them. Whether you choose hyphens or underscores, be consistent in their use.

*Never use whitespace or untypable characters*
> Whitespace in a URL is not recommended. It will usually just be converted to a plus sign (+), leading to confusion. It should be obvious that you should avoid untypable

characters, and I would caution you strongly against using any characters other than alphanumeric characters, numbers, dashes, and underscores. It may feel clever at the time, but "clever" has a way of not standing the test of time. Obviously, if your website is not for an English audience, you may use non-English characters (using percent codes), though that can cause headaches if you ever want to localize your website.

*Use lowercase for your URLs*

This one will cause some debate: there are those who feel that mixed case in URLs is not only acceptable, but preferable. I don't want to get in a religious debate over this, but I will point out that the advantage of lowercase is that it can always automatically be generated by code. If you've ever had to go through a website and sanitize thousands of links, or do string comparisons, you will appreciate this argument. I personally feel that lowercase URLs are more aesthetically pleasing, but in the end, this decision is up to you.

# Routes and SEO

If you want your website to be discoverable (and most people do), then you need to think about SEO, and how your URLs can affect it. In particular, if there are certain keywords that are very important—*and it makes sense*—consider making it part of the URL. For example, Meadowlark Travel offers several Oregon Coast vacations: to ensure high search engine ranking for these vacations, we use the string "Oregon Coast" in the title, header, body, and meta description, and the URLs start with */vacations/oregon-coast*. The Manzanita vacation package can be found at */vacations/oregon-coast/manzanita*. If, to shorten the URL, we simply used */vacations/manzanita*, we would be losing out on valuable SEO.

That said, resist the temptation to carelessly jam keywords into URLs in an attempt to improve your rankings: it will fail. For example, changing the Manzanita vacation URL to */vacations/oregon-coast-portland-and-hood-river/oregon-coast/manzanita* in an effort to say "Oregon Coast" one more time, and also work the "Portland" and "Hood River" keywords in at the same time, is wrong-headed. It flies in the face of good IA, and will likely backfire.

# Subdomains

Along with the path, subdomains are the other part of the URL that is commonly used to route requests. Subdomains are best reserved for significantly different parts of your application—for example, a REST API (*api.meadowlarktravel.com*) or an admin interface (*admin.meadowlarktravel.com*). Sometimes subdomains are used for technical reasons. For example, if we were to build our blog with WordPress (while the rest of our site uses Express), it can be easier to use *blog.meadowlarktravel.com* (a better solution would be to use a proxy server, such as Nginx). There are usually SEO consequences to partitioning your content using subdomains, which is why you should generally reserve them for areas of your site that aren't important to SEO, such as admin areas and APIs. Keep this in mind and make sure there's no other option before using a subdomain for content that is imporant to your SEO plan.

The routing mechanism in Express does not take subdomains into account by default: `app.get(/about)` will handle requests for *http://meadowlarktravel.com/about, http:// www.meadowlarktravel.com/about,* and *http://admin.meadowlarktravel.com/about*. If you want to handle a subdomain separately, you can use a package called `vhost` (for "virtual host," which comes from an Apache mechanism commonly used for handling subdomains). First, install the package (`npm install --save vhost`), then edit your application file to create a subdomain:

```
// create "admin" subdomain...this should appear
// before all your other routes
var admin = express.Router();
app.use(vhost('admin.*', admin));

// create admin routes; these can be defined anywhere
admin.get('/', function(req, res){
        res.render('admin/home');
});
admin.get('/users', function(req, res){
        res.render('admin/users');
});
```

`express.Router()` essentially creates a new instance of the Express router. You can treat this instance just like your original instance (`app`): you can add routes and middleware just as you would to `app`. However, it won't do anything until you add it to `app`. We add it through `vhost`, which binds that router instance to that subdomain.

# Route Handlers Are Middleware

We've already seen very basic route: simply matching a given path. But what does `app.get('/foo',...)` actually *do*? As we saw in Chapter 10, it's simply a specialized piece of middleware, down to having a `next` method passed in. Let's look at some more sophisticated examples:

```
app.get('/foo', function(req,res,next){
        if(Math.random() < 0.5) return next();
        res.send('sometimes this');
});
app.get('/foo', function(req,res){
        res.send('and sometimes that');
});
```

In the previous example, we have two handlers for the same route. Normally, the first one would win, but in this case, the first one is going to pass approximately half the time, giving the second one a chance. We don't even have to use `app.get` twice: you can use as many handlers as you want for a single `app.get` call. Here's an example that has an approximately equal chance of three different responses:

```
app.get('/foo',
        function(req,res, next){
                if(Math.random() < 0.33) return next();
                res.send('red');
        },
        function(req,res, next){
                if(Math.random() < 0.5) return next();
                res.send('green');
        },
        function(req,res){
                res.send('blue');
        },
    )
```

While this may not seem particularly useful at first, it allows you to create generic functions that can be used in any of your routes. For example, let's say we have a mechanism that shows special offers on certain pages. The special offers change frequently, and they're not shown on every page. We can create a function to inject the specials into the `res.locals` property (which you'll remember from Chapter 7):

```
function specials(req, res, next){
        res.locals.specials = getSpecialsFromDatabase();
        next();
}

app.get('/page-with-specials', specials, function(req,res){
        res.render('page-with-specials');
});
```

We could also implement an authorization mechanism with this approach. Let's say our user authorization code sets a session variable called `req.session.authorized`. We can use the following to make a reusable authorization filter:

```
function authorize(req, res, next){
        if(req.session.authorized) return next();
        res.render('not-authorized');
}

app.get('/secret', authorize, function(){
        res.render('secret');
})

app.get('/sub-rosa', authorize, function(){
        res.render('sub-rosa');
});
```

# Route Paths and Regular Expressions

When you specify a path (like */foo*) in your route, it's eventually converted to a regular expression by Express. Some regular expression metacharacters are available in route paths: +, ?, *, (, and ). Let's look at a couple of examples. Let's say you want the URLs */user* and */username* to be handled by the same route:

```
app.get('/user(name)?', function(req,res){
        res.render('user');
});
```

One of my favorite novelty websites is *http://khaaan.com*. Go ahead: I'll wait while you visit it. Feel better? Good. Let's say we want to make our own "KHAAAAAAAAN" page, but we don't want our users to have to remember if it's 2 *a*'s or 3 or 10. The following will get the job done:

```
app.get('/khaa+n', function(req,res){
        res.render('khaaan');
});
```

Not all normal regex metacharacters have meaning in route paths, though—only the ones listed earlier. This is important, because periods, which are normally a regex metacharacter meaning "any character," can be used in routes unescaped.

Lastly, if you really need the full power of regular expressions for your route, that is supported:

```
app.get(/crazy|mad(ness)?|lunacy/, function(req,res){
        res.render('madness');
});
```

I have yet to find a good reason for using regex metacharacters in my route paths, much less full regexes, but it's good to know the functionality is there.

# Route Parameters

Where regex routes may find little day-to-day use in your Expression toolbox, you'll most likely be using route parameters quite frequently. In short, it's a way to make part of your route into a variable parameter. Let's say in our website we want to have a page for each staff member. We have a database of staff members with bios and pictures. As our company grows, it becomes more and more unwieldy to add a new route for each staff member. Let's see how route parameters can help us:

```
var staff = {
        mitch: { bio: 'Mitch is the man to have at your back in a bar fight.' },
        madeline: { bio: 'Madeline is our Oregon expert.' },
        walt: { bio: 'Walt is our Oregon Coast expert.' },
};
```

```
app.get('/staff/:name', function(req, res){
        var info = staff[req.params.name];
        if(!info) return next();        // will eventually fall through to 404
        res.render('staffer', info);
})
```

Note how we used *:name* in our route. That will match any string (that doesn't include a forward slash) and put it in the `req.params` object with the key `name`. This is a feature we will be using often, especially when creating a REST API. You can have multiple parameters in our route. For example, if we want to break up our staff listing by city:

```
var staff = {
        portland: {
                mitch: { bio: 'Mitch is the man to have at your back.' },
                madeline: { bio: 'Madeline is our Oregon expert.' },
        },
        bend: {
                walt: { bio: 'Walt is our Oregon Coast expert.' },
        },
};

app.get('/staff/:city/:name', function(req, res){
        var info = staff[req.params.city][req.params.name];
        if(!info) return next();        // will eventually fall through to 404
        res.render('staffer', info);
});
```

# Organizing Routes

It may be clear to you already that it would be unwieldy to define all of our routes in the main application file. Not only will that file grow over time, it's also not a great separation of functionality: there's a lot going on in that file already. A simple site may have only a dozen routes or fewer, but a larger site could have hundreds of routes.

So how to organize your routes? Well, how do you *want* to organize your routes? Express is not opinionated about how you organize your routes, so how you do it is limited only by your own imagination.

I'll cover some popular ways to handle routes in the next sections, but at the end of the day, I recommend four guiding principles for deciding how to organize your routes:

*Use named functions for route handlers*

Up to now, we've been writing our route handlers inline, by actually defining the function that handles the route right then and there. This is fine for small applications or prototyping, but it will quickly become unwieldy as your website grows.

*Routes should not be mysterious*

This principle is intentionally vague, because a large, complex website may by necessity require a more complicated organizational scheme than a 10-page website.

At one end of the spectrum is simply putting *all* of the routes for your website in one single file so you know where they are. For large websites, this may be undesirable, so you break the routes out by functional areas. However, even then, it should be clear where you should go to look for a given route. When you need to fix something, the last thing you want to do is have to spend an hour figuring out where the route is being handled. I have an ASP.NET MVC project at work that is a nightmare in this respect: the routes are handled in at least 10 different places, and it's not logical or consistent, and it's often contradictory. Even though I am intimately familiar with that (very large) website, I still have to spend a significant amount of time tracking down where certain URLs are handled.

*Route organization should be extensible*

If you have 20 or 30 routes now, defining them all in one file is probably fine. What about in three years when you have 200 routes? It can happen. Whatever method you choose, you should ensure you have room to grow.

*Don't overlook automatic view-based route handlers*

If your site consists of many pages that are static and have fixed URLs, all of your routes will end up looking like this: app.get('/static/thing', function(req, res){ res.render('static/thing'); }. To reduce needless code repetition, consider using an automatic view-based route handler. This approach is described later in this chapter and can be used together with custom routes.

# Declaring Routes in a Module

The first step to organizing our routes is getting them all into their own module. There are multiple ways to do this. One approach is to make your module a function that returns an array of objects containing "method" and "handler" properties. Then you could define the routes in your application file thusly:

```
var routes = require('./routes.js')();

routes.forEach(function(route){
        app[route.method](route.handler);
})
```

This method has its advantages, and could be well suited to storing our routes dynamically, such as in a database or a JSON file. However, if you don't need that functionality, I recommend passing the app instance to the module, and letting it add the routes. That's the approach we'll take for our example. Create a file called *routes.js* and move all of our existing routes into it:

```
module.exports = function(app){

        app.get('/', function(req,res){
                app.render('home');
        }))

        //...

};
```

If we just cut and paste, we'll probably run into some problems. For example, our /about handler uses the fortune object that isn't available in this context. We could add the necessary imports, but hold off on that: we'll be moving the handlers into their own module soon, and we'll solve the problem then.

So how do we link our routes in? Simple: in *meadowlark.js*, we simply import our routes:

```
require('./routes.js')(app);
```

# Grouping Handlers Logically

To meet our first guiding principle (use named functions for route handlers), we'll need somewhere to put those handlers. One rather extreme option is to have a separate Java-Script file for every handler. It's hard for me to imagine a situation in which this approach would have benefit. It's better to somehow group related functionality together. Not only does that make it easier to leverage shared functionality, but it makes it easier to make changes in related methods.

For now, let's group our functionality into separate files: *handlers/main.js*, where we'll put the home page handler, the "about" handler, and generally any handler that doesn't have another logical home; *handlers/vacations.js*, where vacation-related handlers will go; and so on.

Consider *handlers/main.js*:

```
var fortune = require('../lib/fortune.js');

exports.home = function(req, res){
        res.render('home');
};

exports.about = function(req, res){
        res.render('about', {
                fortune: fortune.getFortune(),
                pageTestScript: '/qa/tests-about.js'
        } );
};

//...
```

Now let's modify *routes.js* to make use of this:

```
var main = require('./handlers/main.js');

module.exports = function(app){

    app.get('/', main.home);
    app.get('/about', main.about);
    //...

};
```

This satisfies all of our guiding principles. */routes.js* is *very* straightforward. It's easy to see at a glance what routes there are in your site and where they are being handled. We've also left ourselves plenty of room to grow. We can group related functionality in as many different files as we need. And if *routes.js* ever gets unwieldy, we can use the same technique again, and pass the app object on to another module that will in turn register more routes (though that is starting to veer into the "overcomplicated" territory—make sure you can really justify an approach that complicated!).

# Automatically Rendering Views

If you ever find yourself wishing for the days of old where you could just put an HTML file in a directory and—presto!—your website would serve it, then you're not alone. If your website is very content-heavy without a lot of functionality, you may find it a needless hassle to add a route for every view. Fortunately, we can get around this problem.

Let's say you just want to add the file *views/foo.handlebars* and just magically have it available on the route */foo*. Let's see how we might do that. In our application file, right before the 404 handler, add the following middleware:

```
var autoViews = {};
var fs = require('fs');

app.use(function(req,res,next){
    var path = req.path.toLowerCase();
    // check cache; if it's there, render the view
    if(autoViews[path]) return res.render(autoViews[path]);
    // if it's not in the cache, see if there's
    // a .handlebars file that matches
    if(fs.existsSync(__dirname + '/views' + path + '.handlebars')){
        autoViews[path] = path.replace(/^\//, '');
        return res.render(autoViews[path]);
    }
    // no view found; pass on to 404 handler
    next();
});
```

Now we can just add a *.handlebars* file to the *view* directory and have it magically render on the appropriate path. Note that regular routes will circumvent this mechanism (because we placed the automatic view handler after all other routes), so if you have a route that renders a different view for the route */foo*, that will take precedence.

# Other Approaches to Route Organization

I've found that the approach I've outlined here offers a great balance between flexibility and effort. However, there are some other popular approaches to route organization. The good news is that they don't conflict with the technique I have described here. So you can mix and match techniques if you find certain areas of your website work better when organized differently (though you run the danger of confusing your architecture).

The two most popular approaches to route organization are *namespaced routing* and *resourceful routing*. Namespaced routing is great when you have many routes that all start with the same prefix (for example, */vacations*). There's a Node module called express-namespace that makes this approach easy. Resourceful routing automatically adds routes based on the methods in an object. It can be a useful technique if your site logic is naturally object-oriented. The package express-resource is an example of how to implement this style of route organization.

Routing is an important part of your project, and if the module-based routing technique I've described in this chapter doesn't seem right for you, I recommend you check out the documentation for express-namespace or express-resource.

# CHAPTER 15
# REST APIs and JSON

So far, we've been designing a website to be consumed by browsers. Now we turn our attention to making data and functionality available to other programs. Increasingly, the Internet is no longer a collections of siloed websites, but a true web: websites communicate freely with each other in order to provide a richer experience for the user. It's a programmer's dream come true: the Internet is becoming as accessible to your code as it has traditionally been to real people.

In this chapter, we'll add a web service to our app (there's no reason that a web server and a web service can't coexist in the same application). The term "web service" is a general term that means any application programming interface (API) that's accessible over HTTP. The idea of web services has been around for quite some time, but until recently, the technologies that enabled them were stuffy, byzantine, and overcomplicated. There are still systems that use those technologies (such as SOAP and WSDL), and there are Node packages that will help you interface with these systems. We won't be covering those, though: instead, we will be focused on providing so-called "RESTful" services, which are much more straightforward to interface with.

The acronym REST stands for "representational state transfer," and the grammatically troubling "RESTful" is used as an adjective to describe a web service that satisfies the principles of REST. The formal description of REST is complicated, and steeped in computer science formality, but the basics are that REST is a stateless connection between a client and a server. The formal definition of REST also specifies that the service can be cached and that services can be layered (that is, when you use a REST API, there may be other REST APIs beneath it).

From a practical standpoint, the constraints of HTTP actually make it difficult to create an API that's not RESTful; you'd have to go out of your way to establish state, for example. So our work is mostly cut out for us.

We'll be adding a REST API to the Meadowlark Travel website. To encourage travel to Oregon, Meadowlark Travel maintains a database of attractions, complete with interesting historical facts. An API allows the creation of apps that enable visitors to go on self-guided tours with their phones or tablets: if the device is location-aware, the app can let them know if they are near an interesting site. So that the database can grow, the API also supports the addition of landmarks and attractions (which go into an approval queue to prevent abuse).

# JSON and XML

Vital to providing an API is having a common language to speak in. Part of the communication is dictated for us: we must use HTTP methods to communicate with the server. But past that, we are free to use whatever data language we choose. Traditionally, XML has been a popular choice, and it remains an important markup language. While XML is not particularly complicated, Douglas Crockford saw that there was room for something more lightweight, and JavaScript object notation (JSON) was born. In addition to being very JavaScript-friendly (though it is by no means proprietary: it is an easy format for any language to parse), it also has the advantage of being generally easier to write by hand than XML.

I prefer JSON over XML for most applications: there's better JavaScript support, and it's a simpler, more compact format. I recommend focusing on JSON and providing XML only if existing systems require XML to communicate with your app.

# Our API

We'll plan our API out before we start implementing it. We will want the following functionality:

GET /api/attractions
> Retrieves attractions. Takes lat, lng, and radius as querystring parameters and returns a list of attractions.

GET /api/attraction/:id
> Returns an attraction by ID.

POST /api/attraction
> Takes lat, lng, name, description, and email in the request body. The newly added attraction goes into an approval queue.

PUT /api/attraction/:id
> Updates an existing attraction. Takes an attraction ID, lat, lng, name, description, and email. Update goes into approval queue.

```
DEL /api/attraction/:id
```
    Deletes an attraction. Takes an attraction ID, `email`, and `reason`. Delete goes into approval queue.

There are many ways we could have described our API. Here, we've chosen to use combinations of HTTP methods and paths to distinguish our API calls, and a mix of querystring and body parameters for passing data. As an alternative, we could have had different paths (such as */api/attractions/delete*) with all the same method.[1] We could also have passed data in a consistent way. For example, we might have chosen to pass all the necessary information for retrieving parameters in the URL instead of using a querystring: `GET /api/attractions/:lat/:lng/:radius`. To avoid excessively long URLs, I recommend using the request body to pass large blocks of data (for example, the attraction description).

> It has become a standard to use `POST` for *creating* something, and `PUT` for *updating* (or modifying) something. The English meaning of these words doesn't support this distinction in any way, so you may want to consider using the path to distinguish between these two operations to avoid confusion.

For brevity, we will implement only three of these functions: adding an attraction, retrieving an attraction, and listing attractions. If you download the book source, you can see the whole implementation.

# API Error Reporting

Error reporting in HTTP APIs is usually achieved through HTTP status codes: if the request returns 200 (OK), the client knows the request was successful. If the request returns 500 (Internal Server Error), the request failed. In most applications, however, not everything can (or should be) categorized coarsely into "success" or "failure." For example, what if you request something by an ID, but that ID doesn't exist? This does not represent a server error: the client has asked for something that doesn't exist. In general, errors can be grouped into the following categories:

*Catastrophic errors*
    Errors that result in an unstable or unknown state for the server. Usually, this is the result of an unhandled exception. The only safe way to recover from a catastrophic error is to restart the server. Ideally, any pending requests would receive a 500 response code, but if the failure is severe enough, the server may not be able to respond at all, and the request will time out.

---

1. If your client can't use different HTTP methods, see *https://github.com/expressjs/method-override*, which allows you to "fake" different HTTP methods.

*Recoverable server errors*

Recoverable errors do not require a server restart, or any other heroic action. The error is a result of an unexpected error condition on the server (for example, a database connection being unavailable). The problem may be transient or permanent. A 500 response code is appropriate in this situation.

*Client error*

Client errors are a result of the client making the mistake, usually missing or invalid parameters. It isn't appropriate to use a 500 response code: after all, the server has not failed. Everything is working normally, the client just isn't using the API correctly. You have a couple of options here: you could respond with a status code of 200 and describe the error in the response body, or you could additionally try to describe the error with an appropriate HTTP status code. I recommend the latter approach. The most useful response codes in this case are 404 (Not Found), 400 (Bad Request), and 401 (Unauthorized). Additionally, the response body should contain an explanation of the specifics of the error. If you want to go above and beyond, the error message would even contain a link to documentation. Note that if the user requests a list of things, and there's nothing to return, this is not an error condition: it's appropriate to simply return an empty list.

In our application, we'll be using a combination of HTTP response codes and error messages in the body. Note that this approach is compatible with jQuery, which is an important consideration given the prevalance of API access using jQuery.

# Cross-Origin Resource Sharing (CORS)

If you're publishing an API, you'll likely want to make the API available to others. This will result in a *cross-site HTTP request*. Cross-site HTTP requests have been the subject of many attacks and have therefore been restricted by the *same-origin policy*, which restricts where scripts can be loaded from. Specifically, the protocol, domain, and port must match. This makes it impossible for your API to be used by another site, which is where CORS comes in. CORS allows you to lift this restriction on a case-by-case basis, even allowing you to list which domains specifically are allowed to access the script. CORS is implemented through the `Access-Control-Allow-Origin` header. The easiest way to implement it in an Express application is to use the `cors` package (`npm install --save cors`). To enable CORS for your application:

```
app.use(require('cors')());
```

Because the same-origin API is there for a reason (to prevent attacks), I recommend applying CORS only where necessary. In our case, we want to expose our entire API (but only the API), so we're going to restrict CORS to paths starting with */api*:

```
app.use('/api', require('cors')());
```

See the package documentation (*https://www.npmjs.org/package/cors*) for information about more advanced use of CORS.

# Our Data Store

Once again, we'll use Mongoose to create a schema for our attraction model in the database. Create the file *models/attraction.js*:

```
var mongoose = require('mongoose');

var attractionSchema = mongoose.Schema({
    name: String,
    description: String,
    location: { lat: Number, lng: Number },
    history: {
        event: String,
        notes: String,
        email: String,
        date: Date,
    },
    updateId: String,
    approved: Boolean,
});
var Attraction = mongoose.model('Attraction', attractionSchema);
module.exports = Attraction;
```

Since we wish to approve updates, we can't let the API simply update the original record. Our approach will be to create a new record that references the original record (in its `updateId` property). Once the record is approved, we can update the original record with the information in the update record and then delete the update record.

# Our Tests

If we use HTTP verbs other than `GET`, it can be a hassle to test our API, since browsers only know how to issue `GET` requests (and `POST` requests for forms). There are ways around this, such as the excellent "Postman - REST Client" Chrome plugin. However, whether or not you use such a utility, it's good to have automated tests. Before we write tests for our API, we need a way to actually *call* a REST API. For that, we'll be using a Node package called `restler`:

```
npm install --save-dev restler
```

We'll put the tests for the API calls we're going to implement in *qa/tests-api.js*:

```
var assert = require('chai').assert;
var http = require('http');
var rest = require('restler');

suite('API tests', function(){
```

```
var attraction = {
    lat: 45.516011,
    lng: -122.682062,
    name: 'Portland Art Museum',
    description: 'Founded in 1892, the Portland Art Museum\'s colleciton ' +
        'of native art is not to be missed.  If modern art is more to your ' +
        'liking, there are six stories of modern art for your enjoyment.',
    email: 'test@meadowlarktravel.com',
};

var base = 'http://localhost:3000';

test('should be able to add an attraction', function(done){
    rest.post(base+'/api/attraction', {data:attraction}).on('success',
        function(data){
        assert.match(data.id, /\w/, 'id must be set');
        done();
    });
});

test('should be able to retrieve an attraction', function(done){
    rest.post(base+'/api/attraction', {data:attraction}).on('success',
        function(data){
        rest.get(base+'/api/attraction/'+data.id).on('success',
            function(data){
            assert(data.name===attraction.name);
            assert(data.description===attraction.description);
            done();
        })
    })
});

});
```

Note that in the test that retrieves an attraction, we add an attraction first. You might think that we don't need to do this because the first test already does that, but there are two reasons for this. The first is practical: even though the tests appear in that order in the file, because of the asynchronous nature of JavaScript, there's no guarantee that the API calls will execute in that order. The second reason is a matter of principle: any test should be completely standalone and not rely on any other test.

The syntax should be straightforward: we call rest.get or rest.put, pass it the URL, and an options object containing a data property, which will be used for the request body. The method returns a promise that raises events. We're concerned with the success event. When using restler in your application, you may want to also listen for other events, like fail (server responded with 4xx status code) or error (connection or parsing error). See the restler documentation (*https://github.com/danwrong/rest ler*) for more information.

# Using Express to Provide an API

Express is quite capable of providing an API. Later on in this chapter, we'll learn how to do it with a Node module that provides some extra functionality, but we'll start with a pure Express implementation:

```
var Attraction = require('./models/attraction.js');

app.get('/api/attractions', function(req, res){
    Attraction.find({ approved: true }, function(err, attractions){
        if(err) return res.status(500).send('Error occurred: database error.');
        res.json(attractions.map(function(a){
            return {
                name: a.name,
                id: a._id,
                description: a.description,
                location: a.location,
            }
        }));
    });
});

app.post('/api/attraction', function(req, res){
    var a = new Attraction({
        name: req.body.name,
        description: req.body.description,
        location: { lat: req.body.lat, lng: req.body.lng },
        history: {
            event: 'created',
            email: req.body.email,
            date: new Date(),
        },
        approved: false,
    });
    a.save(function(err, a){
        if(err) return res.status(500).send('Error occurred: database error.');
        res.json({ id: a._id });
    });
});

app.get('/api/attraction/:id', function(req,res){
    Attraction.findById(req.params.id, function(err, a){
        if(err) return res.status(500).send('Error occurred: database error.');
        res.json({
            name: a.name,
            id: a._id,
            description: a.description,
            location: a.location,
        });
    });
});
```

Note that when we return an attraction, we don't simply return the model as returned from the database. That would expose internal implementation details. Instead, we pick the information we need and construct a new object to return.

Now if we run our tests (either with Grunt, or `mocha -u tdd -R spec qa/tests-api.js`), we should see that our tests are passing.

## Using a REST Plugin

As you can see, it's easy to write an API using only Express. However, there are advantages to using a REST plugin. Let's use the robust `connect-rest` to future-proof our API. First, install it:

```
npm install --save connect-rest
```

And import it in *meadowlark.js*:

```
var rest = require('connect-rest');
```

Our API shouldn't conflict with our normal website routes (make sure you don't create any website routes that start with */api*). I recommend adding the API routes after the website routes: the `connect-rest` module will examine every request and add properties to the request object, as well as do extra logging. For this reason, it fits better after you link in your website routes, but before your 404 handler:

```
// website routes go here

// define API routes here with rest.VERB....

// API configuration
var apiOptions = {
    context: '/api',
    domain: require('domain').create(),
};

// link API into pipeline
app.use(rest.rester(apiOptions));

// 404 handler goes here
```

> If you're looking for maximum separation between your website and your API, consider using a subdomain, such as *api.meadowlark.com*. We will see an example of this later.

Already, connect-rest has given us a little efficiency: it's allowed us to automatically prefix all of our API calls with /api. This reduces the possibility of typos, and enables us to easily change the base URL if we wanted to.

Let's now look at how we add our API methods:

```
rest.get('/attractions', function(req, content, cb){
    Attraction.find({ approved: true }, function(err, attractions){
        if(err) return cb({ error: 'Internal error.' });
        cb(null, attractions.map(function(a){
            return {
                name: a.name,
                description: a.description,
                location: a.location,
            };
        }));
    });
});

rest.post('/attraction', function(req, content, cb){
    var a = new Attraction({
        name: req.body.name,
        description: req.body.description,
        location: { lat: req.body.lat, lng: req.body.lng },
        history: {
            event: 'created',
            email: req.body.email,
            date: new Date(),
        },
        approved: false,
    });
    a.save(function(err, a){
        if(err) return cb({ error: 'Unable to add attraction.' });
        cb(null, { id: a._id });
    });
});

rest.get('/attraction/:id', function(req, content, cb){
    Attraction.findById(req.params.id, function(err, a){
        if(err) return cb({ error: 'Unable to retrieve attraction.' });
        cb(null, {
            name: attraction.name,
            description: attraction.description,
            location: attraction.location,
        });
    });
});
```

REST functions, instead of taking the usual request/response pair, take up to three pa-rameters: the request (as normal); a *content* object, which is the parsed body of the request; and a callback function, which can be used for asynchronous API calls. Since we're using a database, which is asynchronous, we have to use the callback to send a response to the client (there is a synchronous API, which you can read about in the `connect-rest` documentation (*https://github.com/imrefazekas/connect-rest*)).

Note also that when we created the API, we specified a domain (see Chapter 12). This allows us to isolate API errors and take appropriate action. `connect-rest` will automatically send a response code of 500 when an error is detected in the domain, so all that remains for you to do is logging and shutting down the server. For example:

```
apiOptions.domain.on('error', function(err){
    console.log('API domain error.\n', err.stack);
    setTimeout(function(){
        console.log('Server shutting down after API domain error.');
        process.exit(1);
    }, 5000);
    server.close();
    var worker = require('cluster').worker;
    if(worker) worker.disconnect();
});
```

# Using a Subdomain

Because an API is substantially different from a website, it's a popular choice to use a subdomain to partition the API from the rest of your website. This is quite easy to do, so let's refactor our example to use *api.meadowlarktravel.com* instead of *meadowlark-travel.com/api*.

First, make sure the `vhost` middleware is installed (`npm install --save vhost`). In your development environment, you probably don't have your own domain nameserver (DNS) set up, so we need a way to trick Express into thinking that you're connecting to a subdomain. To do this, we'll add an entry to our *hosts file*. On Linux and OS X systems, your hosts file is */etc/hosts*; for Windows, it's located at *%SystemRoot%\system32\drivers \etc\hosts*. If the IP address of your test server is 192.168.0.100, you would add the following line to your hosts file:

```
192.168.0.100   api.meadowlark
```

If you're working directly on your development server, you can use 127.0.0.1 (the numeric equivalent of *localhost*) instead of the actual IP address.

Now we simply link in a new `vhost` to create our subdomain:

```
app.use(vhost('api.*', rest.rester(apiOptions)));
```

You'll also need to change the context:

```
var apiOptions = {
    context: '/',
    domain: require('domain').create(),
};
```

That's all there is to it. All of the API routes you defined via rest.VERB calls will now be available on the *api* subdomain.

# CHAPTER 16

# Static Content

Static content refers to the resources your app will be serving that don't change on a per-request basis. Here are the usual suspects:

*Multimedia*

Images, videos, and audio files. It's quite possible to generate image files on the fly, of course (and video and audio, though that's far less common), but most multimedia resources are static.

*CSS*

Even if you use an abstracted CSS language like LESS, Sass, or Stylus, at the end of the day, your browser needs plain CSS,[1] which is a static resource.

*JavaScript*

Just because the server is running JavaScript doesn't mean there won't be client-side JavaScript. Client-side JavaScript is considered a static resource. Of course, now the line is starting to get a bit hazy: what if there was common code that we wanted to use on the backend and client side? There are ways to solve this problem, but at the end of the day, the JavaScript that gets sent to the client is generally static.

*Binary downloads*

This is the catch-all category: any PDFs, ZIP files, installers, and the like.

You'll note that HTML doesn't make the list. What about HTML pages that are static? If you have those, it's fine to treat them as a static resource, but then the URL will end in *.html*, which isn't very "modern." While it is possible to create a route that simply serves a static HTML file without the *.html* extension, it's generally easier to create a view (a view doesn't have to have any dynamic content).

---

1. It is possible to use uncompiled LESS in a browser, with some JavaScript magic. There are performance consequences to this approach, so I don't recommend it.

Note that if you are building an API only, there may be no static resources. If that's the case, you may skip this chapter.

## Performance Considerations

How you handle static resources has a significant impact on the real-world performance of your website, especially if your site is multimedia-heavy. The two primary performance considerations are *reducing the number of requests* and *reducing content size*.

Of the two, reducing the number of (HTTP) requests is more critical, especially for mobile (the overhead of making an HTTP request is significantly higher over a cellular network). Reducing the number of requests can be accomplished in two ways: combining resources and browser caching.

Combining resources is primarily an architectural and frontend concern: as much as possible, small images should be combined into a single sprite. Then use CSS to set the offset and size to display only the portion of the image you want. For creating sprites, I highly recommend the free service SpritePad (*http://wearekiss.com/spritepad*). It makes generating sprites incredibly easy, and it generates the CSS for you as well. Nothing could be easier. SpritePad's free functionality is probably all you'll ever need, but if you find yourself creating a lot of sprites, you might find their premium offerings worth it.

Browser caching helps reduce HTTP requests by storing commonly used static resources in the client's browser. Though browsers go to great lengths to make caching as automatic as possible, it's not magic: there's a lot you can and should do to enable browser caching of your static resources.

Lastly, we can increase performance by reducing the size of static resources. Some techniques are *lossless* (size reduction can be achieved without losing any data), and some techniques are *lossy* (size reduction is achieved by reducing the quality of static resources). Lossless techniques include minification of JavaScript and CSS, and optimizing PNG images. Lossy techniques include increasing JPEG and video compression levels. We'll be discussing minification and bundling (which also reduces HTTP requests) in this chapter.

 You generally don't have to worry about cross-domain resource sharing (CORS) when using a CDN. External resources loaded in HTML aren't subject to CORS policy: you only have to enable CORS for resources that are loaded via AJAX (see Chapter 15).

## Future-Proofing Your Website

When you move your website into production, the static resources must be hosted on the Internet *somewhere*. You may be used to hosting them on the same server where all your dynamic HTML is generated. Our example so far has also taken this approach: the Node/Express server we spin up when we type `node meadowlark.js` serves all of the HTML as well as static resources. However, if you want to maximize the performance of your site (or allow for doing so in the future), you will want to make it easy to host your static resources on a *content delivery network* (CDN). A CDN is a server that's optimized for delivering static resources. It leverages special headers (that we'll learn about soon) that enable browser caching. Also, CDNs can enable *geographic optimization*; that is, they can deliver your static content from a server that is geographically closer to your client. While the Internet is very fast indeed (not operating at the speed of light, exactly, but close enough), it is still faster to deliver data over a hundred miles than a thousand. Individual time savings may be small, but if you multiply across all of your users, requests, and resources, it adds up fast.

It's quite easy to "future-proof" your website so that you can move your static content to a CDN when the time comes, and I recommend that you get in the habit of always doing it. What it boils down to is creating an abstraction layer for your static resources so that relocating them all is as easy as flipping a switch.

Most of your static resources will be referenced in HTML views (`<link>` elements to CSS files, `<script>` references to JavaScript files, `<img>` tags referencing images, and multimedia embedding tags). Then, it is common to have static references in CSS, usually the `background-image` property. Lastly, static resources are sometimes referenced in JavaScript, such as JavaScript code that dynamically changes or inserts `<img>` tags or the `background-image` property.

## Static Mapping

At the heart of our strategy for making static resources relocatable, and friendly to caching, is the concept of mapping: when we're writing our HTML, we really don't want to have to worry about the gory details of where our static resources are going to be hosted. What we *are* concerned with is the logical organization of our static resources. That is to say, it's important that photos of our Hood River vacations go in */img/vacations/hood-river* and photos of Manzanita in */img/vacations/manzanita*. So we'll focus on making it easy to use only this organization when specifying static resources. For example, in HTML, you want to be able to write `<img src="/img/meadowlark_logo.png" alt="Meadowlark Travel Logo">`, not `<img src="//s3-us-west-2.amazonaws.com/meadowlark/img/meadowlark_logo-3.png" alt="Meadowlark Travel Logo">` (as it might look if you're using Amazon's cloud storage).

We will be using "protocol-relative URLs" to reference our static resources. This refers to URLs that begin only with // not *http://* or *https://*. This allows the browser to use whatever protocol is appropriate. If the user is viewing a secure page, it will use HTTPS; otherwise, it will use HTTP. Obviously, your CDN must support HTTPS, and I haven't found one that doesn't.

So this boils down to a mapping problem: we wish to map less specific paths (*/img/meadowlark_logo.png*) to more specific paths (*//s3-us-west-2.amazonaws.com/meadowlark/img/meadowlark_logo-3.png*). Furthermore, we wish to be able to change that mapping at will. For example, before you sign up for an Amazon S3 account, you may wish to host your images locally (*//meadowlarktravel.com/img/meadowlark_logo.png*).

In these examples, all we're doing to achieve our mapping is adding something to the start of the path, which we'll call a *base URL*. However, your mapping scheme could be more sophisticated than that: essentially the sky's the limit here. For example, you could employ a database of digital assets to map `"Meadowlark Logo"` to *http://meadowlark-travel.com/img/meadowlark_logo.png*. While that's possible, I would warn you away from it: using filenames and paths is a pretty standard and ubiquitous way to organize content, and you should have a compelling reason to deviate from that. A more practical example of a more sophisticated mapping scheme is to employ asset versioning (which we'll be discussing later). For example, if the Meadowlark Travel logo has undergone five revisions, you could write a mapper that would map */img/meadowlark_logo.png* to */img/meadowlark_logo-5.png*.

For now, we're going to be sticking with a very simple mapping scheme: we just add a base URL. We're assuming all static assets begin with a slash. Since we'll be using our mapper for several different types of files (views, CSS, and JavaScript), we'll want to modularize it. Let's create a file called *lib/static.js*:

```
var baseUrl = '';

exports.map = function(name){
        return baseUrl + name;
}
```

Not very exciting, is it? And right now, it doesn't do anything at all: it just returns its argument unmodified (assuming the argument is a string, of course). That's okay; right now, we're in development, and it's fine to have our static resources hosted on *localhost*. Note that also we'll probably want to read the value of `baseUrl` from a configuration file; for now, we'll just leave it in the module.

It's tempting to add some functionality that checks for the presence of a beginning slash in the asset name and adds it if it isn't present, but keep in mind that your asset mapper is going to be used *every-where*, and therefore should be as fast as possible. We can statically analyze our code as part of our QA toolchain to make sure our asset names always start with a slash.

## Static Resources in Views

Static resources in views are the easiest to deal with, so we'll start there. We can create a Handlebars helper (see Chapter 7) to give us a link to a static resource:

```
// set up handlebars view engine
var handlebars = require('express-handlebars').create({
    defaultLayout:'main',
    helpers: {
        static: function(name) {
            return require('./lib/static.js').map(name);
        }
    }
});
```

We added a Handlebars helper called `static`, which simply calls our static mapper. Now let's modify *main.layout* to use this new helper for the logo image:

```
<header><img src="{{static '/img/logo.jpg'}}"
    alt="Meadowlark Travel Logo"></header>
```

If we run the website, we'll see that absolutely nothing has changed: if we inspect the source, we'll see that the URL of the logo image is still */img/meadowlark_logo.jpg*, as expected.

Now we'll take some time and replace all of our references to static resources in our views and templates. Now static resources in all of our HTML should be ready to be moved to a CDN.

## Static Resources in CSS

CSS is going to be slightly more complicated, because we don't have Handlebars to help us out (it is possible to configure Handlebars to generate CSS, but it's not supported—it's not what Handlebars was designed for). However, CSS preprocessors like LESS, Sass, and Stylus all support variables, which is what we need. Of these three popular prepro-cessors, I prefer LESS, which is what we'll be using here. If you use Sass or Stylus, the technique is very similar, and it should be clear how to adapt this technique to a different preprocessor.

We'll add a background image to our site to provide a little texture. Create a directory called *less*, and a file in it called *main.less*:

```
body {
        background-image: url("/img/backgrouind.png");
}
```

This looks exactly like CSS so far, and that's not by accident: LESS is backward compatible with CSS, so any valid CSS is also valid LESS. As a matter of fact, if you already have any CSS in your *public/css/main.css* file, you should move it into *less/main.less*. Now we need a way to compile the LESS to generate CSS. We'll use a Grunt task for that:

```
npm install --save-dev grunt-contrib-less
```

Then modify *Gruntfile.js*. Add `grunt-contrib-less` to the list of Grunt tasks to load, then add the following section to `grunt.initConfig`:

```
less: {
    development: {
        files: {
            'public/css/main.css': 'less/main.less',
        }
    }
}
```

The syntax essentially reads "generate *public/css/main.css* from *less/main.less*." Now run `grunt less`, and you'll see you now have a CSS file. Let's link it into our layout, in the `<head>` section:

```
        <!-- ... -->
    <link rel="stylesheet" href="{{static /css/main.css}}">
</head>
```

Note that we're using our newly minted `static` helper! This is not going to solve the problem of the link to */img/background.png* inside the generated CSS file, but it will create a relocatable link to the CSS file itself.

Now that we've got the framework set up, let's make the URL used in the CSS file relocatable. First, we'll link in our static mapper as a LESS custom function. This can all be accomplished in *Gruntfile.js*:

```
less: {
    development: {
        options: {
            customFunctions: {
                static: function(lessObject, name) {
                    return 'url("' +
                        require('./lib/static.js').map(name.value) +
                        '")';
                }
            }
        },
```

```
    files: {
        'public/css/main.css': 'less/main.less',
    }
  }
}
```

Note that we add the standard CSS url specifier and double quotes to the output of the mapper: that will ensure that our CSS is valid. Now all we have to do is modify our LESS file, *less/main.less*:

```
body {
        background-image: static("/img/background.png");
}
```

Notice that all that really changed was that we replaced url with static; it's as easy as that.

# Static Resources in Server-Side JavaScript

Using our static mapper in server-side JavaScript is really easy, as we've already written a module to do our mapping. For example, let's say we want to add an easter egg to our application. At Meadowlark Travel, we're huge fans of Bud Clark (a former Portland mayor). We want our logo replaced with a logo with a picture of Mr. Clark on his birthday. Modify *meadowlark.js*:

```
var static = require('./lib/static.js').map;

app.use(function(req, res, next){
        var now = new Date();
        res.locals.logoImage = now.getMonth()==11 && now.getDate()==19 ?
                static('/img/logo_bud_clark.png') :
                static('/img/logo.png');
        next();
});
```

Then in *views/layouts/main.handlebars*:

```
<header><img src="{{logoImage}}" alt="Meadowlark Travel Logo"></header>
```

Note that we don't use the static Handlebars helper in the view: that's because we already used it in the route handler, and if we used it here, we'd be double-mapping the file, which would be no good!

# Static Resources in Client-Side JavaScript

Your first instinct might simply be to make the static mapper available to the client, and for our simple case, it would work fine (although we would have to use *browserify*, which allows you to use Node-style modules in the browser). However, I am going to recommend against this approach because it will quickly fall apart as our mapper gets more sophisticated. For example, if we start to use a database for more sophisticated mapping, that will no longer work in the browser. Then we would have to get into the business of making an AJAX call so the server could map a file for us, which will slow things down considerably.

So what to do? Fortunately, there's a simple solution. It's not quite as elegant as having access to the mapper, but it won't cause problems for us down the line.

Let's say you use jQuery to dynamically change the shopping cart image: when it's empty, the visual representation of the shopping cart is empty. After the user has added items to it, a box appears in the cart. (We would really want to use a sprite for this, but for the sake of the example, we will use two different images).

Our two images are called */img/shop/cart_empty.png* and */img/shop/cart_full.png*. Without mapping, we might use something like this:

```
$(document).on('meadowlark_cart_changed'){
        $('header img.cartIcon').attr('src', cart.isEmpty() ?
                '/img/shop/cart_empty.png' : '/img/shop/cart_full.png' );
}
```

This will fall apart when we move our images to a CDN, so we want to be able to map these images too. The solution is just to do the mapping on the server, and set custom JavaScript variables. In *views/layouts/main.handlebars*, we can do that:

```
<!-- ... -->
<script>
    var IMG_CART_EMPTY = '{{static '/img/shop/cart_empty.png'}}';
    var IMG_CART_FULL = '{{static '/img/shop/cart_full.png'}}';
</script>
```

Then our jQuery simply uses those variables:

```
$(document).on('meadowlark_cart_changed', function(){
        $('header img.cartIcon').attr('src', cart.isEmpty() ?
                IMG_CART_EMPTY : IMG_CART_FULL );
});
```

If you do a lot of image swapping on the client side, you'll probably want to consider organizing all of your image variables in an object (which itself becomes something of a map). For example, we might rewrite the previous code as:

```
<!-- ... -->
<script>
        var static = {
                IMG_CART_EMPTY: '{{static '/img/shop/cart_empty.png'}}',
                IMG_CART_FULL: '{{static '/img/shop/cart_full.png'}}
        }
</script>
```

# Serving Static Resources

Now that we've seen how we can create a framework that allows us to easily change where our static resources are served from, what is the best way to actually store the assets? It helps to understand the headers that your browser uses to determine how (and whether) to cache a resource:

Expires/Cache-Control

These two headers tell your browser the maximum amount of time a resource can be cached. They are taken seriously by the browser: if they inform the browser to cache something for a month, it simply won't redownload it for a month, as long as it stays in the cache. It's important to understand that a browser may remove the image from the cache prematurely, for reasons you have no control over. For example, the user could clear the cache manually, or the browser could clear your resource to make room for other resources the user is visiting more frequently. You only need one of these headers, and Expires is more broadly supported, so it's preferable to use that one. If the resource is in the cache, and it has not expired yet, the browser will not issue a GET request at all, which improves performance, especially on mobile.

Last-Modified/ETag

These two tags provide a versioning of sorts: if the browser needs to fetch the resource, it will examine these tags *before* downloading the content. A GET request is still issued to the server, but if the values returned by these headers satisfy the browser that the resource hasn't changed, it will not proceed to download the file. As the name implies, Last-Modified allows you to specify the date the resource was last modified. ETag allows you to use an arbitrary string, which is usually a version string or a content hash.

When serving static resources, you should use the Expires header *and* either Last-Modified or ETag. Express's built-in static middleware sets Cache-Control, but doesn't handle either Last-Modified or ETag. So, while it's suitable for development, it's not a great solution for deployment.

If you choose to host your static resources on a CDN, such as Amazon CloudFront, Microsoft Azure, or MaxCDN, the advantage is that they will handle most of these details for you. You will be able to fine-tune the details, but the defaults provided by any of these services are already good.

If you don't want to host your static resources on a CDN, but want something more robust than Express's built-in connect middleware, consider using a proxy server, such as Nginx (see Chapter 12), which is quite capable.

# Changing Your Static Content

Caching significantly improves the performance of your website, but it isn't without its consequences. In particular, if you change any of your static resources, clients may not see them until the cached versions expire in your browser. Google recommends you cache for a month, preferably a year. Imagine a user who uses your website every day on the same browser: that person might not see your updates for a whole year!

Clearly this is an undesirable situation, and you can't just tell your users to clear their cache. The solution is *fingerprinting*. Fingerprinting simply decorates the name of the resource with some kind of version information. When you update the asset, the resource name changes, and the browser knows it needs to download it.

Let's take our logo, for example (*/img/meadowlark_logo.png*). If we host it on a CDN for maximum performance, specifying an expiration of one year, and then go and change the logo, your users may not see the updated logo for up to a year. However, if you rename your logo */img/meadowlark_logo-1.png* (and reflect that name change in your HTML), the browser will be forced to download it, because it looks like a new resource.

If you consider the dozens—or even hundreds or thousands—of images on your site, this approach may seem very daunting. If you're in that situation (large numbers of images hosted on a CDN), this is where you might consider making your static mapper more sophisticated. For example, you might store the current version of all your digital assets in a database, and the static mapper could look up the asset name (*/img/meadowlark_logo.png*, for example) and return a URL to the *most recent version* of the asset (*/img/meadowlark_logo-12.png*).

At the very least, you should fingerprint your CSS and JavaScript files. It's one thing if your logo is not current, but it's incredibly frustrating to roll out a new feature, or change the layout on a page, only to find that your users aren't seeing the changes because the resources are cached.

A popular alternative to fingerprinting individual files is to *bundle* your resources. Bundling takes all of your CSS and smashes it into one file that's impossible for a human to read, and does the same for your client-side JavaScript. Since new files are being created anyway, it's usually easy and common to fingerprint those files.

# Bundling and Minification

In an effort to reduce HTTP requests *and* reduce the data sent over the wire, "bundling and minification" has become popular. Bundling takes like files (CSS or JavaScript) and bundles multiple files into one (thereby reducing HTTP requests). Minification removes anything unnecessary from your source, such as whitespace (outside of strings), and it can even rename your variables to something shorter.

One additional advantage of bundling and minification is that it reduces the number of assets that need to be fingerprinted. Still, things are getting complicated quick! Fortunately, there are some Grunt tasks that will help us manage the madness.

Since our project doesn't currently have any client-side JavaScript, let's create two files: one will be for "contact us" form submission handling, and the other will be for shopping cart functionality. We'll just put some logging in there for now so we can verify that the bundling and minification is working:

*public/js/contact.js*:

```
$(document).ready(function(){
    console.log('contact forms initialized');
});
```

*public/js/cart.js*:

```
$(document).ready(function(){
    console.log('shopping cart initialized');
});
```

We've already got a CSS file (generated from a LESS file), but let's add another one. We'll put our cart-specific styles in their own CSS file. Call it *less/cart.less*:

```
div.cart {
    border: solid 1px black;
}
```

Now in *Gruntfile.js* add it to the list of LESS files to compile:

```
files: {
    'public/css/main.css': 'less/main.less',
    'public/css/cart.css': 'less/cart.css',
}
```

We'll use no fewer than three Grunt tasks to get where we're going: one for the JavaScript, one for the CSS, and another to fingerprint the files. Let's go ahead and install those modules now:

```
npm install --save-dev grunt-contrib-uglify
npm install --save-dev grunt-contrib-cssmin
npm install --save-dev grunt-hashres
```

Then load these tasks in the Gruntfile:

```
[
    // ...
    'grunt-contrib-less',
    'grunt-contrib-uglify',
    'grunt-contrib-cssmin',
    'grunt-hashres',
].forEach(function(task){
    grunt.loadNpmTasks(task);
});
```

And set up the tasks:

```
grunt.initConfig({
    // ...
    uglify: {
        all: {
            files: {
                'public/js/meadowlark.min.js': ['public/js/**/*.js']
            }
        }
    },
    cssmin: {
        combine: {
            files: {
                'public/css/meadowlark.css': ['public/css/**/*.css',
                    '!public/css/meadowlark*.css']
            }
        },
        minify: {
            src: 'public/css/meadowlark.css',
            dest: 'public/css/meadowlark.min.css',
        }
    },
    hashres: {
        options: {
            fileNameFormat: '${name}.${hash}.${ext}'
        },
        all: {
            src: [
                'public/js/meadowlark.min.js',
                'public/css/meadowlark.min.css',
            ],
            dest: [
                'views/layouts/main.handlebars',
            ]
        },
    }
});
};
```

Let's look at what we just did. In the `uglify` task (minification is often called "uglifying" because…well, just look at the output, and you'll understand), we take all the site Java-Script and combine it into one file called *meadowlark.min.js*. For `cssmin`, we have two tasks: we first combine all the CSS files into one called *meadowlark.css* (note the second element in that array: the exclamation point at the beginning of the string says *not* to include these files…this will prevent it from circularly including the files it generates itself!). Then we minify the combined CSS into a file called *meadowlark.min.css*.

Before we get to `hashres`, let's pause for a second. We've now taken all of our JavaScript and put it in *meadowlark.min.js* and all of our CSS and put it in *meadowlark.min.css*.

Now, instead of referencing individual files in our HTML, we'll want to reference them in our layout file. So let's modify our layout file:

```
<!-- ... -->
<script src="http://code.jquery.com/jquery-2.0.2.min.js"></script>
<script src="{{static '/js/meadowlark.min.js'}}"></script>
<link rel="stylesheet" href="{{static '/css/meadowlark.min.css'}}">
</head>
```

So far, it may seem like a lot of work for a small payoff. However, as your site grows, you will find yourself adding more and more JavaScript and CSS. I've seen projects that have had a dozen or more JavaScript files and five or six CSS files. Once you reach that point, bundling and minification will yield impressive performance improvements.

Now on to the `hashres` task. We want to fingerprint these bundled and minified CSS and JavaScript files so that when we update our website, our clients see the changes immediately, instead of waiting for their cached version to expire. The `hashres` task handles the complexities of that for us. Note that we tell it that we want to rename the *public/js/meadowlark.min.js* and *public/css/meadowlark.min.css* file. `hashres` will generate a hash of the file (a mathematical fingerprinting) and append it to the file. So now, instead of */js/meadowlark.min.js*, you'll have */js/meadowlark.min.62a6f623.js* (the actual value of the hash will be different if your version differs by even a single character). If you had to remember to change the references in *views/layout/main.handlebars* every time, well…you would probably forget sometimes. Fortunately, the `hashres` task comes to the rescue: it can automatically change the references for you. See in the configuration how we specified *views/layouts/main.handlebars* in the `dest` section? That will automatically change the references for us.

So now let's give it a try. It's important that we do things in the right order, because these tasks have dependencies:

```
grunt less
grunt cssmin
grunt uglify
grunt hashres
```

That's a lot of work every time we want to change our CSS or JavaScript, so let's set up a Grunt task so we don't have to remember all that. Modify *Gruntfile.js*:

```
grunt.registerTask('default', ['cafemocha', 'jshint', 'exec']);
grunt.registerTask('static', ['less', 'cssmin', 'uglify', 'hashres']);
```

Now all we have to do is type `grunt static`, and everything will be taken care of for us.

## Skipping Bundling and Minification in Development Mode

One problem with bundling and minification is that it makes frontend debugging all but impossible. All of your JavaScript and CSS are smashed into their own bundles, and the situation can even be worse if you choose extremely aggressive options for your minification. What would be ideal is a way to disable bundling and minification in development mode. Fortunately, I've written just the module for you: connect-bundle.

Before we get started with that module, let's create a configuration file. We'll be defining our bundles now, but we will also use this configuration file later to specify database settings. It's common to specify your configuration in a JSON file, and it's a little known but very useful trick that you can read and parse a JSON file using require, just as if it were a module:

```
var config = require('./config.json');
```

However, because I get tired of typing quotation marks, I generally prefer to put my configuration in a JavaScript file (which is almost identical to a JSON file, minus a few quotation marks). So let's create *config.js*:

```
module.exports = {
    bundles: {

        clientJavaScript: {
            main: {
                file: '/js/meadowlark.min.js',
                location: 'head',
                contents: [
                    '/js/contact.js',
                    '/js/cart.js',
                ]
            }
        },

        clientCss: {
            main: {
                file: '/css/meadowlark.min.css',
                contents: [
                    '/css/main.css',
                    '/css/cart.css',
                ]
            }
        }
    }
}
```

We're defining bundles for JavaScript and CSS. We could have multiple bundles (one for desktop and one for mobile, for example), but for our example, we just have one bundle, which we call "main." Note that in the JavaScript bundle, we can specify a location. For reasons of performance and dependency, it may be desirable to put your JavaScript in different locations. In the <head>, right after the open <body> tag, and right before the close <body> tag are all common locations to include a JavaScript file. Here, we're just specifying "head" (we can call it whatever we want, but JavaScript bundles must have a location).

Now we modify *views/layouts/main.handlebars*:

```
<!-- ... -->
{{#each _bundles.css}}
    <link rel="stylesheet" href="{{static .}}">
{{/each}}
{{#each _bundles.js.head}}
    <script src="{{static .}}"></script>
{{/each}}
</head>
```

Now if we want to use a fingerprinted bundle name, we have to modify *config.js* instead of *views/layouts/main.handlebars*. Modify *Gruntfile.js* accordingly:

```
hashres: {
    options: {
        fileNameFormat: '${name}.${hash}.${ext}'
    },
    all: {
        src: [
            'public/js/meadowlark.min.js',
            'public/css/meadowlark.min.css',
        ],
        dest: [
            'config.js',
        ]
    },
}
```

Now you can run `grunt static`; you'll see that *config.js* has been updated with the fingerprinted bundle names.

# A Note on Third-Party Libraries

You'll notice I haven't included jQuery in any bundles in these examples. jQuery is so incredibly ubiquitous, I find that there is dubious value in including it in a bundle: the chances are, your browser probably has a cached copy. The gray area would be libraries such as Handlebars, Backbone, or Bootstrap: they're quite popular, but not as likely to be always cached in the browser. If you're using only one or two third-party libraries, it's probably not worth bundling them with your scripts. If you've got five or more libraries, though, you might see a performance gain by bundling the libraries.

# QA

Instead of waiting for the inevitable bug, or hoping that code reviews will catch the problem, why not add a component to our QA toolchain to fix the problem? We'll use a Grunt plugin called `grunt-lint-pattern`, which simply searches for a pattern in source files and generates an error if it's found. First, install the package:

```
npm install --save-dev grunt-lint-pattern
```

Then add `grunt-lint-pattern` to the list of modules to be loaded in *Gruntfile.js*, and add the following configuration:

```
lint_pattern: {
    view_statics: {
        options: {
            rules: [
                {
                    pattern: /<link [^>]*href=["'](?!\{\{static )/,
                    message: 'Un-mapped static resource found in <link>.'
                },
                {
                    pattern: /<script [^>]*src=["'](?!\{\{static )/,
                    message: 'Un-mapped static resource found in <script>.'
                },
                {
                    pattern: /<img [^>]*src=["'](?!\{\{static )/,
                    message: 'Un-mapped static resource found in <img>.'
                },
            ]
        },
        files: {
            src: [
                'views/**/*.handlebars'
            ]
        }
    },
    css_statics: {
        options: {
            rules: [
                {
                    pattern: /url\(/,
                    message: 'Un-mapped static found in LESS property.'
                },
            ]
        },
        files: {
            src: [
                'less/**/*.less'
            ]
        }
    }
}
```

And add `lint_pattern` to your default rule:

```
grunt.registerTask('default', ['cafemocha', 'jshint', 'exec', 'lint_pattern']);
```

Now when we run `grunt` (*which we should be doing regularly*), we will catch any instances of unmapped statics.

# Summary

For what seems like such a simple thing, static resources are a lot of trouble. However, they probably represent the bulk of the data actually being transferred to your visitors, so spending some time optimizing them will yield substantial payoff.

Depending on the size and complexity of your website, the techniques for static mapping I've outlined here may be overkill. For those projects, the other viable solution is to simply host your static resources on a CDN from the start, and always use the full URL to the resource in your views and CSS. You will probably still want to run some kind of linting to make sure you're not hosting static resources locally: you can use `grunt-lint-pattern` to search for links that don't start with `(?:https?:)?//`; that will prevent you from accidentally using local resources.

Elaborate bundling and minification is another area in which you can save time if the payoff isn't worth it for your application. In particular, if your site includes only one or two JavaScript files, and all of your CSS lives in a single file, you could probably skip bundling altogether, and minification will produce only modest gains, unless your JavaScript or CSS is massive.

Whatever technique you choose to use to serve your static resources, I highly recommend hosting them separately, preferably on a CDN. If it sounds like a hassle to you, let me assure that it's not nearly as difficult as it sounds, especially if you spend a little time on your deployment system, so deploying static resources to one location and your application to another is automatic.

If you're concerned about the hosting costs of CDNs, I encourage you to take a look at what you're paying now for hosting. Most hosting providers essentially charge for bandwidth, even if you don't know it. However, if all of a sudden your site is mentioned on Slashdot, and you get "Slashdotted," you may find yourself with a hosting bill you didn't expect. CDN hosting is usually set up so that you pay for what you use. To give you an example, a website that I manage for a medium-sized regional company, which uses about 20 GB a month of bandwidth, pays only a few dollars per month to host static resources (and it's a very media-heavy site).

The performance gains you realize by hosting your static resources on a CDN are significant, and the cost and inconvenience of doing so is minimal, so I highly recommend going this route.

# CHAPTER 17

# Implementing MVC in Express

We've covered a lot of ground by now, and if you're feeling a little overwhelmed, you're not alone. This chapter will discuss some techniques to bring a little order to the madness.

One of the more popular development paradigms to come to prominence in recent years is the model-view-controller (MVC) pattern. This is quite an old concept, actually, dating back to the 1970s. It's experienced a resurgence thanks to its suitability for web development.

One of the biggest advantages of MVC that I've observed is a reduced ramp-up time on projects. For example, a PHP developer who's familiar with MVC frameworks can jump into a .NET MVC project with surprising ease. The actual programming language is usually not so much a barrier as just *knowing where to find stuff*. MVC breaks down functionality into very well-defined realms, giving us a common framework for developing software.

In MVC, the *model* is a "pure" view of your data and logic. It does not concern itself with user interaction at all. *Views* convey models to the user, and the controller accepts user input, manipulates models, and chooses what view(s) to display. (I've often thought "coordinator" would be a better term than "controller": after all, a controller does not sound like something that accepts user input, and yet this is one of the main responsibilities of the controller in an MVC project.)

MVC has spawned what seems like countless variations. Microsoft's "model-view-view model" (MVVM) in particular introduces a valuable concept: the view model (it also rolls the controller into the view, a simplification I find less interesting). The idea of a *view model* is that it is a transformation of a model. Furthermore, a single view model may combine more than one model, or parts of models, or parts of a single model. At first blush, it may seem like an unnecessary complication, but I've found it to be a very valuable concept. Its value lies in "protecting" the model. In pure MVC, it's tempting (or even necessary) to contaminate your model with transformations or enhancements that are necessary only for the views. Model views give you an "out": if you need a view of your data that's only needed for presentation, it belongs in a view model.

Like any pattern, you have to decide how rigid you want to be about it. Too much rigidity leads to heroic efforts to accomplish edge cases "the right way," and too little rigidity leads to maintenance issues and technical debt. My preference is to lean more toward the side of rigidity. Fortunately, MVC (with view models) provides very natural areas of responsibility, and I find it's very rare to run into a situation that can't easily be accommodated by this pattern.

# Models

To me, the models are far and away the most important components. If your model is robust and well designed, you can always scrap the presentation layer (or add an additional presentation layer). Going the other way is harder, though: your models are the foundations of your project.

It is vitally important that you don't contaminate your models with any presentation or user-interaction code. Even if it seems easy or expedient, I assure you that you are only making trouble for yourself in the future. A more complicated—and contentious—issue is the relationship between your models and your persistence layer.

In an ideal world, your models and the persistence layer could be completely separate. And certainly this is achievable, but usually at significant cost. Very often, the logic in your models is heavily dependent on persistence, and separating the two layers may be more trouble than it's worth.

In this book, we've taken the path of least resistance by using Mongoose (which is specific to MongoDB) to define our models. If being tied to a specific persistence technology makes you nervous, you might want to consider using the native MongoDB driver (which doesn't require any schemas or object mapping) and separating your models from your persistence layer.

There are those who submit that models should be *data only*. That is, they contain no logic, only data. While the word "model" does conjure the idea of data more than functionality, I don't find this to be a useful restriction, and prefer to think of a model as combining data and logic.

I recommend creating a subdirectory in your project called *models* that you can keep your models in. Whenever you have logic to implement, or data to store, you should do so in a file within the *models* directory. For example, we might keep our customer data and logic in a file called *models/customer.js*:

```
var mongoose = require('mongoose');
var Order = require('./order.js');
```

```
var customerSchema = mongoose.Schema({
        firstName: String,
        lastName: String,
        email: String,
        address1: String,
        address2: String,
        city: String,
        state: String,
        zip: String,
        phone: String,
        salesNotes: [{
                date: Date,
                salespersonId: Number,
                notes: String,
        }],
});

customerSchema.methods.getOrders = function(cb){
        return Order.find({ customerId: this._id }, cb);
};

var Customer = mongoose.model('Customer', customerSchema);
module.exports = Customer;
```

# View Models

While I prefer not to be dogmatic about passing models directly to views, I definitely recommend creating a view model if you're tempted to modify your model *just because you need to display something in a view*. View models give you a way to keep your model abstract, while at the same time providing meaningful data to the view.

Take the previous example. We have a model called Customer. Now we want to create a view showing customer information, along with a list of orders. Our Customer model doesn't quite work, though. There's data in it we don't want to show the customer (sales notes), and we may want to format the data that is there differently (for example, correctly formatting mailing address and phone number). Furthermore, we want to display data that isn't even *in* the Customer model, such as the list of customer orders. This is where view models come in handy. Let's create a view model in *viewModels/customer.js*:

```
// convenience function for joining fields
function smartJoin(arr, separator){
        if(!separator) separator = ' ';
        return arr.filter(function(elt){
                return elt!==undefined &&
                        elt!==null &&
                        elt.toString().trim() !== '';
        }).join(separator);
}
```

```
module.exports = function(customer, orders){
    return {
        firstName: customer.firstName,
        lastName: customer.lastName,
        name: smartJoin([customer.firstName, customer.lastName]),
        email: customer.email,
        address1: customer.address1,
        address2: customer.address2,
        city: customer.city,
        state: customer.state,
        zip: customer.zip,
        fullAddress: smartJoin([
            customer.address1,
            customer.address2,
            customer.city + ', ' +
                customer.state + ' ' +
                customer.zip,
        ], '<br>'),
        phone: customer.phone,
        orders: orders.map(function(order){
            return {
                orderNumber: order.orderNumber,
                date: order.date,
                status: order.status,
                url: '/orders/' + order.orderNumber,
            }
        }),
    }
}
```

In this code example, you can see how we're discarding the information we don't need, reformatting some of our info (such as fullAddress), and even constructing additional information (such as the URL that can be used to get more order details).

The concept of view models is essential to protecting the integrity and scope of your model. If you find all of the copying (such as firstname: customer.firstName), you might want to look into *Underscore* (*http://underscorejs.org*), which gives you the ability to do more elaborate composition of objects. For example, you can clone an object, picking only the properties you want, or go the other way around and clone an object while omitting only certain properties. Here's the previous example rewritten with Underscore (install with npm install --save underscore):

```
var _ = require('underscore');

// get a customer view model
function getCustomerViewModel(customer, orders){
    var vm = _.omit(customer, 'salesNotes');
    return _.extend(vm, {
        name: smartJoin([vm.firstName, vm.lastName]),
        fullAddress: smartJoin([
            customer.address1,
```

```
                    customer.address2,
                    customer.city + ', ' +
                            customer.state + ' ' +
                            customer.zip,
            ], '<br>'),
            orders: orders.map(function(order){
                    return {
                            orderNumber: order.orderNumber,
                            date: order.date,
                            status: order.status,
                            url: '/orders/' + order.orderNumber,
                    };
            }),
        });
    }
```

Note that we are also using JavaScript's `.map` method to set the order list for the customer view model. In essence, what we're doing is creating an ad hoc (or anonymous) view model. The alternate approach would be to create a "customer order view model" object. That would be a better approach if we needed to use that view model in multiple places.

# Controllers

The controller is responsible for handling user interaction and choosing the appropriate views to display based on that user interaction. Sounds a lot like request routing, doesn't it? In reality, the only difference between a controller and a router is that controllers typically group related functionality. We've already seen some ways we can group related routes: now we're just going to make it more formal by calling it a controller.

Let's imagine a "customer controller": it would be responsible for viewing and editing a customer's information, including the orders a customer has placed. Let's create such a controller, *controllers/customer.js*:

```
var Customer = require('../models/customer.js');
var customerViewModel = require('../viewModels/customer.js');

exports = {

        registerRoutes: function(app) {
                app.get('/customer/:id', this.home);
                app.get('/customer/:id/preferences', this.preferences);
                app.get('/orders/:id', this.orders);

                app.post('/customer/:id/update', this.ajaxUpdate);
        },

    home: function(req, res, next) {
        Customer.findById(req.params.id, function(err, customer) {
            if(err) return next(err);
```

```
            if(!customer) return next();      // pass this on to 404 handler
            customer.getOrders(function(err, orders) {
                if(err) return next(err);
                res.render('customer/home',
                                        customerViewModel(customer, orders));
            });
        });
    },

    preferences: function(req, res, next) {
        Customer.findById(req.params.id, function(err, customer) {
            if(err) return next(err);
            if(!customer) return next();      // pass this on to 404 handler
            customer.getOrders(function(err, orders) {
                if(err) return next(err);
                res.render('customer/preferences',
                                        customerViewModel(customer, orders));
            });
        });
    },

    orders: function(req, res, next) {
        Customer.findById(req.params.id, function(err, customer) {
            if(err) return next(err);
            if(!customer) return next();      // pass this on to 404 handler
            customer.getOrders(function(err, orders) {
                if(err) return next(err);
                res.render('customer/preferences',
                                        customerViewModel(customer, orders));
            });
        });
    },

    ajaxUpdate: function(req, res) {
        Customer.findById(req.params.id, function(err, customer) {
            if(err) return next(err);
            if(!customer) return next();      // pass this on to 404 handler
            if(req.body.firstName){
                if(typeof req.body.firstName !== 'string' ||
                    req.body.firstName.trim() === '')
                    return res.json({ error: 'Invalid name.'});
                customer.firstName = req.body.firstName;
            }
            // and so on....
            customer.save(function(err) {
                return err ? res.json({ error: 'Unable to update customer.' }) :
                                res.json({ success: true });
            });
        });
    },
};
```

Note that in our controller, we separate route management from actual functionality. In this case, the `home`, `preferences`, and `orders` methods are identical except for the choice of view. If that's all we were doing, I would probably combine those into a generic method, but the idea here is that they might be further customized.

The most complicated method in this controller is `ajaxUpdate`. It's clear from the name that we'll be using AJAX to do updates on the frontend. Notice that we don't just blindly update the customer object from the parameters passed in the request body: that would open us up to possible attacks. It's more work, but much safer, to handle the fields individually. Also, we want to perform validation here, even if we're doing it on the frontend as well. Remember that an attacker can examine your JavaScript and construct an AJAX query that bypasses your frontend validation in attempt to compromise your application, so always do validation on the server, even if it's redundant.

Your options are once again limited by your imagination. If you wanted to completely separate controllers from routing, you could certainly do that. In my opinion, that would be an unnecessary abstraction, but it might make sense if you were trying to write a controller that could also handle different kinds of UIs attached to it (like a native app, for example).

# Conclusion

Like many programming paradigms or patterns, MVC is more of a general concept than a specific technique. As you've seen in this chapter, the approach we've been taking is already mostly there: we just made it a little more formal by calling our route handler a "controller" and separating the routing from the functionality. We also introduced the concept of a view model, which I feel is critical to preserving the integrity of your model.

# CHAPTER 18

# Security

Most websites and applications these days have some kind of security requirement. If you are allowing people to log in, or if you're storing personally identifiable information (PII), you'll want to implement some kind of security for your site.

In this chapter, we'll be discussing HTTP Secure (HTTPS), which establishes a foundation on which you can build a secure website, and authentication mechanisms, with a focus on third-party authentication.

Security is a big topic that could fill up an entire book itself. For that reason, the focus in this book is going to be leveraging existing authentication modules. Writing your own authentication system is certainly possible, but is a large and complicated undertaking. Furthermore, there are good reasons to prefer a third-party login approach, which we will discuss later in this chapter.

## HTTPS

The first step in providing secure services is using HTTP Secure (HTTPS). The nature of the Internet makes it possible for a third party to intercept packets being transmitted between clients and servers. HTTPS encrypts those packets, making it extremely difficult for an attacker to get access to the information being transmitted. (I say very difficult, not impossible, because there's no such thing as perfect security. However, HTTPS is considered sufficiently secure for banking, corporate security, and healthcare.)

You can think of HTTPS as sort of a foundation for securing your website. It does not provide authentication, but it lays the groundwork for authentication. For example, your authentication system probably involves transmitting a password: if that password is transmitted unencrypted, no amount of authentication sophistication will secure your system. Security is as strong as the weakest link, and the first link in that chain is the network protocol.

The HTTPS protocol is based on the server having a *public key certificate*, sometimes called an SSL certificate. The current standard format for SSL certificates is called X. 509. The idea behind certificates is that there are *certificate authorities* (CAs) that issue certificates. A certificate authority makes *trusted root certificates* available to browser vendors. Browsers include these trusted root certificates when you install a browser, and that's what establishes the chain of trust between the CA and the browser. For this chain to work, your server must use a certificate issued by a CA.

The upshot of this is that to provide HTTPS, you need a certificate from a CA, so how does one go about acquiring such a thing? Broadly speaking, you can generate your own, get one from a free CA, or purchase one from a commercial CA.

## Generating Your Own Certificate

Generating your own certificate is easy, but generally suitable only for development and testing purposes (and possibly for intranet deployment). Due to the hierarchical nature established by certificate authorities, browsers will trust only certificates generated by a known CA (and that's probably not you). If your website uses a certificate from a CA that's not known to the browser, the browser will warn you in very alarming language that you're establishing a secure connection with an unknown (and therefore untrusted) entity. In development and testing, this is fine: you and your team know that you generated your own certificate, and you expect this behavior from browsers. If you were to deploy such a website to production for consumption by the public, they would turn away in droves.

 If you control the distribution and installation of browsers, you can automatically install your own root certificate when you install the browser: this will prevent people using that browser from being warned when they connect to your website. This is not trivial to set up, however, and applies only to environments in which you control the browser(s) being used. Unless you have a very solid reason to take this approach, it's generally more trouble than it's worth.

To generate your own certificate, you'll need an OpenSSL implementation. Table 18-1 shows how to acquire an implementation:

*Table 18-1. Acquiring an implementation for different platforms*

| Platform | Instructions |
| --- | --- |
| OS X | `brew install openssl` |
| Ubuntu, Debian | `sudo apt-get install openssl` |
| Other Linux | Download from *http://www.openssl.org/source/*; extract tarball and follow instructions |
| Windows | Download from *http://gnuwin32.sourceforge.net/packages/openssl.htm* |

If you are a Windows user, you may need to specify the location of the OpenSSL configuration file, which can be tricky due to Windows pathnames. The surefire way is to locate the *openssl.cnf* file (usually in the *share* directory of the installation), and before you run the `openssl` command, set the `OPENSSL_CNF` environment variable: `SET OPENSSL_CONF=openssl.cnf`.

Once you've installed OpenSSL, you can generate a private key and a public certificate:

```
openssl req -x509 -nodes -days 365 -newkey rsa:2048 -keyout meadowlark.pem
    -out meadowlark.crt
```

You will be asked for some details, such as your country code, city, and state, fully qualified domain name (FQDN), and email address. Since this certificate is for development/testing purposes, the values you provide are not particularly important (in fact, they're all optional, but leaving them out will result in a certificate that will be regarded with even more suspicion by a browser). The common name (FQDN) is what the browser uses to identify the domain. So if you're using *localhost*, you can use that for your FQDN, or you can use the IP address of the server, or the server name, if available. The encryption will still work if the common name and domain you use in the URL don't match, but your browser will give you an additional warning about the discrepancy.

If you're curious about the details of this command, you can read about them on the OpenSSL documentation page (*http://www.openssl.org/docs/apps/req.html*). It is worth pointing out that the `-nodes` option doesn't have anything to do with Node, or even the plural word "nodes": it actually means "no DES," meaning the private key is not DES-encrypted.

The result of this command is two files, *meadowlark.pem* and *meadowlark.crt*. The PEM (Privacy-enhanced Electronic Mail) file is your private key, and should not be made available to the client. The CRT file is the self-signed certificate that will be sent to the browser to establish a secure connection.

Alternatively, there are websites that will provide free self-signed certificates, such as *http://www.selfsignedcertificate.com*.

## Using a Free Certificate Authority

HTTPS is based on trust, and it's an uncomfortable reality that one of the easiest ways to gain trust on the Internet is to buy it. And it's not all snake oil, either: establishing the security infrastructure, insuring certificates, and maintaining relationships with browser vendors is expensive. However, buying a certificate is not your only legitimate option for production-ready certificates: CACert (*http://www.cacert.org*) employs a point-based "web of trust" to ensure you are who you say you are. To get enough points to be issued a certificate, you have to meet with a CACert member who is qualified as an "assurer." Or you can attend events at which you can get points.

Unfortunately, you get what you pay for: CACert is not currently supported by any major browser. It is likely that they will eventually be supported by Mozilla Firefox, but given the nonprofit nature of CACert, it's unlikely that it will ever be supported for Google Chrome, Internet Explorer, or Apple Safari.

For this reason, I can really only recommend using a CACert certificate for development or testing purposes, or if your service is specifically for consumption by the open source crowd, who will not be as intimidated by an untrusted certificate.

All of the major certificate vendors (such as Comodo and Symantec) offer free trial certificates that last anywhere from 30 to 90 days. This is a valid option if you want to test a commercial certificate, but you will need to purchase a certificate before the trial period is up if you want to ensure continuity of service.

## Purchasing a Certificate

Currently, 90% of the approximately 50 root certificates distributed with every major browser are owned by four companies: Symantec (who purchased VeriSign), Comodo Group, Go Daddy, and GlobalSign. Purchasing directly from a CA can be quite expensive: it usually starts around $300 per year (though some offer certificates less than $100 per year). A less expensive option is going through a reseller, from whom you can get an SSL certificate for as little as $10 per year or less.

It's important to understand exactly what it is you're paying for, and why you would pay $10, $150, or $300 (or more) for a certificate. The first important point to understand is that there is no difference whatsoever in the level of encryption offered between a $10 certificate and a $1,500 certificate. This is something that expensive certificate authorities would rather you not know: their marketing tries hard to obscure this fact.

There are four considerations I use in selecting a certificate vendor:

*Customer support*
> If you ever have problems with your certificate, whether it be browser support (customers will let you know if your certificate is flagged by their browser as not trustworthy), installation issues, or renewal hassles, you will appreciate good customer support. This is one reason why you might purchase a more expensive certificate. Often, your hosting provider will resell certificates, and in my experience, they provide a higher level of customer support, because they want to keep you as a hosting client as well.

*Avoid chained root certificates*
> It is common to *chain* certificates, meaning you actually require multiple certificates to establish a secure connection. Chained certificates result in additional

installation effort, and for this reason, I will spend a little more to purchase a certificate that relies on a single root certificate. Often it's difficult (or impossible) to determine what you're getting, and this is another reason to look for good customer support. If you ask whether the root certificate is chained, and they can't or won't tell you, you should look elsewhere.

### Single-domain, multisubdomain, multidomain, and wildcard certificates

The most inexpensive certificates are usually *single domain*. That may not sound so bad, but remember that it means that if you purchase a certificate for *meadowlarktravel.com*, then the certificate will not work for *www.meadowlarktravel.com*, or vice versa. For this reason, I tend to avoid single-domain certificates, though it can be a good option for the extremely budget conscious (you can always set up redirects to funnel requests to the proper domain). Multisubdomain certificates are good in that you can purchase a single certificate that covers *meadowlarktravel.com*, *www.meadowlark.com*, *blog.meadowlarktravel.com*, *shop.meadowlarktravel.com*, etc. The downside is that you have to know in advance what subdomains you want to use. If you see yourself adding or using different subdomains over the course of a year (that need to support HTTPS), you might be better off going with a *wildcard* certificate, which are generally more expensive. But they will work for *any* subdomain, and you never have to specify what the subdomains are. Lastly, there are multidomain certificates which, like wildcard certificates, tend to be more expensive. These certificates support whole multiple domains so, for example, you could have *meadowlarktravel.com*, *meadowlarktravel.us*, *meadowlarktravel.com*, and the *www* variants.

### Domain, organization, and extended validation certificates

There are three kinds of certificates: domain, organization, and extended validation. Domain certificates, as the name implies, simply provide confidence that you're doing business with the *domain* that you think you are. Organization certificates, on the other hand, provide some assurance about the actual organization you're dealing with. They're more difficult to get: there's usually paperwork involved, and you must provide things like state and/or federal business name records, physical addresses, etc. Different certificate vendors will require different documentation, so make sure to ask your certificate vendor what's required to get one of these certificates. Lastly are *extended validation* certificates, which are the Rolls Royce of SLL certificates. They are like organization certificates in that they verify the existence of the organization, but they require a higher standard of proof, and can even require expensive audits to establish your data security practices (though this seems to be increasingly rare). They can be had for as little as $150 for a single domain. I recommend either the less expensive domain certificates or the extended validation certificates. Organization certificates, while they verify the existence of your organization, are not displayed any differently than browsers, so in my experience, unless the user actually examines the certificate (which is rare) there will be no apparent difference between this and a domain certificate. Extended validation certificates, on the other hand, usually display some clues to users that they are dealing with a legitimate business (such as the URL bar being displayed in green, and the organization name being displayed next to the SSL icon).

If you've dealt with SSL certificates before, you might be wondering why I didn't mention certificate insurance. I've omitted that price differentiator because essentially it's insurance against something that's almost impossible. The idea is that if someone suffers financial loss due to a transaction on your website, and they can *prove it was due to inadequate encryption*, the insurance is there to cover your damages. While it is certainly possible that, if your application involves financial transactions, someone may attempt to take legal action against you for financial loss, the likelihood of it being due to inadequate encryption is essentially zero. If I were to attempt to seek damages from a company due to financial loss linked to their online services, the absolute last approach I would take is to attempt to prove that the SSL encryption was broken. If you're faced with two certificates that differ only in price and insurance coverage, buy the cheaper certificate.

The process of purchasing a certificate starts with the creation of a private key (as we did above for the self-signed certificate). You will then generate a *certificate signing request* (CSR), that will be uploaded during the certificate purchase process (the certificate issuer will provide instructions for doing this). Note that the certificate issuer never has access to your private key, nor is your private key transmitted over the Internet, which protects the security of the private key. The issuer will then send you the certificate, which will have an extension of *.crt*, *.cer*, or *.der* (the certificate will be in a format called "Distinguished Encoding Rules" or DER, hence the less common *.der* extension). You will also receive any certificates in the certificate chain. It is safe to email this certificate because it won't work without the private key you generated.

## Enabling HTTPS for Your Express App

Once you have your private key and certificate, using them in your app is easy. Let's revisit how we've been creating our server:

```
app.listen(app.get('port'), function() {
        console.log('Express started in ' + app.get('env') +
                ' mode on port ' + app.get('port') + '.');
});
```

Switching over to HTTPS is simple. I recommend that you put your private key and SSL cert in a subdirectory called *ssl* (though it's quite common to keep it in your project root). Then you just use the https module instead of http, and pass an options object along to the createServer method:

```
var https = require('https');   // usually at top of file
```

```
var options = {
        key: fs.readFileSync(__dirname + '/ssl/meadowlark.pem'),
        cert: fs.readFileSync(__dirname + '/ssl/meadowlark.crt'),
};

https.createServer(options, app).listen(app.get('port'), function(){
        console.log('Express started in ' + app.get('env') +
                ' mode on port ' + app.get('port') + ' using HTTPS.');
});
```

That's all there is to it. Assuming you're still running your server on port 3000, you can now connect to *https://localhost:3000*. If you try to connect to *http://localhost:3000*, it will simply time out.

## A Note on Ports

Whether you know it or not, when you visit a website, you're *always* connecting to a specific port, even though it's not specified in the URL. If you don't specify a port, port 80 is assumed for HTTP. As a matter of fact, most browsers will simply not display the port number if you explicitly specify port 80. For example, navigate to *http://www.apple.com:80*; chances are, when the page loads, the browser will simply strip off the *:80*. It's still connecting on port 80, it's just implicit.

Similarly, there's a standard port for HTTPS, 443. Browser behavior is similar: if you connect to *https://www.google.com:443*, most browsers will simply not display the *:443*, but that's the port they're connecting over.

If you're not using port 80 for HTTP or port 443 for HTTPS, you'll have to explicitly specify the port *and* the protocol to connect correctly. There's no way to run HTTP and HTTPS on the same port (technically, it's possible, but there's no good reason to do it, and the implementation would be very complicated).

If you want to run your HTTP app on port 80, or your HTTPS app on port 443 so you don't have to specify the port explicitly, you have two things to consider. First is that many systems already have a default web server running on port 80. For example, if you're using OS X and you have web sharing enabled, Apache will be running on port 80, and you won't be able to start your app on port 80.

The other thing to know is that on most operating systems, ports 1–1024 require elevated privileges to open. For example, on a Linux or OS X machine, if you attempt to start your app on port 80, it will fail with an EACCES error. To run on port 80 or 443 (or any port under 1025), you'll need to elevate your privileges by using the sudo command. If you don't have administrator rights, you will be unable to start the server directly on port 80 or 443.

Unless you're managing your own servers, you probably don't have root access to your hosted account: so what happens when you want to run on port 80 or 443? Generally, hosting providers have some kind of proxy service that runs with elevated privileges that will pass requests through to your app, which is running on a nonprivileged port. We'll learn more about this in the next section.

## HTTPS and Proxies

As we've seen, it's very easy to use HTTPS with Express, and for development, it will work fine. However, when you want to scale your site out to handle more traffic, you will want to use a proxy server such as Nginx (see Chapter 12). If your site is running in a shared hosting environment, it is almost certain that there will be a proxy server that will route requests to your application.

If you're using a proxy server, then the client (the user's browser) will communicate with the *proxy server*, not your server. The proxy server, in turn, will most likely communicate with your app over regular HTTP (since your app and the proxy server will be running together on a trusted network). You will often hear people say that the HTTPS *terminates* at the proxy server.

For the most part, once you or your hosting provider has correctly configured the proxy server to handle HTTPS requests, you won't need to do any additional work. The exception to that rule is if your application needs to handle both secure and insecure requests.

There are three solutions to this problem. The first is simply to configure your proxy to redirect all HTTP traffic to HTTPS, in essence forcing all communication with your application to be over HTTPS. This approach is becoming much more common, and it's certainly an easy solution to the problem.

The second approach is to somehow communicate the protocol used in the client-proxy communication to the server. The usual way to communicate this is through the X-Forwarded-Proto header. For example, to set this header in Nginx:

```
proxy_set_header X-Forwarded-Proto $scheme;
```

Then, in your app, you could test to see if the protocol was HTTPS:

```
app.get('/', function(req, res){
        // the following is essentially
        // equivalent to: if(req.secure)
        if(req.headers['x-forwarded-proto']==='https') {
                res.send('line is secure');
        } else {
                res.send('you are insecure!');
        }
});
```

In Nginix, there is a separate `server` configuration block for HTTP and HTTPS. If you fail to set the `X-Forwarded-Protocol` in the configuration block corresponding to HTTP, you open yourself up to the possibility of a client spoofing the header and thereby fooling your application into thinking that the connection is secure even though it isn't. If you take this approach, make sure you *always* set the `X-Forwarded-Protocol` header.

Express provides some convenience properties that change behavior (quite correctly) when you're using a proxy. Don't forget to tell Express to trust the proxy by using `app.enable('trust proxy')`. Once you do, `req.protocol`, `req.secure`, and `req.ip` will refer to the client's connection to the proxy, not to your app.

# Cross-Site Request Forgery

Cross-site request forgery (CSRF) attacks exploit the fact that users generally trust their browser and visit multiple sites in the same session. In a CSRF attack, script on a malicious site makes requests of another site: if you are logged in on the other site, the malicious site can successfully access secure data from another site.

To prevent CSRF attacks, you must have a way to make sure a request legitimately came from your website. The way we do this is to pass a unique token to the browser. When the browser then submits a form, the server checks to make sure the token matches. The `csurf` middleware will handle the token creation and verification for you; all you'll have to do is make sure the token is included in requests to the server. Install the `csurf` middleware (`npm install --save csurf`), then link it in and add a token to `res.lo cals`:

```
// this must come after we link in body-parser, cookie-parser, express-session
app.use(require('csurf')());
app.use(function(req, res, next){
        res.locals._csrfToken = req.csrfToken();
        next();
});
```

The `csurf` middleware adds the `csurfToken` method to the request object. We don't have to assign it to `res.locals`; we could just pass `req.csurfToken()` explicitly to every view that needs it, but this is generally less work.

Now on all of your forms (and AJAX calls), you'll have to provide a field called `_csrf`, which must match the generated token. Let's see how we would add this to one of our forms:

```
<form action="/newsletter" method="POST">
        <input type="hidden" name="_csrf" value="{{_csrfToken}}">
        Name: <input type="text" name="name"><br>
```

```
        Email: <input type="email" name="email"><br>
        <button type="submit">Submit</button>
</form>
```

The csurf middleware will handle the rest: if the body contains fields, but no valid _csrf field, it will raise an error (make sure you have an error route in your middleware!). Go ahead and remove the hidden field and see what happens.

 If you have an API, you probably don't want the csurf middleware interfering with it. If you want to restrict access to your API from other websites, you should look into the "API key" functionality of connect-rest. To prevent csurf from interfering with your middleware, link it in before you link in csurf.

# Authentication

Authentication is a big, complicated topic. Unfortunately, it's also a vital part of most nontrivial web applications. The most important piece of wisdom I can impart to you is *don't try to do it yourself*. If you look at your business card and it doesn't say "Security Expert," you probably aren't prepared for the complex considerations involved in designing a secure authentication system.

Note that I'm not saying that you shouldn't try to understand the security systems in your application. I'm just recommending that you don't try to build it yourself. Feel free to study the open source code of the authentication techniques I'm going to recommend. It will certainly give you some insight as to why you might not want to take on this task unaided!

## Authentication Versus Authorization

While the two terms are often used interchangeably, there is a subtle difference. *Authentication* refers to verifying users' identities. That is, they are who they say they are. Authorization refers to determining what a user is authorized to access, modify, or view. For example, customers might be authorized to access their account information, whereas an Meadowlark Travel employee would be authorized to access another person's account information or sales notes.

Usually (but not always), authentication comes first, and then authorization is determined. Authorization can be very simple (authorized/not authorized), broad (user/administrator), or very fine-grained, specifying read, write, delete, and update privileges against different account types. The complexity of your authorization system is dependent on the type of application you're writing.

Because authorization is so dependent on the details of your application, I'll be giving only a rough outline in this book, using a very broad authentication scheme (customer/ employee).

I will often use the abbreviation "auth," but only when it is clear from the context whether it means "authentication" or "authorization," or when it doesn't matter.

## The Problem with Passwords

The problem with passwords is that every security system is as strong as its weakest link. And passwords require the user to invent a password—and there's your weakest link. Humans are notoriously bad at coming up with secure passwords. As I write this, in an analysis of security breaches in 2013, the most popular password is "12345." "password" is #2 (it was #1 the previous year). Even in the security conscious year of 2013, people are still choosing abysmally bad passwords. Having password policies requiring, for example, a capital letter, a number, and a punctuation mark is just going to result in a password of "Password1!".

Even analyzing passwords against a list of common passwords doesn't do much to stop the problem. Then people start writing down their higher quality passwords on note pads, leaving them in unencrypted files on their computers, or emailing them to themselves.

At the end of the day, it's a problem that you, the app designer, cannot do much to fix. However, there are things you can do that promote more secure passwords. One is to pass the buck and rely on a third party for authentication. The other is to make your login system friendly to password management services, like LastPass, RoboForm, and PasswordBox.

## Third-Party Authentication

Third-party authentication takes advantage of the fact that pretty much everyone on the Internet has an account on at least one major service, such as Google, Facebook, Twitter, or LinkedIn. All of these services provide a mechanism to authenticate and identify your users through their service.

Third-party authentication is often referred to as *federated authentication* or *delegated authentication*. The terms are largely interchangeable, though federated authentication is usually associated with Security Assertion Markup Language (SAML) and OpenID, and delegated authentication is often associated with OAuth.

Third-party authentication has three major advantages. First, your authentication burden is lowered. You do not have to worry about authenticating individual users, only interacting with a trusted third party. The second advantage is that it reduces "password fatigue": the stress associated with having too many accounts. I use LastPass (*http://lastpass.com*), and I just checked my password vault: I have almost 400 passwords. As a technology professional, I may have more than your average Internet user, but it's not uncommon for even a casual Internet user to have dozens or even hundreds of accounts. Lastly, third-party authentication is "frictionless": it allows your users to start using your site more quickly, with credentials they already have. Often, if users see that they have to create yet *another* username and password, they will simply move on.

If you don't use a password manager, the chances are, you're using the same password for most of those sites (most people have a "secure" password they use for banking and the like, and an "insecure" password they use for everything else). The problem with this approach is that if even *one* of the sites you use that password for is breached, and your password becomes known, then hackers will try using that same password with other services. It's like putting all of your eggs in one basket.

Third-party authentication has its downsides. Hard as it is to believe, there *are* folks out there who don't have an account on Google, Facebook, Twitter, or LinkedIn. Then, among the people who *do* have such accounts, suspicion (or a desire for privacy) may make them unwilling to use those credentials to log onto your website. Many websites solve this particular problem by encouraging users to use an existing account, but those who don't have them (or are unwilling to use them to access your service) can create a new login for your service.

## Storing Users in Your Database

Whether or not you rely on a third party to authenticate your users, you will want to store a record of users in your own database. For example, if you're using Facebook for authentication, that only verifies a user's identity. If you need to save settings specific to that user, you can't reasonably use Facebook for that: you have to store information about that user in your own database. Also, you probably want to associate an email address with your users, and they may not wish to use the same email address they use for Facebook (or whatever third-party authentication service you use). Lastly, storing user information in your database allows you to perform authentication yourself, should you wish to provide that option.

So let's create a model for our users, *models/user.js*:

```
var mongoose = require('mongoose');

var userSchema = mongoose.Schema({
        authId: String,
        name: String,
        email: String,
        role: String,
        created: Date,
```

```
});

var User = mongoose.model('User', userSchema);
module.exports = User;
```

Recall that every object in a MongoDB database has its own unique ID, stored in its `_id` property. However, that ID is controlled by MongoDB, and we need some way to map a user record to a third-party ID, so we have our own ID property, called `authId`. Since we'll be using multiple authentication strategies, that ID will be a combination of a strategy type and a third-party ID, to prevent collisions. For example, a Facebook user might have an `authId` of `facebook:525764102`, whereas a Twitter user would have an `authId` of `twitter:376841763`.

We will be using two roles in our example: "customer" and "employee."

## Authentication Versus Registration and the User Experience

Authentication refers to verifying a user's identity, either with a trusted third party, or through credentials you've provided the user (such as a username and password). Registration is the process by which a user gets an account on your site (from our perspective, registration is when we create a `User` record for that user in the database).

When users join your site for the first time, it should be clear to them that they're registering. Using a third-party authentication system, we could register them without their knowledge if they successfully authenticate through the third party. This is not generally considered a good practice, and it should be clear to users that they're registering for your site (whether they're authenticating through a third party or not), and provide a clear mechanism for canceling their membership.

One user experience situation to consider is "third-party confusion." If a user registers in January for your service using Facebook, then returns in July, and is confronted with a screen offering the choices of logging in with Facebook, Twitter, Google, or LinkedIn, the user may very well have forgotten what registration service was originally used. This is one of the pitfalls of third-party authentication, and there is precious little you can do about it. It's another good reason to ask the user to provide an email address: this way, you can give the user an option to look up an account by email, and send an email to that address specifying what service was used for authentication.

If you feel that you have a firm grasp on the social networks your users use, you can ease this problem by having a "primary" authentication service. For example, if you feel pretty confident that the majority of your users have a Facebook account, you could have a big button that says, "Log in with Facebook." Then, using smaller buttons or even just text links, say, "or log in with Google, Twitter, or LinkedIn." This approach can cut down on the instance of third-party confusion.

# Passport

Passport is a very popular and robust authentication module for Node/Express. It is not tied to any one authentication mechanism; rather, it is based on the idea of pluggable authentication *strategies* (including a local strategy if you don't want to use third-party authentication). Understanding the flow of authentication information can be overwhelming, so we'll start with just one authentication mechanism and add more later.

The detail that's important to understand is that, with third-party authentication, your app *never receives a password*. That is handled entirely by the third party. This is a good thing: it's putting the burden of secure handling and storage of passwords on the third party.[1]

The whole process, then, relies on redirects (it must, if your application is never to receive the user's third-party password). At first, you might be confused about why you can pass *localhost* URLs to the third party and still successfully authenticate (after all, the third-party server handling your request doesn't know about *your localhost*). It works because the third party simply instructs *your browser* to redirect, and your browser is inside your network, and can therefore redirect to local addresses.

The basic flow is shown in Figure 18-1. This diagram shows the important flow of functionality, making it clear that the authentication actually occurs on the third-party website. Enjoy the simplicity of the diagram—things are about to get a lot more complicated.

When you use Passport, there are four steps that your app will be responsible for. Consider a more detailed view of the third-party authentication flow, as shown in Figure 18-2.

---

1. It is unlikely that the third party is storing passwords either. A password can be verified by storing something called a *salted hash*, which is a one-way transformation of the password. That is, once you generate a hash from a password, you can't recover the password. *Salting* the hash provides additional protection against certain kinds of attacks.

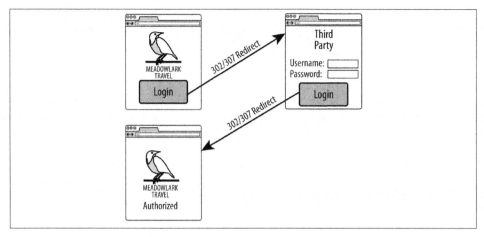

*Figure 18-1. Third-party authentication flow*

For simplicity, we are using Meadowlark Travel to represent your app, and Facebook for the third-party authentication mechanism. Figure 18-2 illustrates how the user goes from the login page to the secure "account info" page (the "account info" page is just used for illustration purposes: this could be any page on your website that requires authentication).

This diagram shows detail you don't normally think about, but is important to understand in this context. In particular, when you visit a URL, *you* aren't making the request of the server: the browser is actually doing that. That said, the browser can do three things: make an HTTP request, display the response, and perform a redirect (which is essentially making another request and displaying another response...which in turn could be another redirect).

In the "Meadowlark" column, you can see the four steps your application is actually responsible for. Fortunately, we'll be leveraging Passport (and pluggable strategies) to perform the details of those steps; otherwise, this book would be much, much longer.

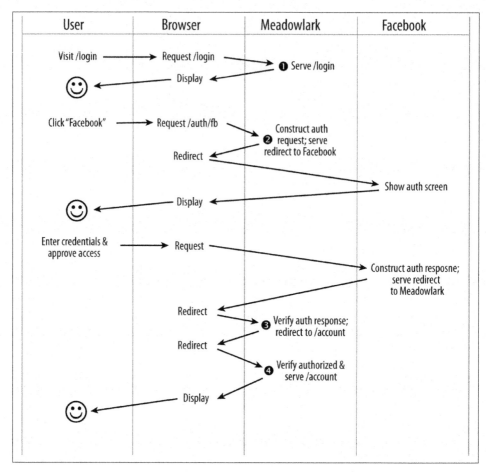

*Figure 18-2. Detailed view of third-party authentication flow*

Before we get into implementation details, let's consider each of the steps in a little more detail:

*Login page*

The login page is where the user can choose the login method. If you're using a third-party authentication, it's usually just a button or a link. If you're using local authentication, it will include username and password fields. If the user attempts to access a URL requiring authentication (such as /account in our example) without being logged in, this is probably the page you will want to redirect to (alternatively, you could redirect to a "Not Authorized" page with a link to the login page).

*Construct authentication request*

In this step, you'll be constructing a request to be sent to a third party (via a redirect). The details of this request are complicated and specific to the authentication strategy. Passport (and the strategy plugin) will be doing all the heavy lifting here. The auth request includes protection against "man in the middle" attacks, as well as other vectors an attacker might exploit. Usually the auth request is short-lived, so you can't store it and expect to use it later: this helps prevent attacks by limiting the window in which an attacker has time to act. This is where you can request additional information from the third-party authorization mechanism. For example, it's common to request the user's name, and possibly email address. Keep in mind that the more information you request from users, the less likely they are to authorize your application.

*Verify authentication response*

Assuming the user authorized your application, you'll get back a valid auth response from the third party, which is proof of the user's identity. Once again, the details of this validation are complicated and will be handled by Passport (and the strategy plugin). If the auth response indicates that the user is not authorized (if invalid credentials were entered, or your application wasn't authorized by the user), you would then redirect to an appropriate page (either back to the login page, or to a "Not Authorized" or "Unable to Authorize" page). Included in the auth response will be an ID for the user that is unique *to that specific third party*, as well as any additional details you requested in step 2. To enable step 4, we must "remember" that the user is authorized. The usual way to do this is to set a session variable containing the user's ID, indicating that this session has been authorized (cookies can also be used, though I recommend using sessions).

*Verify authorization*

In step 3, we stored a user ID in the session. The presence of that user ID allows us to retrieve a user object from the database that contains information about what the user is authorized to do. In this manner, we don't have to authenticate with the third party for every request (which would result in a slow and painful user experience). This task is simple, and we no longer need Passport for this: we have our own User object that contains our own authentication rules. (If that object isn't available, it indicates the request isn't authorized, and we can redirect to the login or "Not Authorized" page.)

 Using Passport for authentication is a fair amount of work, as you'll see in this chapter. However, authentication is an important part of your application, and I feel that it is wise to invest some time in getting it right. There are projects such as LockIt (*http://bit.ly/lock_it*) that try to provide a more "off the shelf" solution. To make the most effective use of LockIt (or similar solutions), however, it behooves you to understand the details of authentication and authorization, which is what this chapter is designed to do. Also, if you ever need to customize an authentication solution, Passport is a great place to start.

## Setting up Passport

To keep things simple, we'll start with a single authentication provider. Arbitrarily, we'll choose Facebook. Before we can set up Passport and the Facebook strategy, we'll need to do a little configuration in Facebook. For Facebook authentication, you'll need a *Facebook app*. If you already have a suitable Facebook app, you can use that, or you can create a new one specifically for authentication. If possible, you should use your organization's official Facebook account to create the app. That is, if you worked for Meadowlark Travel, you would use the Meadowlark Travel Facebook account to create the app (you can always add your personal Facebook account as an administrator of the app for ease of administration). For testing purposes, it's fine to use your own Facebook account, but using a personal account for production will appear unprofessional and suspicious to your users.

The details of Facebook app administration seem to change fairly frequently, so I am not going to explain the details here. Consult the Facebook developer documentation (*https://developers.facebook.com/docs*) if you need details on creating and administering your app.

For development and testing purposes, you will need to associate the development/testing domain name with the app. Facebook allows you to use *localhost* (and port numbers), which is great for testing purposes. Alternatively, you can specify a local IP address, which can be helpful if you're using a virtualized server, or another server on your network for testing. The important thing is that the URL you enter into your browser to test the app (for example, *http://localhost:3000*) is associated with the Facebook app. Currently, you can only associate one domain with your app: if you need to be able to use multiple domains, you will have to create multiple apps (for example, you could have "Meadowlark Dev," "Meadowlark Test," and "Meadowlark Staging"; your production app can simply be called "Meadowlark Travel").

Once you've configured your app, you will need its unique app ID, and its app secret, both of which can be found on the Facebook app management page for that app.

 One of the biggest frustrations you'll probably face is receiving a message from Facebook such as "Given URL is not allowed by the Application configuration." This indicates that the hostname and port in the callback URL do not match what you've configured in your app. If you look at the URL in your browser, you will see the encoded URL, which should give you a clue. For example, if I'm using 192.168.0.103:3443, and I get that message, I look at the URL. If I see *redirect_uri=https%3A%2F%2F192.68.0.103%3A3443%2Fauth %2Ffacebook%2Fcallback* in the querystring, I can quickly spot the mistake: I used "68" instead of "168" in my hostname.

Now let's install Passport, and the Facebook authentication strategy:

```
npm install --save passport passport-facebook
```

Before we're done, there's going to be a lot of authentication code (especially if we're supporting multiple strategies), and we don't want to clutter up *meadowlark.js* with all that code. Instead, we'll create a module called *lib/auth.js*. This is going to be a large file, so we're going to take it piece by piece. We'll start with the imports and two methods that Passport requires, `serializeUser` and `deserializeUser`:

```
var User = require('../models/user.js'),
        passport = require('passport'),
        FacebookStrategy = require('passport-facebook').Strategy;

passport.serializeUser(function(user, done){
        done(null, user._id);
});

passport.deserializeUser(function(id, done){
        User.findById(id, function(err, user){
                if(err || !user) return done(err, null);
                done(null, user);
        });
});
```

Passport uses `serializeUser` and `deserializeUser` to map requests to the authenticated user, allowing you to use whatever storage method you want. In our case, we are only going to store the MongoDB-assigned ID (the `_id` property of `User` model instances) in the session. The way we're using it here makes "serialize" and "deserialize" a bit of a misnomer: we're actually just storing a user ID in the session. Then, when needed, we can get a `User` model instance by finding that DB in the database.

Once these two methods are implemented, as long as there is an active session, and the user has successfully authenticated, `req.session.passport.user` will be the corresponding `User` model instance.

Next, we're going to choose what to export. To enable Passport's functionality, we'll need to do two distinct activities: initialize Passport and register routes that will handle authentication and the redirected callbacks from our third-party authentication services. We don't want to combine these two in one function because in our main application file, we may want to choose when Passport is linked into the middleware chain (remember that order is significant when adding middleware). So, instead of having our module export function that does either of these things, we're going to have it return a function that returns an object that has the methods we need. Why not just return an object to start with? Because we need to bake in some configuration values. Also, since we need to link the Passport middleware into our application, a function is an easy way to pass in the Express application object:

```
module.exports = function(app, options){

        // if success and failure redirects aren't specified,
        // set some reasonable defaults
        if(!options.successRedirect)
                options.successRedirect = '/account';
        if(!options.failureRedirect)
                options.failureRedirect = '/login';

        return {

                init: function() { /* TODO */ },

                registerRoutes: function() { /* TODO */ },

        };
};
```

Before we get into the details of the `init` and `registerRoutes` methods, let's look at how we'll use this module (hopefully that will make this business of returning a function that returns an object a little more clear):

```
var auth = require('./lib/auth.js')(app, {
        // baseUrl is optional; it will default to localhost if you omit it;
        // it can be helpful to set this if you're not working on
        // your local machine.  For example, if you were using a staging server,
        // you might set the BASE_URL environment variable to
        // https://staging.meadowlark.com
    baseUrl: process.env.BASE_URL,
    providers: credentials.authProviders,
    successRedirect: '/account',
    failureRedirect: '/unauthorized',
});
// auth.init() links in Passport middleware:
auth.init();

// now we can specify our auth routes:
auth.registerRoutes();
```

Notice that, in addition to specifying the success and failure redirect paths, we also specify a property called `providers`, which we've externalized in the *credentials.js* file (see Chapter 13). We'll need to add the `authProviders` property to *credentials.js*:

```
module.exports = {
        mongo: {
                //...
        },

        authProviders: {
            facebook: {
                development: {
                    appId: 'your_app_id',
```

```
                    appSecret: 'your_app_secret',
                },
            },
        },
    }
```

Notice that we put the app details in a property called development; this will allow us to specify both development and production apps (remember that Facebook does not allow you to associate more than one URL with an application).

 Another reason to bundle our authentication code in a module like this is that we can reuse it for other projects...as a matter of fact, there are already some authentication packages that do essentially what we're doing here. However, it's important to understand the details of what's going on, so even if you end up using a module someone else wrote, this will help you understand everything that's going on in your authentication flow.

Now let's take care of our init method:

```
init: function() {
    var env = app.get('env');
    var config = options.providers;

    // configure Facebook strategy
    passport.use(new FacebookStrategy({
        clientID: config.facebook[env].appId,
        clientSecret: config.facebook[env].appSecret,
        callbackURL: (options.baseUrl || '') + '/auth/facebook/callback',
    }, function(accessToken, refreshToken, profile, done){
        var authId = 'facebook:' + profile.id;
        User.findOne({ authId: authId }, function(err, user){
            if(err) return done(err, null);
            if(user) return done(null, user);
            user = new User({
                authId: authId,
                name: profile.displayName,
                created: Date.now(),
                role: 'customer',
            });
            user.save(function(err){
                if(err) return done(err, null);
                done(null, user);
            });
        });
    }));

    app.use(passport.initialize());
    app.use(passport.session());
},
```

This is a pretty dense bit of code, but most of it is actually just Passport boilerplate. The important bit is inside the function that gets passed to the FacebookStrategy instance. When this function gets called (after the user has successfully authenticated), the profile parameter contains information about the Facebook user. Most important, it includes a Facebook ID: that's what we'll use to associate a Facebook account to our own User model. Note that we namespace our authId property by prefixing *facebook:*. Slight as the chance may be, this prevents the possibility of a Facebook ID colliding with a Twitter or Google ID (it also allows us to examine user models to see what authentication method a user is using, which could be useful). If the database already contains an entry for this namespaced ID, we simply return it (this is when serializeUser gets called, which will put the MongoDB ID into the session). If no user record is returned, we create a new User model and save it to the database.

The last thing we have to do is create our registerRoutes method (don't worry, this one is much shorter):

```
registerRoutes: function(){
    // register Facebook routes
    app.get('/auth/facebook', function(req, res, next){
        if(req.query.redirect) req.session.authRedirect = req.query.redirect;
        passport.authenticate('facebook')(req, res, next);
    });
    app.get('/auth/facebook/callback', passport.authenticate('facebook',
        { failureRedirect: options.failureRedirect }),
        function(req, res){
            // we only get here on successful authentication
            var redirect = req.session.authRedirect;
            if(redirect) delete req.session.authRedirect;
            res.redirect(303, redirect || options.successRedirect);
        }
    );
},
```

Now we have the path */auth/facebook*; visiting this path will automatically redirect the visitor to Facebook's authentication screen (this is done by passport.authenticate('facebook')), step 2 in Figure 18-1. Note that we check to see if there's a query-string parameter redirect; if there is, we save it in the session. This is so we can automatically redirect to the indended destination after completing authentication. Once the user authorizes with Twitter, the browser will be redirected back to your site. Specifically, to the */auth/facebook/callback* path (with the optional redirect querystring indicating where the user was originally). Also on the querystring are authentication tokens that Passport will verify. If the verification fails, Passport will redirect the browser to options.failureRedirect. If the verification is successful, Passport will call next(), which is where your application comes back in. Note how the middleware is chained in the handler for */auth/facebook/callback*: passport.authenticate is called first. If it calls next(), control passes over to your function, which then redirects to either the original location or `options.successRedirect`, if the `redirect` querystring parameter wasn't specified.

> Omitting the `redirect` querystring parameter can simplify your authentication routes, which may be tempting if you only have one URL that requires authentication. However, having this functionality available will eventually come in handy and provide a better user experience. No doubt you've experienced this yourself before: you've found the page you want, and you're instructed to log in. You do, and you're redirected to a default page, and you have to navigate back to the original page. It's not a very satisfying user experience.

The "magic" that Passport is doing during this process is saving the user (in our case, just a MongoDB database user ID) to the session. This is a good thing, because the browser is *redirecting*, which is a different HTTP request: without having that information in the session, we wouldn't have any way to know that the user had been authenticated! Once a user has been successfully authenticated, `req.session.pass port.user` will be set, and that's how future requests will know that the user has been authenticated.

Let's look at our `/account` handler to see how it checks to make sure the user is authenticated (this route handler will be in our main application file, or in a separate routing module, not in */lib/auth.js*):

```
app.get('/account', function(req, res) {
    if(!req.user)
        return res.redirect(303, '/unauthorized');
    res.render('account', { username: req.user.name });
});
// we also need an 'unauthorized' page
app.get('/unauthorized', function(req, res) {
    res.status(403).render('unauthorized');
});
```

Now only authenticated users will see the account page; everyone else will be redirected to a "Not Authorized" page.

## Role-Based Authorization

So far, we're not technically doing any authorization (we're only differentiating between authorized and unauthorized users). However, let's say we only want customers to see their account views (employees might have an entirely different view where they can see user account information).

Remember that in a single route, you can have multiple functions, which get called in order. Let's create a function called `customerOnly` that will allow only customers:

```
function customerOnly(req, res, next){
    if(req.user && req.user.role==='customer') return next();
    // we want customer-only pages to know they need to logon
    res.redirect(303, '/unauthorized');
}
```

Let's also create a employeeOnly function that will operate a little differently. Let's say we have a path /sales that we want to be available only to employees. Furthermore, we don't want nonemployees to even be aware of its existence, even if they stumble on it by accident. If a potential attacker went to the /sales path, and saw a "Not Authorized" page, that is a little information that might make an attack easier (simply by knowing that the page is there). So, for a little added security, we want nonemployees to see a regular 404 page when they visit the /sales page, giving potential attackers nothing to work with:

```
function employeeOnly(req, res, next){
    if(req.user && req.user.role==='employee') return next();
    // we want employee-only authorization failures to be "hidden", to
    // prevent potential hackers from even knowhing that such a page exists
    next('route');
}
```

Calling next('route') will not simply execute the next handler in the route: it will skip this route altogether. Assuming there's not a route further on down the line that will handle /account, this will eventually pass to the 404 handler, giving us the desired result.

Here's how easy it is to put these functions to use:

```
// customer routes

app.get('/account', customerOnly, function(req, res){
        res.render('account');
});
app.get('/account/order-history', customerOnly, function(req, res){
        res.render('account/order-history');
});
app.get('/account/email-prefs', customerOnly, function(req, res){
        res.render('account/email-prefs');
});

// employer routes
app.get('/sales', employeeOnly, function(req, res){
        res.render('sales');
});
```

It should be clear that role-based authorization can be as simple or as complicated as you wish. For example, what if you want to allow multiple roles? You could use the following function and route:

```
function allow(roles) {
    return function(req, res, next) {
        if(req.user && roles.split(',').indexOf(req.user.role)!==-1) return next();
```

```
        res.redirect(303, '/unauthorized');
    };
}

app.get('/account', allow('customer,employee'), function(req, res){
    res.render('account');
});
```

Hopefully that example gives you an idea of how creative you can be with role-based authorization. You could even authorize on other properties, such as the length of time a user has been a member or how many vacations that user has booked with you.

## Adding Additional Authentication Providers

Now that our framework is in place, adding additional authentication providers is easy. Let's say we want to authenticate with Google. Before we start adding code, you'll have to set up a project on your Google account. Go to your Google Developers Console (*https://console.developers.google.com*), and choose a project (if you don't already have a project, click "Create Project" and follow the instructions. Once you've selected a project, navigate to the "APIs & Auth" section, then "Credentials", and click the "Create New Client ID" button. Enter the appropriate URLs for your app (it works with localhost), and then copy the client ID and client secret into your *credentials.js* file, as we did for Facebook. One more thing is required for the Google authentication package we're using here: you have to go to "APIs" and enable the "Google+ API" (under "Social APIs").

Once you've got everything set up on the Google side, run npm install --save passport-google-oauth, and add the following code to *lib/auth.js*:

```
passport.use(new GoogleStrategy({
    clientID: config.google[env].clientID,
    clientSecret: config.google[env].clientSecret,
    callbackURL: (options.baseUrl || '') + '/auth/google/callback',
}, function(token, tokenSecret, profile, done){
    var authId = 'google:' + profile.id;
    User.findOne({ authId: authId }, function(err, user){
        if(err) return done(err, null);
        if(user) return done(null, user);
        user = new User({
            authId: authId,
            name: profile.displayName,
            created: Date.now(),
            role: 'customer',
        });
        user.save(function(err){
            if(err) return done(err, null);
            done(null, user);
        });
    });
}));
```

And the following to the `registerRoutes` method:

```
// register Google routes
app.get('/auth/google', function(req, res, next){
    if(req.query.redirect) req.session.authRedirect = req.query.redirect;
    passport.authenticate('google', { scope: 'profile' })(req, res, next);
});
app.get('/auth/google/callback', passport.authenticate('google',
    { failureRedirect: options.failureRedirect }),
    function(req, res){
        // we only get here on successful authentication
        var redirect = req.session.authRedirect;
        if(redirect) delete req.session.authRedirect;
        res.redirect(303, req.query.redirect || options.successRedirect);
    }
);
```

## Conclusion

Congratulations on making it through the most intricate chapter! It's unfortunate that such an important feature (authentication and authorization) is so complicated, but in a world rife with security threats, it's an unavoidable complexity. Fortunately, projects like Passport (and the excellent authentication schemes based on it) lessen our burden somewhat. Still, I encourage you not to give short shrift to this area of your application: exercising diligence in the area of security will make you a good Internet citizen. Your users may never thank you for it, but woe be to the owners of an application who allow user data to be compromised due to poor security.

# CHAPTER 19

# Integrating with Third-Party APIs

Increasingly, successful websites are not completely standalone. To engage existing users and find new users, integration with social networking is a must. To provide store locators or other location-aware services, using geolocation and mapping services is essential. It doesn't stop there: more and more organizations are realizing that providing an API helps expand their service and makes it more useful.

In this chapter, we'll be discussing the two most common integration needs: social media and geolocation.

## Social Media

Social media is a great way to promote your product or service: if that's your goal, the ability for your users to easily share your content on social media sites is essential. As I write this, the dominant social networking services are Facebook and Twitter. Google+ may be struggling for a piece of the pie, but don't count them out: they are, after all, backed by one of the largest, most savvy Internet companies in the world. Sites like Pinterest, Instagram, and Flickr have their place, but they are usually a little more audience specific (for example, if your website is about DIY crafting, you would absolutely want to support Pinterest). Laugh if you will, but I predict that MySpace will make a comeback. Their site redesign is inspired, and it's worth noting that they built it on Node.

### Social Media Plugins and Site Performance

Most social media integration is a frontend affair. You reference the appropriate JavaScript files in your page, and it enables both incoming content (the top three stories from your Facebook page, for example) and outgoing content (the ability to tweet about the page you're on, for example). While this often represents the easiest path to social media integration, it comes at a cost: I've seen page load times double or even triple thanks to the additional HTTP requests. If page performance is important to you (and it should be, especially for mobile users), you should carefully consider how you integrate social media.

That said, the code that enables a Facebook "Like" button or a "Tweet" button leverages in-browser cookies to post on the user's behalf. Moving this functionality to the backend would be difficult (and, in some instances, impossible). So if that is functionality you need, linking in the appropriate third-party library is your best option, even though it can affect your page performance. One saving grace is that the Facebook and Twitter APIs are so ubiquitous that there's a high probability that your browser already has them cached, in which case there will be little effect on performance.

## Searching for Tweets

Let's say that we want to mention the top 10 most recent tweets that contain the hashtag #meadowlarktravel. We could use a frontend component to do this, but it will involve additional HTTP requests. Furthermore, if we do it on the backend, we have the option of caching the tweets for performance. Also, if we do the searching on the backend, we can "blacklist" uncharitable tweets, which would be more difficult on the frontend.

Twitter, like Facebook, allows you to create *apps*. It's something of a misnomer: a Twitter app doesn't *do* anything (in the traditional sense). It's more like a set of credentials that you can use to create the actual app on your site. The easiest and most portable way to access the Twitter API is to create an app and use it to get access tokens.

Create a Twitter app by going to *http://dev.twitter.com*. Click your user icon in the upper-lefthand corner, and then select "My applications." Click "Create a new application," and follow the instructions. Once you have an application, you'll see that you now have a *consumer key* and a *consumer secret*. The consumer secret, as the name implies, should be kept secret: do not ever include this in responses sent to the client. If a third party were to get access to this secret, they could make requests on behalf of your application, which could have unfortunate consequences for you if the use is malicious.

Now that we have a consumer key and consumer secret, we can communicate with the Twitter REST API.

To keep our code tidy, we'll put our Twitter code in a module called *lib/twitter.js*:

```
var https = require('https');

module.exports = function(twitterOptions){

    return {
        search: function(query, count, cb){
            // TODO
        }
    };
};
```

This pattern should be starting to become familiar to you. Our module exports a function into which the caller passes a configuration object. What's returned is an object containing methods. In this way, we can add functionality to our module. Currently, we're only providing a search method. Here's how we will be using the library:

```
var twitter = require('./lib/twitter')({
        consumerKey: credentials.twitter.consumerKey,
        consumerSecret: credentials.twitter.consumerSecret,
});

twitter.search('#meadowlarktravel', 10, function(result){
        // tweets will be in result.statuses
});
```

(Don't forget to put a twitter property with consumerKey and consumerSecret in your *credentials.js* file.)

Before we implement the search method, we must provide some functionality to authenticate ourselves to Twitter. The process is simple: we use HTTPS to request an access token based on our consumer key and consumer secret. We only have to do this once: currently, Twitter does not expire access tokens (though you can invalidate them manually). Since we don't want to request an access token every time, we'll cache the access token so we can reuse it.

The way we've constructed our module allows us to create private functionality that's not available to the caller. Specifically, the only thing that's available to the caller is module.exports. Since we're returning a function, only that function is available to the caller. Calling that function results in an object, and only the properties of that object are available to the caller. So we're going to create a variable accessToken, which we'll use to cache our access token, and a getAccessToken function that will get the access token. The first time it's called, it will make a Twitter API request to get the access token. Subsequent calls will simply return the value of accessToken:

```
var https = require('https');

module.exports = function(twitterOptions){

        // this variable will be invisible outside of this module
        var accessToken;

        // this function will be invisible outside of this module
        function getAccessToken(cb){
                if(accessToken) return cb(accessToken);
                // TODO: get access token
        }

        return {
                search: function(query, count, cb){
                        // TODO
```

```
            },
        };
    };
```

Because `getAccessToken` may require an asynchronous call to the Twitter API, we have to provide a callback, which will be invoked when the value of `accessToken` is valid. Now that we've established the basic structure, let's implement `getAccessToken`:

```
function getAccessToken(cb){
    if(accessToken) return cb(accessToken);

    var bearerToken = Buffer(
        encodeURIComponent(twitterOptions.consumerKey) + ':' +
        encodeURIComponent(twitterOptions.consumerSecret)
    ).toString('base64');

    var options = {
        hostname: 'api.twitter.com',
        port: 443,
        method: 'POST',
        path: '/oauth2/token?grant_type=client_credentials',
        headers: {
            'Authorization': 'Basic ' + bearerToken,
        },
    };

    https.request(options, function(res){
        var data = '';
        res.on('data', function(chunk){
            data += chunk;
        });
        res.on('end', function(){
            var auth = JSON.parse(data);
            if(auth.token_type!=='bearer') {
                console.log('Twitter auth failed.');
                return;
            }
            accessToken = auth.access_token;
            cb(accessToken);
        });
    }).end();
}
```

The details of constructing this call are available on Twitter's developer documentation page for application-only authentication (*http://bit.ly/application-only-auth*). Basically, we have to construct a bearer token that's a base64-encoded combination of the consumer key and consumer secret. Once we've constructed that token, we can call the /oauth2/token API with the `Authorization` header containing the bearer token to request an access token. Note that we must use HTTPS: if you attempt to make this call over HTTP, you are transmitting your secret key unencrypted, and the API will simply hang up on you.

Once we receive the full response from the API (we listen for the end event of the response stream), we can parse the JSON, make sure the token type is bearer, and be on our merry way. We cache the access token, then invoke the callback.

Now that we have a mechanism for obtaining an access token, we can make API calls. So let's implement our search method:

```
search: function(query, count, cb){
        getAccessToken(function(accessToken){
                var options = {
                        hostname: 'api.twitter.com',
                        port: 443,
                        method: 'GET',
                        path: '/1.1/search/tweets.json?q=' +
                                encodeURIComponent(query) +
                                '&count=' + (count || 10),
                        headers: {
                                'Authorization': 'Bearer ' + accessToken,
                        },
                };
                https.request(options, function(res){
                        var data = '';
                        res.on('data', function(chunk){
                                data += chunk;
                        });
                        res.on('end', function(){
                                cb(JSON.parse(data));
                        });
                }).end();
        });
},
```

# Rendering Tweets

Now we have the ability to search tweets...so how do we display them on our site? Largely, it's up to you, but there are some things to consider. Twitter has an interest in making sure its data is used in a manner consistent with the brand. To that end, it does have display requirements (*https://dev.twitter.com/terms/display-requirements*), which employ functional elements you must include to display a tweet.

There is some wiggle room in the requirements (for example, if you're displaying on a device that doesn't support images, you don't have to include the avatar image), but for the most part, you'll end up with something that looks very much like an embedded tweet. It's a lot of work, and there is a way around it...but it involves linking to Twitter's widget library, which is the very HTTP request we're trying to avoid.

If you need to display tweets, your best bet is to use the Twitter widget library, even though it incurs an extra HTTP request (again, because of Twitter's ubiquity, that resource is probably already cached by the browser, so the performance hit may be negligible). For more complicated use of the API, you'll still have to access the REST API from the backend, so you will probably end up using the REST API in concert with frontend scripts.

Let's continue with our example: we want to display the top 10 tweets that mention the hashtag #meadowlarktravel. We'll use the REST API to search for the tweets and the Twitter widget library to display them. Since we don't want to run up against usage limits (or slow down our server), we'll cache the tweets and the HTML to display them for 15 minutes.

We'll start by modifying our Twitter library to include a method embed, which gets the HTML to display a tweet (make sure you have var querystring = require('query string'); at the top of the file):

```
embed: function(statusId, options, cb){
    if(typeof options==='function') {
        cb = options;
        options = {};
    }
    options.id = statusId;
    getAccessToken(function(accessToken){
        var requestOptions = {
            hostname: 'api.twitter.com',
            port: 443,
            method: 'GET',
            path: '/1.1/statuses/oembed.json?' +
                querystring.stringify(options),
            headers: {
                'Authorization': 'Bearer ' + accessToken,
            },
        };
        https.request(requestOptions, function(res){
            var data = '';
            res.on('data', function(chunk){
                data += chunk;
            });
            res.on('end', function(){
                cb(JSON.parse(data));
            });
        }).end();
    });
},
```

Now we're ready to search for, and cache, tweets. In our main app file, let's create an object to store the cache:

```
var topTweets = {
        count: 10,
        lastRefreshed: 0,
        refreshInterval: 15 * 60 * 1000,
```

```
        tweets: [],
    };
```

Next we'll create a function to get the top tweets. If they're already cached, and the cache hasn't expired, we simply return topTweets.tweets. Otherwise, we perform a search and then make repeated calls to embed to get the embeddable HTML. Because of this last bit, we're going to introduce a new concept: *promises*. A promise is a technique for managing asynchronous functionality. An asynchronous function will return immediately, but we can create a promise that will *resolve* once the asynchronous part has been completed. We'll use the Q promises library (*https://npmjs.org/package/q*), so make sure you run npm install --save q and put var Q = require(q); at the top of your app file. Here's the function:

```
function getTopTweets(cb){
        if(Date.now() < topTweets.lastRefreshed + topTweets.refreshInterval)
                return cb(topTweets.tweets);

        twitter.search('#meadowlarktravel', topTweets.count, function(result){
                var formattedTweets = [];
                var promises = [];
                var embedOpts = { omit_script: 1 };
                result.statuses.forEach(function(status){
                        var deferred = Q.defer();
                        twitter.embed(status.id_str, embedOpts, function(embed){
                                formattedTweets.push(embed.html);
                                deferred.resolve();
                        });
                        promises.push(deferred.promise);
                });
                Q.all(promises).then(function(){
                        topTweets.lastRefreshed = Date.now();
                        cb(topTweets.tweets = formattedTweets);
                });
        });
}
```

If you're new to asynchronous programming, this may seem very alien to you, so let's take a moment and analyze what's happening here. We'll examine a simplified example, where we do something to each element of a collection asynchronously.

In Figure 19-1, I've assigned arbitrary execution steps. They're arbitrary in that the first async block could be step 23 or 50 or 500, depending on how many other things are going on in your application; likewise, the second async block could happen at any time (but, thanks to promises, we know it has to happen *after* the first block).

```
1    var promises = [];
2    things.forEach(function(thing){
3        var deferred = Q.defer();
4        api.async(function(thing){
15           console.log(thing);              Async execution
16           deferred.resolve();
         });
5        promises.push(deferred);
     });
6    Q.all(promises).then(function(){          Async execution
23       console.log('all done!');             after all promises
     });                                       resolve
7    console.log('other stuff...');
```

*Figure 19-1. Promises*

In step 1, we create an array to store our promises, and in step 2, we start iterating over our collection of things. Note that even though forEach takes a function, it is *not* asynchronous: the function will be called synchronously for each item in the collection, which is why we know that step 3 is inside the function. In step 4, we call api.async, which represents a method that works asynchronously. When it's done, it will invoke the callback you pass in. Note that console.log(num) will *not* be step 4: that's because asynchronous function hasn't had a chance to finish and invoke the callback. Instead, step 5 executes (simply adding the promise we've created to the array), and then starts again (step 6 will be the same line as step 3). Once the iteration has completed (for however many elements there are in things), the forEach loop is over, and step 6 executes. Step 6 is special: it says, "when all the promises have resolved, then execute this function." In essence, this is another asynchronous function, but this one won't execute until all three of our calls to api.async complete. Step 7 executes, and something is printed to the console. So even though console.log(num) appears before con sole.log('other stuff…') in the code, "other stuff" will be printed first. After step 13, "other stuff" happens. At some point, there will be nothing left to do, and the Java-Script engine will start looking for other things to do. So it proceeds to execute our first asynchronous function: when that's done, the callback is invoked, and we're at steps 15 and 16. Those two steps will be repeated until there are no more items in things to process. Once all the promises have been resolved, then (and only then) can we get to step 23.

Asynchronous programming (and promises) can take a while to wrap your head around, but the payoff is worth it: you'll find yourself thinking in entirely new, more productive ways.

# Geocoding

Geocoding refers to the process of taking a street address or place name (Bletchley Park, Sherwood Drive, Bletchley, Milton Keynes MK3 6EB, UK) and converting it to geographic coordinates (latitude 51.9976597, longitude –0.7406863). If your application is going to be doing any kind of geographic calculation—distances or directions—or displaying a map, then you'll need geographic coordinates.

> You may be used to seeing geographic coordinates specified in degrees, minutes, and seconds (DMS). Geocoding APIs and mapping services use a single floating-point number for latitude and longitude. If you need to display DMS coordinates, see *http://en.wikipedia.org/wiki/geographic_coordinate_conversion*.

## Geocoding with Google

Both Google and Bing offer excellent REST services for Geocoding. We'll be using Google for our example, but the Bing service is very similar. First, let's create a module *lib/geocode.js*:

```
var http = require('http');

module.exports = function(query, cb){

        var options = {
                hostname: 'maps.googleapis.com',
                path: '/maps/api/geocode/json?address=' +
                        encodeURIComponent(query) + '&sensor=false',
        };

        http.request(options, function(res){
                var data = '';
                res.on('data', function(chunk){
                        data += chunk;
                });
                res.on('end', function(){
                        data = JSON.parse(data);
                        if(data.results.length){
                                cb(null, data.results[0].geometry.location);
                        } else {
                                cb("No results found.", null);
                        }
                });
        }).end();
};
```

Now we have a function that will contact the Google API to geocode an address. If it can't find an address (or fails for any other reason), an error will be returned. The API can return multiple addresses. For example, if you search for "10 Main Street" without specifying a city, state, or postal code, it will return dozens of results. Our implementation simply picks the first one. The API returns a lot of information, but all we're currently interested in are the coordinates. You could easily modify this interface to return more information. See the Google geocoding API documentation (*https://devel opers.google.com/maps/documentation/geocoding*) for more information about the data the API returns. Note that we included &sensor=false in the API request: this is a required field that should be set to true for devices that have a location sensor, such as mobile phones. Your server is probably not location aware, so it should be set to false.

### Usage restrictions

Both Google and Bing have usage limits for their geocoding API to prevent abuse, but they're very high. At the time of writing, Google's limit is 2,500 requests per 24-hour period. Google's API also requires that you use Google Maps on your website. That is, if you're using Google's service to geocode your data, you can't turn around and display that information on a Bing map without violating the terms of service. Generally, this is not an onerous restriction, as you probably wouldn't be doing geocoding unless you intended to display locations on a map. However, if you like Bing's maps better than Google's, or vice versa, you should be mindful of the terms of service and use the appropriate API.

## Geocoding Your Data

Let's say Meadowlark Travel is now selling Oregon-themed products (T-shirts, mugs, etc.) through dealers, and we want "find a dealer" functionality on our website, but we don't have coordinate information for our dealers, only street addresses. This is where we'll want to leverage a geocoding API.

Before we start, there are two things to consider. Initially, we'll probably have some number of dealers already in the database. We'll want to geocode those dealers in bulk. But what happens in the future when we add new dealers, or dealer addresses change?

As it happens, both cases can be handled with the same code, but there are complications to consider. The first is usage limits. If we have more than 2,500 dealers, we'll have to break up our initial geocoding over multiple days to avoid Google's API limits. Also, it may take a long time to do the initial bulk geocoding, and we don't want our users to have to wait an hour or more to see a map of dealers! After the initial bulk geocoding, however, we can handle new dealers trickling in, as well as dealers who have changed addresses. Let's start with our dealer model, in *models/dealer.js*:

```
var mongoose = require('mongoose');

var dealerSchema = mongoose.Schema({
        name: String,
        address1: String,
```

```
            address2: String,
            city: String,
            state: String,
            zip: String,
            country: String,
            phone: String,
            website: String,
            active: Boolean,
            geocodedAddress: String,
            lat: Number,
            lng: Number,
    });

    dealerSchema.methods.getAddress = function(lineDelim){
            if(!lineDelim) lineDelim = '<br>';
            var addr = this.address1;
            if(this.address2 && this.address2.match(/\S/))
                    addr += lineDelim + this.address2;
            addr += lineDelim + this.city + ', ' +
                    this.state + this.zip;
            addr += lineDelim + (this.country || 'US');
            return addr;
    };

    var Dealer = mongoose.model("Dealer", dealerSchema);
    module.exports = Dealer;
```

We can populate the database (either by transforming an existing spreadsheet, or manual data entry) and ignore the geocodedAddress, lat, and lng fields. Now that we've got the database populated, we can get to the business of geocoding.

We're going to take an approach similar to what we did for Twitter caching. Since we were caching only 10 tweets, we simply kept the cache in memory. The dealer information could be significantly larger, and we want it cached for speed, but we don't want to do it in memory. We do, however, want to do it in a way that's super fast on the client side, so we're going to create a JSON file with the data.

Let's go ahead and create our cache:

```
    var dealerCache = {
            lastRefreshed: 0,
            refreshInterval: 60 * 60 * 1000,
            jsonUrl: '/dealers.json',
            geocodeLimit: 2000,
            geocodeCount: 0,
            geocodeBegin: 0,
    };
    dealerCache.jsonFile = __dirname +
            '/public' + dealerCache.jsonUrl;
```

First we'll create a helper function that geocodes a given Dealer model and saves the result to the database. Note that if the current address of the dealer matches what was

last geocoded, we simply do nothing and return. This method, then, is very fast if the
dealer coordinates are up-to-date:

```
function geocodeDealer(dealer){
        var addr = dealer.getAddress(' ');
        if(addr===dealer.geocodedAddress) return;       // already geocoded

        if(dealerCache.geocodeCount >= dealerCache.geocodeLimit){
                // has 24 hours passed since we last started geocoding?
                if(Date.now() > dealerCache.geocodeCount + 24 * 60 * 60 * 1000){
                        dealerCache.geocodeBegin = Date.now();
                        dealerCache.geocodeCount = 0;
                } else {
                        // we can't geocode this now: we've
                        // reached our usage limit
                        return;
                }
        }

        var geocode = require('./lib/geocode.js');
        geocode(addr, function(err, coords){
                if(err) return console.log('Geocoding failure for ' + addr);
                dealer.lat = coords.lat;
                dealer.lng = coords.lng;
                dealer.save();
        });
}
```

We could add `geocodeDealer` as a method of the `Dealer` model.
However, since it has a dependency on our geocoding library, we are
opting to make it its own function.

Now we can create a function to refresh the dealer cache. This operation can take a while
(especially the first time), but we'll deal with that in a second:

```
dealerCache.refresh = function(cb){

        if(Date.now() > dealerCache.lastRefreshed + dealerCache.refreshInterval){
                // we need to refresh the cache
                Dealer.find({ active: true }, function(err, dealers){
                        if(err) return console.log('Error fetching dealers: '+
                                err);

                        // geocodeDealer will do nothing if coordinates
                        // are up-to-date
                        dealers.forEach(geocodeDealer);

                        // we now write all the dealers out to JSON file
                        fs.writeFileSync(dealerCache.jsonFile,
```

```
                              JSON.stringify(dealers));

                    // all done -- invoke callback
                    cb();
          });
    }

};
```

Finally, we need to establish a way to routinely keep our cache up-to-date. We could use `setInterval`, but if a lot of dealers change, it's possible (if unlikely) that it would take more than an hour to refresh the cache. So instead, when one refresh is done, we have it use `setTimeout` to wait an hour before refreshing the cache again:

```
function refreshDealerCacheForever(){
      dealerCache.refresh(function(){
              // call self after refresh interval
              setTimeout(refreshDealerCacheForever,
                      dealerCache.refreshInterval);
      });
}
```

We don't make `refreshDealerCacheForever` a method of `dealerCache` because of a quirk in the way JavaScript handles the `this` object. In particular, when you invoke a function (not a method), `this` does not bind to the context of the calling object.

Now we can finally set our plan in motion. When we first start our app, the cache won't exist, so we simply create an empty one, then start `dealerCache.refreshForever`:

```
// create empty cache if it doesn't exist to prevent 404 errors
if(!fs.existsSync(dealerCache.jsonFile)) fs.writeFileSync(JSON.stringify([]));
// start refreshing cache
refreshDealerCacheForever();
```

Note that the cache file will be updated only after all the dealers have been returned from the database, and any dealers that need to be geocoded have been so. So worst case, if a dealer is added or updated, it will take the refresh interval plus however long it takes to do the geocoding before the updated information shows up on the website.

## Displaying a Map

While displaying a map of the dealers really falls under "frontend" work, it would be very disappointing to get this far and not see the fruits of our labor. So we're going to take a slight departure from the backend focus of this book, and see how to display our newly geocoded dealers on a map.

Unlike the geocoding REST API, using an interactive Google map on your web page requires an API key, which means you'll have to have a Google account. Instructions for obtaining an API key are found on Google's API key documentation page (*https://developers.google.com/maps/documentation/javascript/tutorial#api_key*).

First we'll add some CSS styles to *less/main.less* (don't forget to run grunt `static` to compile the LESS to CSS…otherwise your map won't show up):

```
.dealers #map {
        width: 100%;
        height: 400px;
}
```

This will create a mobile-friendly map that stretches the width of its container, but has a fixed height. Now that we have some basic styling, we can create a view (*views/dealers.handlebars*) that displays the dealers on a map, as well as a list of the dealers:

```
<script src="https://maps.googleapis.com/maps/api/js?key=YOUR_API_KEY↵
&sensor=false"></script>
<script src="https://cdnjs.cloudflare.com/ajax/libs/handlebars.js/1.3.0/↵
handlebars.min.js"></script>

<script id="dealerTemplate" type="text/x-handlebars-template">
    \{{#each dealers}}
        <div class="dealer">
            <h3>\{{name}}</h3>
            \{{address1}}<br>
            \{{#if address2}}\{{address2}}<br>\{{/if}}
            \{{city}}, \{{state}} \{{zip}}<br>
            \{{#if country}}\{{country}}<br>\{{/if}}
            \{{#if phone}}\{{phone}}<br>\{{/if}}
            \{{#if website}}<a href="{{website}}">\{{website}}</a><br>\{{/if}}
        </div>
    \{{/each}}
</script>

<div class="dealers">
    <div id="map"></div>
    <div id="dealerList"></div>
</div>

{{#section 'jquery'}}
        <script>
                var map;
                var dealerTemplate =
                        Handlebars.compile($('#dealerTemplate').html());
                $(document).ready(function(){

                        // center map on US, set zoom to show whole country
                        var mapOptions = {
                                center: new google.maps.LatLng(38.26, -96.06),
```

```
                zoom: 4,
      };

      // initialize map
      map = new google.maps.Map(
            document.getElementById('map'),
            mapOptions);

      // alias for brevity
      var LatLng = google.maps.LatLng;

      // fetch JSON
      $.getJSON('/dealers.json', function(dealers){

            // add markers on map for each dealer
            dealers.forEach(function(d){
                  // skip any dealers without geocoding
                  if(!d.lat || !d.lng) return;
                  var pos = new LatLng(d.lat, d.lng);
                  var marker = new google.maps.Marker({
                        position: pos,
                        map: map,
                        title: d.name
                  });
            });

            // update dealer list using Handlebars
            $('#dealerList').html(dealerTemplate({
                  dealers: dealers
            }));

      });

    });
  </script>
{{/section}}
```

Note that since we wish to use Handlebars on the client side, we have to escape our initial curly braces with a backslash to prevent Handlebars from trying to render the template on the backend. The meat of this bit of code is inside jQuery's `.getJSON` helper (where we fetch the */dealers.json* cache). For each dealer, we create a marker on the map. After we've created all the markers, we use Handlebars to update the list of dealers.

## Improving Client-Side Performance

Our simple display example works for a small number of dealers. But if you have hundreds of markers to display or more, we can squeeze a little bit more performance out of our display. Currently, we're parsing the JSON and iterating over it: we could skip that step.

On the server side, instead of (or in addition to) emitting JSON for our dealers, we could emit JavaScript directly:

```
function dealersToGoogleMaps(dealers){
    var js = 'function addMarkers(map){\n' +
        'var markers = [];\n' +
        'var Marker = google.maps.Marker;\n' +
        'var LatLng = google.maps.LatLng;\n';
    dealers.forEach(function(d){
        var name = d.name.replace(/'/, '\\\'')
            .replace(/\\/, '\\\\');
        js += 'markers.push(new Marker({\n' +
            '\tposition: new LatLng(' +
                d.lat + ', ' + d.lng + '),\n' +
            '\tmap: map,\n' +
            '\ttitle: \'' + name.replace(/'/, '\\')
                            + '\',\n' +
        '}));\n';
    });
    js += '}';
    return js;
}
```

We would then write this JavaScript to a file (*/js/dealers-googleMapMarkers.js*, for example), and include that with a `<script>` tag. Once the map has been initialized, we can just call `addMarkers(map)`, and it will add all of our markers.

The downsides of this approach are that it's now tied to the choice of Google Maps; if we wanted to switch to Bing, we'd have to rewrite our server-side JavaScript generation. But if maximum speed is needed, this is the way to go. Note that we have to be careful when emitting strings. If we were to simply emit "Paddy's Bar and Grill," we would end up with some invalid JavaScript, which would crash our whole page. So whenever you emit a string, make sure to mind what kind of string delimiters you're using, and escape them. While it's less common to encounter backslashes in company names, it's still wise to make sure any backslashes are escaped as well.

## Weather Data

Remember our "current weather" widget from Chapter 7? Let's get that hooked up with some live data! We'll be using Weather Underground's free API to get local weather data. You'll need to create a free account, which you can do at *http://www.wunderground.com/weather/api/*. Once you have your account set up, you'll create an API key (once you get an API key, put it in your *credentials.js* file as `WeatherUnderground.ApiKey`). Use of the free API is subject to usage restrictions (as I write this, you are allowed no more than 500 requests per day, and no more than 10 per minute). To stay under the free usage restrictions, we'll cache the data hourly. In your application file, replace the `get WeatherData` function with the following:

```
var getWeatherData = (function(){
    // our weather cache
    var c = {
        refreshed: 0,
        refreshing: false,
        updateFrequency: 360000, // 1 hour
        locations: [
            { name: 'Portland' },
            { name: 'Bend' },
            { name: 'Manzanita' },
        ]
    };
    return function() {
        if( !c.refreshing && Date.now() > c.refreshed + c.updateFrequency ){
            c.refreshing = true;
            var promises = [];
            c.locations.forEach(function(loc){
                var deferred = Q.defer();
                var url = 'http://api.wunderground.com/api/' +
                    credentials.WeatherUnderground.ApiKey +
                    '/conditions/q/OR/' + loc.name + '.json'
                http.get(url, function(res){
                    var body = '';
                    res.on('data', function(chunk){
                        body += chunk;
                    });
                    res.on('end', function(){
                        body = JSON.parse(body);
                        loc.forecastUrl = body.current_observation.forecast_url;
                        loc.iconUrl = body.current_observation.icon_url;
                        loc.weather = body.current_observation.weather;
                        loc.temp = body.current_observation.temperature_string;
                        deferred.resolve();
                    });
                });
                promises.push(deferred);
            });
            Q.all(promises).then(function(){
                c.refreshing = false;
                c.refreshed = Date.now();
            });
        }
        return { locations: c.locations };
    }
})();
// initialize weather cache
getWeatherData();
```

If you're not used to immediately invoked function expressions (IIFEs), this might look pretty strange. Basically, we're using an IIFE to encapsulate the cache, so we don't contaminate the global namespace with a lot of variables. The IIFE returns a function, which we save to a variable getWeatherData, which replaces the previous version that returns dummy data. Note that we have to use promises again because we're making an HTTP request for each location: because they're asynchronous, we need a promise to know when all three have finished. We also set `c.refreshing` to prevent multiple, redundant API calls when the cahce expires. Lastly, we call the function when the server starts up: if we didn't, the first request wouldn't be populated.

In this example, we're keeping our cache in memory, but there's no reason we couldn't store the cached data in a database instead, which would lend itself better to scaling out (enabling multiple instances of our server to access the same cached data).

## Conclusion

We've really only scratched the surface of what can be done with third-party API integration. Everywhere you look, new APIs are popping up, offering every kind of data imaginable (even the City of Portland is now making a lot of public data available through REST APIs). While it would be impossible to cover even a small percentage of the APIs available to you, this chapter has covered the fundamentals you'll need to know to use these APIs: `http.request`, `https.request`, and parsing JSON.

# CHAPTER 20

# Debugging

"Debugging" is perhaps an unfortunate term, what with its association with defects. The fact is, what we refer to as "debugging" is an activity you will find yourself doing all the time, whether you're implementing a new feature, learning how something works, or actually fixing a bug. A better term might be "exploring," but we'll stick with "debugging," since the activity it refers to is unambiguous, regardless of the motivation.

Debugging is an oft-neglected skill: it seems to be that most programmers are expected to be born knowing how to do it. Perhaps computer science professors and book authors see debugging as such an obvious skill that they overlook it.

The fact is, debugging is a skill that can be taught, and it is an important way by which programmers come to understand not just the framework they are working in, but also their own code and that of their team.

In this chapter, we'll discuss some of the tools and techniques you can use for debugging Node and Express applications effectively.

## The First Principle of Debugging

As the name implies, "debugging" often refers to the process of finding and eliminating defects. Before we talk about tools, let's consider some general debugging principles.

> How often have I said to you that when you have eliminated the impossible, whatever remains, however improbable, must be the truth?
>
> — Sir Authur Conan Doyle

The first and most important principle of debugging is the process of *elimination*. Modern computer systems are incredibly complicated, and if you had to hold the *whole system* in your head, and pluck the source of a single problem out of that vast cloud, you probably wouldn't even know where to start. Whenever you're confronted with a problem that isn't immediately obvious, your *very first thought* should be "What can I *eliminate* as the source of the problem?" The more you can eliminate, the fewer places you have to look.

Elimination can take many forms. Here are some common examples:

- Systematically commenting out or disabling blocks of code.
- Writing code that can be covered by unit tests; the unit tests themselves provide a framework for elimination.
- Analyzing network traffic to determine if the problem is on the client or server side.
- Testing a different part of the system that has similarities to the first.
- Using input that has worked before, and changing that input one piece at a time until the problem exhibits.
- Using version control to go back in time, one step at a time, until the problem disappears.
- "Mocking" functionality to eliminate complex subsystems.

Elimination is not a silver bullet, though. Often, problems are due to complex interactions between two or more components: eliminate (or mock) any one of the components, and the problem could go away, but the problem can't be isolated to any single component. Even in this situation, though, elimination can help narrow down the problem, even if it doesn't light up a neon sign over the exact location.

Elimination is most successful when it's careful and methodical. It's very easy to miss things when you just wantonly eliminate components without considering how those components affect the whole. Play a game with yourself: when you consider a component to eliminate, walk through how the removal of that component will affect the system. This will inform you about what to expect and whether or not removing the component tells you anything useful.

## Take Advantage of REPL and the Console

Both Node and your browser offer you a read-eval-print loop (REPL); this is basically just a way to write JavaScript interactively. You type in some JavaScript, press Enter, and immediately see the output. It's a great way to play around, and is often the quickest and most intuitive way to locate an error in small bits of code.

In a browser, all you have to do is pull up your JavaScript console, and you have a REPL. In Node, all you have to do is type node without any arguments, and you enter REPL mode; you can require packages, create variables and functions, or do anything else you could normally do in your code (except create packages: there's no meaningful way to do that in the REPL).

Console logging is also your friend. It's a crude debugging technique, perhaps, but an easy one (both easy to understand and easy to implement). Calling `console.log` in Node will output the contents of an object in an easy-to-read format, so you can easily spot problems. Keep in mind that some objects are so large that logging them to the console will produce so much output that you'll have a hard time finding any useful information. For example, try `console.log(req)` in one of your path handlers.

# Using Node's Built-in Debugger

Node has a built-in debugger that allows you to step through your application, as if you were going on a ride-along with the JavaScript interpreter. All you have to do to start debugging your app is use the `debug` argument:

```
node debug meadowlark.js
```

When you do, you'll immediately notice a couple of things. First, on your console you will see `debugger listening on port 5858`; this is because the Node debugger works by creating its own web server, which allows you to control the execution of the application being debugged. This may not be impressive right now, but the usefulness of this approach will be clear when we discuss Node Inspector.

When you're in the console debugger, you can type `help` to get a list of commands. The commands you will use most often are `n` (next), `s` (step in), and `o` (step out). `n` will step "over" the current line: it will execute it, but if that instruction calls other functions, they will be executed before control is returned to you. `s`, in contrast, will step *into* the current line: if that line invokes other functions, you will be able to step through them. `o` allows you to step out of the currently executing function. (Note that "stepping in" and "stepping out" refer only to *functions*; they do not step into or out of `if` or `for` blocks or other flow-control statements.)

The command-line debugger has more functionality, but chances are, you won't want to use it that often. The command line is great for many things, but debugging isn't one of them. It's good that it's available in a pinch (for example, if all you have is SSH access to the server, or if your server doesn't even have a GUI installed). More often, you'll want to use a graphical debugger like Node Inspector.

# Node Inspector

While you probably won't want to use the command-line debugger except in a pinch, the fact that Node exposes its debugging controls through a web service gives you other options. In particular, Danny Coates's excellent *Node Inspector* (now maintained by StrongLoop) allows you to debug Node applications with the same interface you use to debug client-side JavaScript.

Node Inspector utilizes the Chromium project's Blink engine, which powers Chrome. If you're already familiar with Chrome's debugger, you will feel right at home. If you're completely new to debugging, buckle up: the first time you see a debugger in action is revelatory.

Obviously, you'll need Chrome (or Opera; the latest versions also use the Blink engine). Go ahead and install one of those browsers if you haven't already. Once you've done that, install Node Inspector:

```
sudo npm install -g node-inspector
```

Once you've installed it, you'll need to start it. You can run it in a separate window if you like, but aside from a helpful startup message, it doesn't log much to the console, so I generally just run it in the background and forget about it:

```
node-inspector&
```

 On Linux or OS X, putting an ampersand at the end of a command will run it in the background. If you need to bring it back to the foreground, simply type fg. If you start something without putting it in the background, you can pause it by pressing Ctrl-Z, then resume it in the background by typing bg.

When you start Node Inspector, you will see the following message: "Visit *http:// 127.0.0.1:8080/debug?port=5858* to start debugging." In addition to telling you how to get started with the debugging, it's telling you that it's expecting the debugging interface to be on port 5858 (which is the default).

Now that Node Inspector is running (and you can just leave it running…on my dev server, it's pretty much constantly running and will automatically attach to whatever app you have running in debug mode), you can start your app in debug mode:

```
node --debug meadowlark.js
```

Note that we used --debug instead of just debug; this runs your program in debug mode without invoking the command-line debugger (which we don't need because we'll be using Node Inspector). Then, before any console output from your application, you'll see debugger listening on port 5858 again, and now we have the whole picture: your app is exposing its debugging interface on port 5858, and Node Inspector is running on port 8080, listening to port 5858. You have three different applications running on three different ports! It may seem dizzying at first, but each server is performing an important function.

Now the fun begins: connect to *http://localhost:8080/debug?port=5858* (remember that *localhost* is an alias for 127.0.0.1). Along the top of your browser, you'll see a menu with Sources and Console. If you select Sources you'll see a small arrow right beneath it. Click that, and you'll see all of the source files that make up your application. Go ahead and navigate to your main app file (*meadowlark.js*); you'll see the source in your browser.

Unlike our previous experience with the commnad-line debugger, your application is already running: all of the middleware has been linked in, and the app is listening. So how do we step through our code? The easiest way (and the method you'll probably use the most often), is to set a *breakpoint*. This just tells the debugger to stop execution on a specific line so you can step through the code. All you have to do to set a breakpoint is click the line number (in the left column); a little blue arrow will appear, indicating there's a breakpoint on that line (click again to turn it off). Go ahead and set a breakpoint inside one of your route handlers. Then, in another browser window, visit that route. You'll find that your browser just spins...that's because the debugger has heeded your breakpoint.

Switch back to the debugger window, and now you can step through the program in a much more visual manner than we did with the command-line debugger. You'll see that the line you set a breakpoint on is highlighted in blue. That means that's the current execution line (which is actually the next line that will execute). From here, you have access to the same commands as we did in the command-line debugger. Similar to the command-line debugger, we have the following actions available to us:

*Resume script execution (F8)*
> This will simply "let it fly"; you will no longer be stepping through the code, unless you stop on another breakpoint. You usually use this when you've seen what you need to see, or you want to skip ahead to another breakpoint.

*Step over next function call (F10)*
> If the current line invokes a function, the debugger will not descend into that function. That is, the function will be executed, and the debugger will advance to the next line after the function invocation. You'll use this when you're on a function call that you're not interested in the details of.

*Step into next function call (F11)*
> This will descend into the function call, hiding nothing from you. If this is the only action you ever used, you would eventually see everything that gets executed—which sounds fun at first, but after you've been at it for an hour, you'll have a newfound respect for what Node and Express are doing for you!

*Step out of current function (Shift-F11)*
> Will execute the rest of the function you're currently in and resume debugging on the next line of the *caller* of this function. Most commonly, you'll use this when you either accidentally step into a function or have seen as much as you need of the function.

In addition to all of the control actions, you have access to a console: that console is executing in the *current context of your application*. So you can inspect variables and even change them, or invoke functions…. This can be incredibly handy for trying out really simple things, but it can quickly get confusing, so I don't encourage you to dynamically modify your running application too much in this manner; it's too easy to get lost.

On the right, you have some useful data. Starting at the top are *watch expressions*; these are JavaScript expressions you can define that will be updated in real time as you step through the application. For example, if there was a specific variable you wanted to keep track of, you could enter it here.

Below watch expressions is the *call stack*; this shows you how you got where you are. That is, the function you're in was called by some function, and that function was called by some function…the call stack lists all of those functions. In the highly asynchronous world of Node, the call stack can be very difficult to unravel and understand, especially when anonymous functions are involved. The topmost entry in that list is where you are now. The one right below it is the function that called the function that you're in now, and so on. If you click any entry in this list, you will be magically transported to that context: all of your watches and your console context will now be in that context. It can be very confusing! It's a great way to learn at a really deep level how your app is working, but it's not for the faint of heart. Because the call stack can be so confusing to unravel, I look at it as a last resort when trying to solve a problem.

Below the call stack are the scope variables. As the name implies, these are the variables that are currently in scope (which includes variables in the parent scope that are visible to us). This section can often provide you a lot of information about the key variables you're interested in at a glance. If you have a lot of variables, this list will become unwieldy, and you might be better off defining just the variables you're interested in as watch expressions.

Next, there is a list of all breakpoints, which is really just bookkeeping: it's handy to have if you're debugging a hairy problem and you have a lot of breakpoints set. Clicking one will take you directly there (but it won't change the context, like clicking something in the call stack; this makes sense because not every breakpoint will represent an active context, whereas everything in the call stack does).

Finally, there are DOM, XHR, and event listener breakpoints. These apply only to JavaScript running in the browers, and you can ignore when debugging Node apps.

Sometimes, what you need to debug is your application setup (when you're linking middleware into Express, for example). Running the debugger as we have been, that will all happen in the blink of an eye before we can even set a breakpoint. Fortunately, there's a way around that. All we have to do is specify --debug-brk instead of simply --debug:

```
node --debug-brk meadowlark.js
```

The debugger will break on the very first line of your application, and then you can step through or set breakpoints as you see fit.

---

For more information on Node Inspector (and some additional tips and tricks), see the project home page (*https://github.com/node-inspector/node-inspector*).

## Debugging Asynchronous Functions

One of the most common frustrations people have when being exposed to asynchronous programming for the first time is in debugging. Consider the following code, for example:

```
1 console.log('Baa, baa, black sheep,');
2 fs.readFile('yes_sir_yes_sir.txt', function(err, data){
3     console.log('Have you any wool?');
4     console.log(data);
5 });
6 console.log('Three bags full;');
```

If you're new to asynchronous programming, you might expect to see:

```
Baa, baa, black sheep,
Have you any wool?
Yes, sir, yes, sir,
Three bags full;
```

But you won't; instead you'll see:

```
Baa, baa, black sheep,
Three bags full;
Have you any wool?
Yes, sir, yes, sir,
```

If you're confused about this, debugging probably won't help. You'll start on line 1, then step over it, which puts you on line 2. You then step in, expecting to enter the function, ending up on line 3, but you actually end up on line 5! That's because `fs.readFile` executes the function only *when it's done reading the file*, which won't happen until your application is idle. So you step over line 5, and you land on line 6...you then keep trying to step, but never get to line 3 (you eventually will, but it could take a while).

If you want to debug lines 3 or 4, all you have to do is set a breakpoint on line 3, and then let the debugger run. When the file is read and the function is invoked, you'll break on that line, and hopefully all will be clear.

## Debugging Express

If, like me, you've seen a lot of overengineered frameworks in your career, the idea of stepping through the framework source code might sound like madness (or torture) to you. And exploring the Express source code is not child's play, but it *is* well within the grasp of anyone with a good understanding of JavaScript and Node. And sometimes, when you are having problems with your code, debugging those problems can best be solved by stepping through the Express source code itself (or third-party middleware).

This section will be a brief tour of the Express source code so that you can be more effective in debugging your Express applications. For each part of the tour, I will give you the filename with respect to the Express root (which you can find in your *node_modules/express* directory), and the name of the function. I'm not using line numbers, because of course they may differ depending on what exact version of Express you're using.

*Express app creation (lib/express.js, `function createApplication()`)*
> This is where your Express app begins its life. This is the function that's being invoked when you call `var app = express()` in your code.

*Express app initialization (lib/application.js, `app.defaultConfiguration`)*
> This is where Express gets initialized: it's a good place to see all the defaults Express starts out with. It's rarely necessary to set a breakpoint in here, but it is useful to step through it at least once to get a feel for the default Express settings.

*Add middleware (lib/application.js, `app.use`)*
> Every time Express links middleware in (whether you do it explicitly, or it's explicitly done by Express or any third parties), this function gets called. It's deceptively simple, but really understanding it takes some effort. It's sometimes useful to put a breakpoint in here (you'll want to use `--debug-brk` when you run your app; otherwise, all the middleware will be added before you can set a breakpoint), but it can be overwhelming: you'll be surprised at how much middleware is linked in in a typical application.

*Render view (lib/application.js, `app.render`)*
> This is another pretty meaty function, but a useful one if you need to debug tricky view-related issues. If you step through this function, you'll see how the view engine is selected and invoked.

*Request extensions (lib/request.js)*
> You will probably be surprised at how sparse and easy to understand this file is. Most of the methods Express adds to the request objects are very simple convenience functions. It's rarely necessary to step through this code or set breakpoints because of the simplicity of the code. It is, however, often helpful to look at this code to understand how some of the Express convenience methods work.

*Send response (lib/response.js, `res.send`)*
> It almost doesn't matter how you construct a response—`.send`, `.render`, `.json`, or `.jsonp`—it will eventually get to this function (the exception is `.sendFile`). So this is a very handy place to set a breakpoint, because it should be called for every response. You can then use the call stack to see how you got there, which can be very handy in figuring out where there might be a problem.

*Response extensions (lib/response.js)*

While there is some meat in `res.send`, most of the other methods in the response object are pretty straightforward. It's occasionally useful to put breakpoints in these functions to see exactly how your app is responding to the request.

*Static middleware (node_modules/serve-static/index.js, `function staticMiddleware`)*

Generally, if static files aren't being served as you expect, the problem is with your routing, not with the static middleware: routing takes precedence over the static middleware. So if you have a file *public/test.jpg*, and a route */test.jpg*, the static middleware will never even get called in deference to the route. However, if you need specifics about how headers are set differently for static files, it can be useful to step through the static middleware.

If you're scratching your head wondering where all the middleware is…that's because there is very little middleware in Express (the static middleware and the router being the notable exceptions). Most of the middleware actually comes from Connect, which is what we'll discuss next.

Since Express 4.0 no longer bundles Connect, you will have Connect installed separately, so you will find the Connect source code (including all its middleware) in *node_modules/connect*. Connect has also been shedding some of its middleware into standalone packages. Here are the locations of some of the more important ones:

*Session middleware (node_modules/express-session/index.js, `function session`)*

A lot goes into making sessions work, but the code is pretty straightforward. You may want to set a breakpoint in this function if you're having issues that are related to sessions. Keep in mind that it is up to you to provide the storage engine for the session middleware.

*Logger middleware (node_modules/morgan/index.js, `function logger`)*

The logger middleware is really there for you as a debugging aid, not to be debugged itself. However, there's some subtlety to the way logging works that you'll get only by stepping through the logger middleware once or twice. The first time I did it, I had a lot of "aha" moments, and found myself using logging more effectively in my applications, so I recommend taking a tour of this middleware at least once.

*URL-encoded body parsing (node_modules/body-parser/index.js, `function urlencoded`)*

The manner in which request bodies are parsed is often a mystery to people. It's not really that complicated, and stepping through this middleware will help you understand the way HTTP requests work. Aside from a learning experience, you won't find that you need to step into this middleware for debugging very often.

We've discussed a *lot* of middleware in this book. I can't reasonably list every landmark you might want to look at on your tour of Express internals, but hopefully these highlights take away some of Express's mystery, and embolden you to explore the framework source code whenever needed. Middleware vary greatly not just in quality but in accessibility: some middleware are wickedly difficult to understand, while some are as clear as a pool of water. Whatever the case, don't be afraid to look: if it's too complicated, you can move on (unless you really need to understand it, of course), and if not, you might learn something.

# CHAPTER 21

# Going Live

The big day is here: you've spent weeks or months toiling over your labor of love, and now your website or service is ready to launch. It's not as easy as just "flipping a switch" and then your website is live…or is it?

In this chapter (which you should really read *weeks* before launch, not the day of!), you'll learn about some of the domain registration and hosting services available to you, techniques for moving from a staging environment to production, deployment techniques, and things to consider when picking production services.

## Domain Registration and Hosting

People are often confused about the difference between *domain registration* and *hosting*. If you're reading this book, you probably aren't, but I bet you know people who are, like your clients or your manager.

Every website and service on the Internet can be identified by an *Internet protocol (IP) address* (or more than one). These numbers are not particularly friendly to humans (and that situation will only get worse as IPv6 adoption improves), but your computer ultimately needs these numbers to show you a web page. That's where *domain names* come in. They map a human-friendly name (like *google.com*) with an IP address (74.125.239.13).

A real-world analogy would be the difference between a business name and a physical address. A domain name is like your business name (Apple), and an IP address is like your physical address (1 Infinite Loop, Cupertino, CA 95014). If you need to actually get in your car and visit Apple's headquarters, you'll need to know the physical address. Fortunately, if you know the business name, you can probably get the physical address. The other reason this abstraction is helpful is that an organization can move (getting a new physical address), and people can still find it even though it's moved.

*Hosting*, on the other hand, describes the actual computers that run your website. To continue the physical analogy, hosting could be compared to the actual buildings you see once you reach the physical address. What is often confusing to people is that domain registration has very little to do with hosting, and rarely do you purchase your domain from the same entity that you pay for hosting (in the same way that you usually buy land from one person and pay another person to build and maintain buildings for you).

While it's certainly possible to host your website without a domain name, it's quite unfriendly: IP addresses aren't very marketable! Usually, when you purchase hosting, you're automatically assigned a subdomain (which we'll cover in a moment), which can be thought of as something between a marketing-friendly domain name and an IP address (for example, *ec2-54-201-235-192.us-west-2.compute.amazonaws.com*).

Once you have a domain, and you go live, you could reach your website with multiple URLs. For example:

- *http://meadowlarktravel.com/*
- *http://www.meadowlarktravel.com/*
- *http://ec2-54-201-235-192.us-west-2.compute.amazonaws.com/*
- *http://54.201.235.192/*

Thanks to domain mapping, all of these addresses point to the same website. Once the requests reach your website, it is possible to take action based on the URL that was used. For example, if someone gets to your website from the IP address, you could automatically redirect to the domain name, though that is not very common as there is little point to it (it is more common to redirect from *http://meadowlarktravel.com/* to *http://www.meadowlarktravel.com/*).

Most domain registrars offer hosting services (or partner with companies that do). I've never found registrar hosting options to be particularly attractive, and I recommend separating domain registration and hosting for reasons of security and flexibility.

## Domain Name System

The Domain Name System (DNS) is what's responsible for mapping domain names to IP addresses. The system is fairly intricate, but there are some things about DNS that you should know as a website owner.

## Security

You should always keep in mind that *domain names are valuable*. If a hacker were to completely compromise your hosting service and take control of your hosting, but you retained control of your domain, you could get new hosting and redirect the domain. If, on the other hand, your *domain* were compromised, you could be in real trouble.

Your reputation is tied to your domain, and good domain names are carefully guarded. People who have lost control of domains have found that it can be devastating, and there are those in the world who will actively try to compromise your domain (especially if it's a particularly short or memorable one) so they can sell it off, ruin your reputation, or blackmail you. The upshot is that *you should take domain security very seriously*, perhaps even more seriously than your data (depending on how valuable your data is). I've seen people spend inordinate amounts of time and money on hosting security while getting the cheapest, sketchiest domain registration they can find. Don't make that mistake. (Fortunately, quality domain registration is not particularly expensive.)

Given the importance of protecting ownership of your domain, you should employ good security practices with respect to your domain registration. At the very least, you should use strong, unique passwords, and employ proper password hygiene (no keeping it on a sticky note attached to your monitor). Preferably, you should use a registrar that offers two-factor authentication. Don't be afraid to ask your registrar pointed questions about what is required to authorize changes to your account. The registrars I recommend are Name.com and Namecheap.com. Both offer two-factor authentication, and I have found their support to be good and their online control panels to be easy and robust.

When you register a domain, you must provide a third-party email address that's associated with that domain (i.e., if you're registering *meadowlarktravel.com*, you shouldn't use *admin@meadowlarktravel.com* as your registrant email). Since any security system is as strong as its weakest link, you should use an email address with good security. It's quite common to use a Gmail or Outlook account, and if you do, you should employ the same security standards as you do with your domain registrar account (good password hygiene and two-factor authentication).

## Top-Level Domains

What your domain ends with (such as *.com* or *.net*) is called a *top-level-domain* (TLD). Generally speaking, there are two types of TLD: country code TLDs and general TLDs. Country code TLDs (such as *.us*, *.es*, and *.uk*) are designed to provide a geographic categorization. However, there are few restrictions on who can acquire these TLDs (the Internet is truly a global network, after all), so they are often used for "clever" domains, such as *placehold.it* and *goo.gl*.

General TLDs (gTLDs) include the familiar *.com*, *.net*, *.gov*, *.fed*, *.mil*, and *.edu*. While anyone can acquire an available *.com* or *.net* domain, there are restrictions in place for the others mentioned. For more information, see Table 21-1.

*Table 21-1. Restricted gTLDs*

| TLD | More information |
| --- | --- |
| .gov, .fed | https://www.dotgov.gov |
| .edu | http://net.educause.edu/edudomain |
| .mil | Military personnel and contractors should contact their IT department, or the DoD Network Information Center (http://www.disa.mil/Services/Network-Services/Service-Support) |

The Internet Corporation for Assigned Names and Numbers (ICANN) is ultimately responsible for management of TLDs, though they delegate much of the actual administration to other organizations. Recently, the ICANN has authorized many new gTLDs, such as *.agency*, *.florist*, *.recipes*, and even *.ninja*. For the foreseeable future, *.com* will probably remain the "premium" TLD, and the hardest one to get real estate in. People who were lucky (or shrewd) enough to purchase *.com* domains in the Internet's formative years received massive payouts for prime domains (for example, Facebook purchased *fb.com* in 2010 for a whopping $8.5 million dollars).

Given the scarcity of *.com* domains, people are turning to alternative TLDs, or using *.com.us* to try to get a domain that accurately reflects their organization. When picking a domain, you should consider how it's going to be used. If you plan on marketing primarily electronically (where people are more likely to click a link than type in a domain), then you should probably focus more on getting a catchy or meaningful domain than a short one. If you're focusing on print advertising, or you have reason to believe people will be entering your URL manually into their devices, you might consider alternative TLDs so you can get a shorter domain name. It's also common practice to have two domains: a short, easy-to-type one, and a longer one more suitable for marketing.

## Subdomains

Where a TLD goes after your domain, a subdomain goes before it. By far, the most common subdomain is *www*. I've never particularly cared for this subdomain. After all, you're at a computer, *using* the World Wide Web; I'm pretty sure you're not going to be confused if there isn't a *www* to remind you of what you're doing. For this reason, I recommend using no subdomain for your primary domain: *http://meadowlarktravel.com/* instead of *http://www.meadowlarktravel.com/*. It's shorter and less busy, and thanks to redirects, there's no danger of losing visits from people who automatically start everything with *www*.

Subdomains are used for other purposes too. I commonly see things like *blogs.meadowlarktravel.com*, *api.meadowlarktravel.com*, and *m.meadowlarktravel.com* (for a mobile site). Often this is done for technical reasons: it can be easier to use a subdomain if, for example, your blog uses a completely different server than the rest of your site. A good proxy, though, can redirect traffic appropriately based on either subdomain or path, so the choice of whether to use a subdomain or a path should be more content-focused than technology-focused (remember what Tim Berners-Lee said about URLs expressing your information architecture, not your technical architecture).

I recommend that subdomains be used to compartmentalize significantly different parts of your website or service. For example, I think it's a good use of subdomains to make your API available at *api.meadowlarktravel.com*. Microsites (sites that have a different appearance than the rest of your site, usually highlighting a single product or subject) are also good candidates for subdomains. Another sensible use for subdomains is to separate admin interfaces from public interfaces (*admin.meadowlarktravel.com*, for employees only).

Your domain registrar, unless you specify otherwise, will redirect all traffic to your server regardless of subdomain. It is up to your server (or proxy), then, to take appropriate action based on the subdomain.

## Nameservers

The "glue" that makes domains work are nameservers, and this is what you'll be asked to provide when you establish hosting for your website. Usually, this is pretty straightforward, as your hosting service will do most of the work for you. For example, let's say we choose to host *meadowlarktravel.com* at WebFaction (*https://www.webfaction.com*). When you set up your hosting account with WebFaction, you'll be given the names of the WebFaction nameservers (there are multiple ones for redundancy). WebFaction, like most hosting providers, calls their nameservers *ns1.webfaction.com*, *ns2.webfaction.com*, and so on. Go to your domain registrar and set the nameservers for the domain you want to host, and you're all set.

The way the mapping works in this case is:

1. Website visitor navigates to *http://meadowlarktravel.com/*.
2. The browser sends the request to the computer's network system.
3. The computer's network system, which has been given an Internet IP address and a DNS server by the Internet provider, asks the DNS resolver to resolve *meadowlarktravel.com*.
4. The DNS resolver is aware that *meadowlarktravel.com* is handled by *ns1.webfaction.com*, so it asks *ns1.webfaction.com* to give it an IP address for *meadowlarktravel.com*.
5. The server at *ns1.webfaction.com* receives the request and recognizes that *meadowlarktravel.com* is indeed an active account, and returns the associated IP address.

While this is the most common case, it's not the only way to configure your domain mapping. Since the server (or proxy) that actually serves your website has an IP address, we can cut out the middleman by registering that IP address with the DNS resolvers (this effectively cuts out the middleman of the nameserver *ns1.webfaction.com* in the previous example). For this approach to work, your hosting service must assign you a *static* IP address. Commonly, hosting providers will give your server(s) a *dynamic* IP address, which means it may change without notice, which would render this scheme ineffective. It can sometimes cost extra to get a static IP address instead of a dynamic one: check with your hosting provider.

If you want to map your domain to your website directly (skipping your host's name-servers), you will either be adding an *A record* or a *CNAME record*. An A record maps a domain name directly to an IP address, whereas a CNAME maps one domain name to another. CNAME records are usually a little less flexible, so A records are generally preferred.

Whatever technique you use, domain mapping is usually aggressively cached, meaning that when you change your domain records, it can take up to 48 hours for your domain to be attached to the new server. Keep in mind that this is also subject to geography: if you see your domain working in Los Angeles, your client in New York may see the domain attached to the previous server. In my experience, 24 hours is usually sufficient for domains to resolve correctly in the continental US, with international resolution taking up to 48 hours.

If you need something to go live precisely at a certain time, you should not rely on DNS changes. Rather, modify your server to redirect to the "coming soon" site or page, and make the DNS changes in advance of the actual switchover. At the appointed moment, then, you can have your server switch over to the live site, and your visitors will see the change immediately, regardless of where they are in the world.

# Hosting

Choosing a hosting service can seem overwhelming at first. Node has taken off in a big way, and everyone's clamoring to offer Node hosting to meet the demand. How you select a hosting provider depends very much on your needs. If you have reason to believe your site will be the next Amazon or Twitter, you'll have a very different set of concerns than you would if you were building a website for your local stamp collector's club.

## Traditional hosting, or cloud hosting?

The term "cloud" is one of the most nebulous tech terms to crop up in recent years. Really, it's just a fancy way to say "the Internet," or "part of the Internet." The term is not entirely useless, though. While not part of the technical definition of the term, hosting in the cloud usually implies a certain commoditizing of computing resources. That is to say, we no longer think about a "server" as a distinct, physical entity: it's simply a homogeneous resource somewhere in the cloud, and one is as good as another. I'm oversimplifying, of course: computing resources are distinguished (and priced) according to their memory, number of CPUs, etc. The difference is between knowing (and caring) what actual server your app is hosted on, and knowing it's hosted on *some* server in the cloud, and it could just as easily be moved over to a different one without you knowing (or caring).

Cloud hosting is also highly *virtualized*. That is, the server(s) your app is running on are not usually physical machines, but virtual machines running on physical servers. This idea was not introduced by cloud hosting, but it has become synonymous with it.

While cloud hosting is not really anything new, it does represent a subtle shift in thinking. It can be a little disconcerting at first, not knowing anything about the actual physical machine your server is running on, trusting that your servers aren't going to be affected by the other servers running on the same computer. Really, though, nothing has changed: when your hosting bill comes, you're still paying for essentially the same thing: someone taking care of the physical hardware and networking that enables your web applications. All that's changed is that you're more removed from the hardware.

I believe that "traditional" hosting (for lack of a better term) will eventually disappear altogether. That's not to say hosting companies will go out of business (though some inevitably will); they will just start to offer cloud hosting themselves.

## XaaS

When considering cloud hosting, you will come across the acronyms SaaS, PaaS, and IaaS:

*Software as a Service (SaaS)*
SaaS generally describes software (websites, apps) that are provided to you: you just use them. An example would be Google Documents or Dropbox.

*Platform as a Service (PaaS)*
PaaS provides all of the infrastructure for you (operating systems, networking—all of that is handled). All you have to do is write your applications. While there is often a blurry line between PaaS and IaaS (and you will often find yourself straddling that line as a developer), this is generally the service model we're discussing in this book. If you're running a website or web service, PaaS is probably what you're looking for.

*Infrastructure as a Service (IaaS)*
IaaS gives you the most flexibility, but at cost. All you get are virtual machines and a basic network connecting them. You are then responsible for installing and maintaining operating systems, databases, and network policies. Unless you need this level of control over your environment, you will generally want to stick with PaaS. (Note that PaaS does allow you to have control over the *choice* of operating systems and network configuration: you just don't have to do it yourself.)

## The behemoths

The companies that essentially run the Internet (or, at least, are heavily invested in the running of the Internet) have realized that with the commoditization of computing resources, they have another viable product to sell. Microsoft, Amazon, and Google all offer cloud computing services, and their services are quite good.

All of these services are priced similarly: if your hosting needs are modest, there will be minimal price difference among the three. If you have very high bandwidth or storage needs, you will have to evaluate the services more carefully, as the cost difference could be greater, depending on your needs.

While Microsoft does not normally leap to mind when we consider open source platforms, I would not overlook Azure. Not only is the platform established and robust, but Microsoft has bent over backward to make it friendly to not just Node, but the open source community. Microsoft offers a one-month Azure trial, which is a great way to determine if the service meets your needs; if you're considering one of the big three, I definitely recommend the free trial to evaluate Azure. Microsoft offers Node APIs for all of their major services, including their cloud storage service. In addition to excellent Node hosting, Azure offers Git-based deployments, an excellent cloud storage system (with a JavaScript API), as well as good support for MongoDB. The downside to Azure is that they don't offer a pricing tier for small projects. You can expect to spend a minimum of $80 a month for production hosting on Azure. Keep in mind that you can easily host multiple projects for that price, so if you're looking to consolidate a bunch of websites, it can be very cost effective.

Amazon offers the most comprehensive set of resources, including SMS (text message), cloud storage, email services, payment services (ecommerce), DNS, and more. In addition, Amazon offers a free usage tier, making it very easy to evaluate.

Google's cloud platform does not yet offer an option for Node hosting, though Node apps can be hosted through their IaaS service. Google does not currently offer a free tier or trial.

In addition to the "big three," it is worth considering Joyent, who is currently heavily involved in Node development. Nodejitsu, a Joyent partner, provides Node-specific hosting and are experts in the field. They offer a unique option for deployment: a private npm repository. If Git-based deployment (which we will be focusing on in this book) doesn't appeal to you, I encourage you to look into Nodejitsu's npm-based deployment.

## Boutique hosting

Smaller hosting services, which I'm going to call "boutique" hosting services (for lack of a better word), may not have the infrastructure or resources of Microsoft, Amazon, or Google, but that doesn't mean they don't offer something valuable.

Because boutique hosting services can't compete in terms of infrastructure, they usually focus on customer service and support. If you need a lot of support, you might want to consider a boutique hosting service. For personal projects, I've been using WebFaction (*http://webfaction.com*) for many years. Their service is extremely affordable, and they have offered Node hosting for some time now. If you have a hosting provider you've been happy with, don't hesitate to ask them if they offer (or plan on offering) Node hosting.

# Deployment

It still surprises me that, in 2014, many people are still using FTP to deploy their applications. If you are, *please stop*. FTP is in no way secure. Not only are all your files transmitted unencrypted, your *username and password* are also. If your hosting provider doesn't give you an option, find a new hosting provider. If you really have no choice, make sure you use a unique password that you're not using for anything else.

At minimum, you should be using SFTP or FTPS (not to be confused), but there's even a better way: Git-based deployment.

The idea is simple: you use Git for version control anyway, and Git is very good at versioning, and deployment is essentially a problem of versioning, making Git a natural fit. (This technique is not restricted to Git; you could use Mercurial or Subversion for deployment if you want to.)

To make this technique work, your development repositories need some way of synchronizing with the deployment repositories. Git offers almost unlimited ways to do this, but the easiest by far is to use an Internet service like GitHub. GitHub is free for public repositories, but you may not want to make the source code for your website public. You can upgrade to a private Git repository for a fee. Alternatively, Atlassian Bitbucket offers free private repository hosting for up to five users.

While Git-based deployments can be set up on almost any service, Azure offers it out of the box, and their implementation is excellent and demonstrates the promise of Git-based deployment. We'll start with that excellent model, then cover how we can partially emulate this with other hosting providers.

## Git deployment

Git's greatest strength (and greatest weakness) is its flexibility. It can be adapted to almost any workflow imaginable. For the sake of deployment, I recommend creating one or more branches *specifically for deployment*. For example, you might have a `production` branch and a `staging` branch. How you use those branches is very much up to your individual workflow. One popular approach is to flow from `master` to `staging` to `production`. So once some changes on `master` are ready to go live, you could merge them into `staging`. Once they have been approved on the staging server, you could then merge staging into production. While this makes logical sense, I dislike the clutter it creates (merges merges everywhere). Also, if you have lots of features that need to be staged and pushed to production in different orders, this can get messy quickly. I feel a better approach is to merge master into staging and, when you're ready to go live with changes, then merge master into production. In this way, staging and production become less associated: you can even have multiple staging branches to experiment with different features before going live (and you can merge things other than master into them). Only when something has been approved for production do you merge it into production.

What happens when you need to roll back changes? This is where things can get complicated. There are multiple techniques for undoing changes, such as applying the inverse of a commit to undo prior commits (git revert), but not only are these techniques complicated, they can also cause problems down the line. The approach I recommend is to treat production (and your staging branches, if you wish) as *disposable*: they are really just reflections of your master branch at different points in time. If you need to roll back changes, then you just do a git reset --hard <old commit id> on your production branch, and then git push origin production --force. In essence, this is "rewriting history," which is often decried by dogmatic Git practitioners as dangerous or "advanced." While it certainly can be, in this case, it is understood that production is a *read-only* branch; developers should never commit to it (which is where rewriting history can get you into trouble).

In the end, it is up to you and your team to decide on a Git workflow. More important than the workflow you pick is the consistency with which you use it, and the training and communication surrounding it.

 We've already discussed the value of keeping your binary assets (multimedia and documents) separate from your code repository. Git-based deployment offers another incentive for this approach. If you have four gigabytes of multimedia data in your repository, they're going to take forever to clone, and you have an unnecessary copy of all of your data for every production server.

## Deployment to Azure

With Azure, you can deploy from a GitHub or Bitbucket repository, or a local repository. I strongly recommend you use either GitHub or Bitbucket; it will make it much easier to add people to your development team. For the following example, we'll be using either GitHub or Bitbucket (the procedure is almost identical for both). You'll need a repository set up in your GitHub or Bitbucket account.

One important note is that Azure expects your main application file to be called *server.js*. We've been using *meadowlarktravel.js* for our main application file, so we'll have to rename it to *server.js* for Azure deployment.

Once you've logged into your Azure portal, you can create a new website:

1. Click the Website icon along the left.
2. Click New along the bottom.
3. Choose Quick Create; choose a name and a region, and click Create Web Site.

Then set up source control deployment:

1. Click your website in the main portal window.
2. Under the "Your site has been created!" message, look for "Set up deployment from source control"; click that link.
3. Choose either GitHub or Bitbucket; if this is your first time, you will be asked to authorize Azure access to your GitHub or Bitbucket account.
4. Choose the repository you want to use and the branch (I recommend `production`).

That's all you have to do...now some amazing stuff happens. If Azure detects that there is an update to the `production` branch, it will automatically update the code on the server (I have done this hundreds of times, and it's never taken more than 30 seconds, though it could take longer if you have very large changes, such as multimedia assets). Even better? If you've added any new dependencies to *package.json*, Azure will automatically install them for you. It will also handle file deletions (unsurprisingly, since this is standard Git behavior). In other words, you have seamless development.

Not only is this the ultimate in seamless, Git-based deployment, but this technique also works well if you scale out your app. So if you have four server instances going, they will all be updated simultaneously with a single push to the appropriate branch.

If you go to the Azure control panel for your website, you will see a tab labeled Deployments. In that tab, you will see information about the history of deployments, which can be helpful in debugging if something goes wrong with your automatic deployment system. Also, you can redeploy previous deployments, which can be a quick way to revert if there's a problem.

## Manual Git-based deployment

If your hosting service does not support any kind of automated Git-based deployment, your approach will involve additional steps. Let's say our setup is the same: we're using GitHub or Bitbucket for version control, and we have a branch called `production`, which is what we want reflected on the production servers.

For each server, you will have to clone the repository, check out the `production` branch, and then set up the infrastructure necessary to start/restart your app (which will be dependent on your choice of platform). When you update the `production` branch, you will have to go to each server, run `git pull --ff-only`, run `npm install` (if you've updated any dependencies), and then restart the app. If your deployments aren't often, and you don't have very many servers, this may not represent a terrible hardship, but if you're updating more often, this will get old fast, and you'll want to find some way to automate the system.

 The `--ff-only` argument to `git pull` allows only fast-forward pulls, preventing automatic merging or rebasing. If you know the pull is fast-forward only, you may safely omit it, but if you get in the habit of doing it, you will never accidentally invoke a merge or rebase!

Unfortunately, automation is not a simple matter. Git has hooks that allow you to take automated action, but not if it's a remote repository that's being updated. If you're looking for automated deployment, the easiest approach is to run an automated job that runs `git pull --ff-only` periodically. If an update occurs, you can then run `npm install` and restart the app.

### Amazon deployment with Elastic Beanstalk

If you're using Amazon AWS, you can use their product *Elastic Beanstalk* (EB) to do automated deployments with Git. EB is a sophisticated product that offers a lot of features that may be attractive if you can't afford to ever make a mistake in deployment. Along with those features comes increased complexity, however: setting up automated deployment with EB is fairly involved. You can find instructions for the various ways to configure EB on the EB documentation page (*http://bit.ly/ebeanstalk*).

# Conclusion

Deploying your website (especially for the first time) should be an exciting occasion. There should be champagne and cheering, but all too often, there is sweating, cursing, and late nights. I've seen far too many websites launched at three in the morning by an irritable, exhausted team. Fortunately, that's changing, partly thanks to cloud deployment. No matter what deployment strategy you choose, the most important thing you can do is to start production deployments early, before the site is ready to go live. You don't have to hook up the domain, so the public doesn't need to know. If you've already deployed the site to production servers half a dozen times before the day of launch, your chances of a successful launch will be much higher. Ideally, your functioning website will already be running on the production server long before launch: all you have to do is flip the switch from the old site to the new site.

# CHAPTER 22

# Maintenance

You launched the site! Congratulations, now you never have to think about it again. What's that? You *do* have to keep thinking about it? Well, in that case, keep reading.

While it has happened a couple of times in my career, it has been the exception to the rule that you finish a site and then never have to touch it again (and when it does happen, it's usually because someone else is doing the work, not that work doesn't need to be done). I distinctly remember one website launch "postmortem." I piped up and said, "Shouldn't we really call it a *postpartum*?"[1] Launching a website really is more of a birth than a death. Once it launches, you're glued to the analytics, anxiously awaiting the client's reaction, waking up at three in the morning to check to see if the site is still up… it's your baby.

Scoping a website, designing a website, building a website: these are all activities that can be planned to death. But what usually receives short shrift is *planning the maintenance* of a website. This chapter will give you some advice on navigating those waters.

## The Principles of Maintenance

### Have a Longevity Plan

It always surprises me when a client agrees on a price to build a website, but it's never discussed how long the site is expected to last. My experience is that if you do good work, clients are happy to pay for it. What clients do *not* appreciate is the unexpected: being told after three years that their site has to be rebuilt when they had an unspoken expectation that it would last five.

---

1. As it happened, the term "postpartum" was a little too visceral. We now call them "retrospectives."

The Internet moves fast. If you built a website with the absolute best and newest technology you could find, it might feel like a creaky relic in two short years. Or it could truck along for seven, aging, but doing so gracefully (this is a lot less common!).

Setting expectations about website longevity is part art, part salesmanship, and part science. The science of it involves something that all scientists, but very few web developers, do: keep records. Imagine if you had a record of every website your team had ever launched, the history of maintenance requests and failures, the technologies used, and how long before each site was rebuilt. There are many variables, obviously, from the team members involved to the economy to the shifting winds of technology, but that doesn't mean that meaningful trends can't be discovered in the data. You may find that certain development approaches work better for your team, or certain platforms or technologies. What I almost guarantee you will find is a correlation between "procrastination" and defects: the longer you put off an infrastructure update or platform upgrade that's causing pain, the worse it will be. Having a good issue tracking system and keeping meticulous records will allow you to give your client a much better (and more realistic) picture of what the life cycle of their project is going to be.

The salesmanship of it boils down to money, of course. If a client can afford to have their website completely rebuilt every three years, then they won't be very likely to suffer from aging infrastructure (they will have other problems, though). On the flip side, there will be clients who need their dollar to stretch as far as possible, wanting a website that will last for five or even seven years (I've known websites that have dragged on for even longer than that, but I feel that seven years is the maximum realistic life expectancy for websites that have any hope of continuing to be useful). You have a responsibility to both of these clients, and both come with their own challenge. With the clients who have a lot of money, don't just take their money because they have it: use that extra money to give them something extraordinary. With the clients on a tight budget, you will have to find creative ways to design their website for greater longevity in the face of constantly changing technology. Both of these extremes have their own challenges, but ones that can be solved. What's important, though is that you *know* what the expectations are.

Lastly, there's the art of the matter. This is what ties it all together: understanding what the client can afford, and where you can honestly convince the client to spend more money so they get value where they need it. It is also the art of understanding technology futures, and being able to predict what technologies will be painfully obsolete in five years and which will be going strong.

There's no way to predict anything with absolute certainty, of course. You could bet wrong on technologies, personnel shifts can completely change the technical culture of your organization, and technology vendors can go out of business (though this is usually less of a problem in the open source world). The technology that you thought would be solid for the lifetime of your product may turn out to be a fad, and you'll find yourself facing the decision to rebuild sooner than you expected. On the flip side, sometimes the exactly right team comes together at the exact right time with the exact right technology, and something is created that far outlives any reasonable expectations. None of this uncertainty should deter you from having a plan, however: better to have a plan that goes awry than to always be rudderless.

It should be clear to you by now that I feel that JavaScript and Node are technologies that are going to be around for a while. The Node community is vibrant and enthusiastic, and wisely based on a language that has clearly *won*. Most important, perhaps, is that JavaScript is a multiparadigm language: object-oriented, functional, procedural, synchronous, asynchronous—it's all there. This makes JavaScript an inviting platform for developers from many different backgrounds, and is in large part responsible for the pace of innovation in the JavaScript ecosystem.

## Use Source Control

This probably seems obvious to you, but it's not just about *using* source control, it's about using it *well*. Why are you using source control? Understand the reasons, and make sure the tools are supporting those reasons. There are many reasons to use source control, but the one that always seems to me to have the biggest payoff is attribution: knowing exactly what change was made when and who did it, so I can ask for more information if necessary. Version control is one of our greatest tools for understanding the history of our projects and how we work together as a team.

## Use an Issue Tracker

Issue trackers go back to the science of development. Without a systematic way to record the history of a project, no insight is possible. You've probably heard it said that the definition of insanity is "doing the same thing over and over again and expecting different results" (often dubiously attributed to Albert Einstein). It does seem crazy to repeat your mistakes over and over again, but how can you avoid it if you don't know what mistakes you're making? Record everything: every defect the client reports; every defect you find before the client sees it; every complaint, every question, every bit of praise. Record how long it took, who fixed it, what Git commits were involved, and who approved the fix. The art here is finding tools that don't make this overly time-consuming or onerous. A bad issue tracking system will languish, unused, and it will be worse than useless. A good issue tracking system will yield vital insights into your business, your team, and your clients.

## Exercise Good Hygiene

I'm not talking about brushing your teeth—though you should do that too—I'm talking about version control, testing, code reviews, and issue tracking. The tools you use are useful only if you use them, and use them correctly. Code reviews are a great way to encourage hygiene because *everything* can be touched on, from discussing the use of the issue tracking system in which the request originated to the tests that had to be added to verify the fix to the version control commit comments.

The data you collect from your issue tracking system should be reviewed on a periodic basis and discussed with the team. From this data, you can gain insights about what's working and what's not. You might be surprised by what you find.

## Don't Procrastinate

Institutional procrastination can be one of the hardest things to combat. Usually it's something that doesn't seem so bad: you notice that your team is routinely eating up a lot of hours on a weekly update that could be drastically improved by a little refactoring. Every week you delay refactoring is another week you're paying the inefficiency cost.[2] Worse, some costs may increase over time. A great example of this is failing to update software dependencies. As the software ages, and team members change, it's harder to find people who remember (or ever understood) the creaky old software. The support community starts to evaporate, and before long, the technology is deprecated and you can't get any kind of support for it. You often hear this described as *technical debt*, and it's a very real thing. While you should avoid procrastinating, understanding the website longevity can factor into these decisions: if you're just about to redesign the whole website, there's little value in eliminating technical debt that's been building up.

## Do Routine QA Checks

For each of your websites, you should have a *documented* routine QA check. That check should include a link checker, HTML and CSS validation, and running your tests. The key here is *documented*: if the items that compose the QA check aren't documented, you will inevitably miss things. A documented QA checklist for each site not only helps prevent overlooked checks, but it allows new team members to be effective immediately. Ideally, the QA checklist can be executed by a nontechnical team member. Not only will this give your (possibly) nontechnical manager confidence in your team, it will allow you to spread QA responsibilities around if you don't have a dedicated QA department. Depending on your relationship with your client, you may also want to share your QA checklist (or part of it) with the client; it's a good way to remind them what they're paying for, and that you are looking out for their best interests.

As part of your routine QA check, I recommend using Google Webmaster Tools (*https://www.google.com/webmasters*) and Bing Webmaster Tools (*http://www.bing.com/toolbox/webmaster*). They are easy to set up, and they give you a very important view of your site: how the major search engines see it. It will alert you to any problems with

---

2. Mike Wilson of Fuel (*http://www.fuelyouth.com*)'s rule of thumb is "the third time you do something, take the time to automate it."

your *robots.txt* file, HTML issues that are interfering with good search results, security issues, and more.

## Monitor Analytics

If you're not running analytics on your website, you need to start now: it provides a vital insight into not just the popularity of your website, but also how your users are using it. Google Analytics (GA) is excellent (and free!), and even if you supplement it with additional analytics services, there's little reason not to include GA on your site. Often, you will be able to spot subtle UX issues by keeping an eye on your analytics. Are there certain pages that are not getting the traffic that you expect? That could indicate a problem with your navigation or promotions, or an SEO issue. Are your bounce rates high? That could indicate the content on your pages needs some tailoring (people are getting to your site by searching, but when they arrive on your site, they realize it's not what they're looking for). You should have an analytics checklist to go along with your QA checklist (it could even be part of your QA checklist). That checklist should be a "living document"; over the lifetime of your website, you or your client may have shifting priorities about what content is most important.

## Optimize Performance

Study after study has shown the dramatic effect of performance on website traffic. It's a fast-paced world, and people expect their content delivered quickly,especially on mobile platforms. The number one principle in performance tuning is to *profile first, then optimize*. "Profiling" means finding out what it actually is that's slowing your site down. If you spend days speeding up your content rendering when the problem is actually your social media plugins, you're wasting precious time and money.

Google PageSpeed is a great way to measure the performance of your website (and now PageSpeed data is recorded in Google Analytics so you can monitor performance trends). Not only will it give you an overall score for mobile and desktop performance, it will also make prioritized suggestions about how to improve performance.

Unless you currently have performance issues, it's probably not necessary to do periodic performance checks (monitoring Google Analytics for significant changes in performance scores should be sufficient); however, it is gratifying to watch your boost in traffic when you improve performance.

## Prioritize Lead Tracking

In the Internet world, the strongest signal your visitors can give you that they are interested in your product or service is to give you contact information: you should treat this information with the utmost care. Any form that collects an email or phone number should be tested routinely as part of your QA checklist, and there should *always* be redundancy when you collect that information. The worst thing you can do to a potential customer is collect contact information and then lose it.

Because lead tracking is so critical to the success of your website, I recommend these five principles for collecting information:

*Have a fallback in case JavaScript fails*
> Collecting customer information via AJAX is fine—it often results in a better user experience. However, if JavaScript should fail for any reason (the user could disable it, or a script on your website could have an error, preventing your AJAX from functioning correctly), the form submission should work anyway. A great way to test this is to disable JavaScript and use your form. It's okay if the user experience is not ideal: the point is that user data is not lost. To implement this, *always* have a valid and working `action` parameter in your `<form>` tag, even if you normally use AJAX.

*If you use AJAX, get the URL from the form's `action` parameter*
> While not strictly necessary, this helps prevent you from accidentally forgetting the `action` parameter on your `<form>` tags. If you tie your AJAX to successful no-JavaScript submission, it's much harder to lose customer data. For example, your form tag could be `<form action="/submit/email" method="POST">`; then in your AJAX handler, you would do the following: `$('form').on('submit', func tion(evt){ evt.preventDefault(); var action = $(this).attr(\'ac tion'); /* perform AJAX submission */ });`.

*Provide at least one level of redundancy*
> You'll probably want to save leads to a database or an external service such as Campaign Monitor. But what if your database fails, or Campaign Monitor goes down, or there's a network issue? You still don't want to lose that lead. A common way to provide redundancy is to send an email in addition to storing the lead. If you take this approach, you should not use a person's email address, but a shared email address (such as *dev@meadowlarktravel.com*): the redundancy does no good if you send it to a person and that person leaves the organization. You could also store the lead in a backup database, or even a CSV file. However, *whenever* your primary storage fails, there should be some mechanism to alert you of the failure. Collecting a redundant backup is the first half of the battle: being aware of failures and taking appropriate action is the second half.

*In case of total storage failure, inform the user*
> Let's say you have three levels of redundancy: your primary storage is Campaign Monitor, and if that fails, you back up to a CSV file and send an email to *dev@meadowlarktravel.com*. If *all* of these channels fail, the user should receive a message that says something like "We're sorry, we're experiencing technical difficulties. Please try again later, or contact *support@meadowlarktravel.com*."

*Check for positive confirmation, not absence of an error*

It's quite common to have your AJAX handler return an object with an `err` property in the case of failure; the client code then has something that looks like this: `if(data.err){ /* inform user of failure */ } else { /* thank user for successful submission */ }`. **Avoid this approach.** There's nothing wrong with setting an `err` property, but if there's an error in your AJAX handler, leading the server to respond with a 500 response code or a response that isn't valid JSON, **this approach will fail silently**. The user's lead will disappear into the void, and they will be none the wiser. Instead, provide a `success` property for successful submission (even if the primary storage failed: if the user's information was recorded by *something*, you may return `success`). Then your client-side code becomes `if(data.success){ /* thank user for successful submission */ } else { /* inform user of failure \*/ }`.

## Prevent "Invisible" Failures

I see it all the time: because developers are in a hurry, they record errors in ways that never get checked. Whether it is a logfile, a table in a database, a client-side console log, or an email that goes to a dead address, the end result is the same: **your website has quality problems that are going unnoticed**. The number one defense you can have against this problem is to **provide an *easy*, standard method for logging errors**. Document it. Don't make it difficult. Don't make it obscure. Make sure every developer that touches your project is aware of it. It can be as simple as exposing a `meadowlarkLog` function (`log` is often used by other packages). It doesn't matter if the function is recording to a database, flat file, email, or some combination thereof: the important thing is that it is standard. It also allows you to improve your logging mechanism (for example, flat files are less useful when you scale out your server, so you would modify your `meadowlarkLog` function to record to a database instead). Once you have the logging mechanism in place, documented, and everyone on your team knows about it, add "check logs" to your QA checklist, and have instructions on how to do that.

# Code Reuse and Refactoring

One tragedy I see all the time is the reinvention of the wheel, over and over and over again. Usually it's just small things: tidbits that feel easier to just rewrite than to dig up in some project that you did months ago. All of those little rewritten snippets add up. Worse, it flies in the face of good QA: you're probably not going to go to the trouble to write tests for all these little snippets (and if you do, you're doubling the time that you're wasting by not reusing existing code). Each snippet—doing the same thing—can have different bugs. It's a bad habit.

Development in Node and Express offers some great ways to combat this problem. Node brought namespacing (via modules) and packages (via npm), and Express brings the concept of middleware (via Connect). With these tools at your disposal, it makes it a lot easier to develop reusable code.

## Private npm Registry

npm registries are a great place to store shared code; it's what npm was designed for, after all. In addition to simple storage, you get versioning, and a convenient way to include those packages in other projects.

There's a fly in the ointment, though: unless you're working in a completely open source organization, you may not want to create npm packages for all of your reusable code. (There can be other reasons than intellectual property protection, too: your packages could be so organization- or project-specific that it doesn't make sense to make them available on a public registry.)

One way to handle this is *private npm registries*. Setting up a private npm registry can be an involved process, but it is possible.

The biggest hurdle to creating your own private registry is that npm currently doesn't allow you to pull from multiple repositories. So if your *package.json* file contains a mix of packages from the public npm registry (and it will) and packages from a private registry, npm will fail (if you specify the public registry, the private dependencies will fail, and if you specify the private registry, the public dependencies will fail). The npm team has said they don't have the resources to implement this feature (see *https:// github.com/npm/npm/issues/1401*), but there are alternatives.

One way to handle that problem is to replicate the entire public npm. If that sounds daunting and expensive (in terms of storage, bandwidth, and maintenance), you're right. A better approach is to provide a proxy to the public npm, which will pass requests for a public package through to the public registry, while serving private packages from its own database. Fortunately, there is just such a project: Sinopia (*https://github.com/ rlidwka/sinopia*).

Sinopia is incredibly easy to install and, in addition to supporting private packages, provides a handy cache of packages for your organization. If you choose to use Sinopia, you should be aware that it uses the local filesystem to store private packages: you would definitely want to add the package directory to your backup plan! Sinopia suggests using the prefix `test-` for local packages: if you're creating a private registry for your orga-nization, I recommend you use the organization's name (`meadowlark-`).

Since npm is configured to support only one registry, once you "switch over" to using Sinopia (using `npm set registry` and `npm adduser`), you will be unable to use the public npm registry (except through Sinopia). To switch back to using the public npm registry, you can either use `npm set registry https://registry.npmjs.org/`, or simply delete the file *~/.npmjs*. You will have to do this if you want to publish packages to the public registry.

A much easier solution is to use a hosted private repository. Nodejitsu (*https://www.nodejitsu.com/*) and Gemfury (*http://www.gemfury.com/l/npm-registry*) both offer private npm repositories. Unfortunately, both these services are rather expensive. Ninjitsu's service starts at $25/month and offers only 10 packages. To get a more manageable number of packages (50), it'll set you back $100/month. Gemfury's pricing is comparable. If budget is not an issue, this is certainly a no-fuss way to go.

# Middleware

As we've seen throughout this book, writing middleware is not some big, scary, complicated thing: we've done it a dozen times in this book and, after a while, you will do it without even thinking about it. The next step, then, is to put reusable middleware in a package and put it in a npm registry.

If you find that your middleware is too project-specific to put in a reusable package, you should consider refactoring the middleware to be configured for more general use. Remember that you can pass configuration objects into middleware to make them useful in a whole range of situations. Here is an overview of the most common ways to expose middleware in a Node module. All of the following assume that you're using exporting these modules as a package, and that package is called `meadowlark-stuff`:

### Module exposes middleware function directly

Use this method if your middleware doesn't need a configuration object:

```
module.exports = function(req, res, next){
    // your middleware goes here...remember to call next()
    // or next('route') unless this middleware is expected
    // to be an endpoint
    next();
}
```

To use this middleware:

```
var stuff = require('meadowlark-stuff');

app.use(stuff);
```

### Module exposes a function that returns middleware

Use this method if your middleware needs a configuration object or other information:

```
module.exports = function(config){
        // it's common to create the config object
        // if it wasn't passed in:
        if(!config) config = {};
```

```
                   return function(req, res, next){
                         // your middleware goes here...remember to call next()
                         // or next('route') unless this middleware is expected
                         // to be an endpoint
                         next();
                   }
         }
```

To use this middleware:

```
         var stuff = require('meadowlark-stuff')({ option: 'my choice' });

         app.use(stuff);
```

### Module exposes an object that contains middleware

Use this option if you want to expose multiple related middleware:

```
         module.exports = function(config){
                   // it's common to create the config object
                   // if it wasn't passed in:
                   if(!config) config = {};

                   return {
                         m1: function(req, res, next){
                               // your middleware goes here...remember to call next()
                               // or next('route') unless this middleware is expected
                               // to be an endpoint
                               next();
                         },
                         m2: function(req, res, next){
                               next();
                         }
                   }
         }
```

To use this middleware:

```
         var stuff = require('meadowlark-stuff')({ option: 'my choice' });

         app.use(stuff.m1);
         app.use(stuff.m2);
```

### Module exposes an object constructor

This is probably the most uncommon method for returning middleware, but is useful if your middleware is well suited for an object-oriented implementation. It is also the trickiest way to implement middleware, because if you expose your middleware as instance methods, they will not be invoked against the object instance by Express, so this will not be what you expect it to be. If you need to access instance properties, see m2:

```
         function Stuff(config){
                   this.config = config || {};
```

```
}
Stuff.prototype.m1 = function(req, res, next){
        // BEWARE: 'this' will not be what you expect; don't use it
        next();
};
Stuff.prototype.m2 = function(){
        // we use Function.prototype.bind to associate this instance
        // to the 'this property
        return (function(req, res, next){
                // 'this' will now be the Stuff instance
                next();
        }).bind(this);
);

module.exports = Stuff;
```

To use this middleware:

```
var Stuff = require('meadowlark-stuff');

var stuff = new Stuff({ option: 'my choice' });

app.use(stuff.m1);
app.use(stuff.m2());
```

Note that we can link in the m1 middleware directly, but we have to invoke m2 (which then returns middleware that we can link in).

# Conclusion

When you're building a website, the focus is often on the launch, and for good reason: there's a lot of excitement surrounding a launch. However, a client that is delighted by a newly launched website will quickly become a dissatisfied customer if care isn't taken in maintaining the website. Approaching your maintenance plan with the same care with which you launch websites will provide the kind of experience that keeps clients coming back.

# CHAPTER 23

# Additional Resources

In this book, I have tried to give you a comprehensive overview of building websites with Express. And we have covered a remarkable amount of ground, but we've still only scratched the surface of the packages, techniques, and frameworks that are available to you. In this chapter, we'll discuss where you can go for additional resources.

## Online Documentation

For JavaScript, CSS, and HTML documentation, the Mozilla Developer Network (MDN) (*https://developer.mozilla.org*) is without equal. If I need JavaScript documentation, I either search directly on MDN or append "mdn" to my search query. Otherwise, inevitably, w3schools appears in the search. Whoever is managing SEO for w3schools is a genius, but I recommend avoiding this site: I find the documentation is often severely lacking.

Where MDN is a great HTML reference, if you're new to HTML5 (or even if you're not), you should read Mark Pilgrim's *Dive Into HTML5* (*http://diveintohtml5.info*). WHATWG maintains an excellent "living standard" HTML5 specification (*http://devel opers.whatwg.org*); it is usually where I turn to first for really hard-to-answer HTML questions. Finally, the official specifications for HTML and CSS are located on the W3C website (*http://www.w3.org*); they are dry, difficult-to-read documents, but sometimes it's your only recourse for the very hardest problems.

JavaScript adheres to the ECMA-262 ECMAScript language specification (*http://bit.ly/ ECMA-262_specs*). Information about the next version of JavaScript, called ES6 (code-named *Harmony*) can be found at *http://bit.ly/es6_harmony*. To track the availability of ES6 features in Node (and various browsers), see the excellent guide maintained by @kangax (*http://kangax.github.io/es5-compat-table/es6*).

Both jQuery (*http://api.jquery.com*) and Bootstrap (*http://getbootstrap.com*) have extremely good online documentation.

The Node documentation (*http://nodejs.org/api*) is very good, and comprehensive, and it should be your first choice for authoritative documentation about Node modules (such as `http`, `https`, and `fs`). The Express documentation (*http://expressjs.com*) is quite good, but not as comprehensive as one might like. The npm documentation (*https://npmjs.org/doc*) is comprehensive and useful, particularly the page on the *package.json* file (*https://npmjs.org/doc/json.html*).

# Periodicals

There are three free periodicals you should absolutely subscribe to and read dutifully every week:

- JavaScript Weekly (*http://javascriptweekly.com*)
- Node Weekly (*http://nodeweekly.com*)
- HTML5 Weekly (*http://html5weekly.com*)

These three periodicals will keep you informed of the latest news, services, blogs, and tutorials as they become available.

# Stack Overflow

Chances are good that you've already used Stack Overflow (SO): since its inception in 2008, it has become the dominant online Q&A site, and is your best resource to get your JavaScript, Node, and Express questions answered (and any other technology covered in this book). Stack Overflow is a community-maintained, reputation-based Q&A site. The reputation model is what's responsible for the quality of the site and its continued success. Users can gain reputation by having their questions or answers "upvoted" or having an accepted answer. You don't have to have any reputation to ask a question, and registration is free. However, there are things you can do to increase the chances of getting your question answered in a useful manner, which we'll discuss in this section.

Reputation is the currency of Stack Overflow, and while there are people out there who genuinely want to help you, it's the chance to gain reputation that's the icing on the cake that motivates good answers. There are a lot of really smart people on SO, and they're all competing to provide the first and/or best correct answer to your question (there's a strong disincentive to provide a quick but bad answer, thankfully). Here are things you can do to increase the chances of getting a good answer for your question:

*Be an informed SO user*
   Take the SO tour (*http://stackoverflow.com/tour*), then read "How do I ask a good question?" (*http://stackoverflow.com/help/how-to-ask*) If you're so inclined, you can go on to read all of the help documentation (*http://stackoverflow.com/help*)—you'll earn a badge if you read it all!

*Don't ask questions that have already been answered*

Do your due diligence, and try to find out of someone has already asked your question. If you ask a question that has an easily found answer already on SO, your question will quickly be closed as a duplicate, and people will often downvote you for this, negatively affecting your reputation.

*Don't ask people to write your code for you*

You will quickly find your question downvoted and closed if you simply ask "How do I do $X$?" The SO community expects you to make an effort to solve your own problem before resorting to SO. Describe in your question what you've tried and why it isn't working.

*Ask one question at a time*

Questions that are asking five things—"How do I do this, then that, then the other things, and what's the best way to do this?"—are difficult to answer, and are discouraged.

*Craft a minimal example of your issue*

I answer a lot of SO questions, and the ones I almost automatically skip over are those where I see three pages of code (or more!). Just taking your 5,000-line file and pasting into an SO question is not a great way to get your question answered (but people do it all the time). It's a lazy approach that isn't often rewarded. Not only are you less likely to get a useful answer, but the very process of eliminating things that *aren't* causing the problem can lead you to solving the problem yourself (then you don't even need to ask a question on SO). Crafting a minimal example is good for your debugging skills and for your critical thinking ability, and makes you a good SO citizen.

*Learn Markdown*

Stack Overflow uses Markdown for formatting questions and answers. A well-formatted question has a better chance of being answered, so you should invest the time to learn this useful and increasingly ubiquitous markup language (*http://stack overflow.com/help/formatting*).

*Accept and upvote answers*

If someone answers your question satisfactorily, you should upvote and accept it; it boosts the reputation of the answerer, and reputation is what drives SO. If multiple people provide acceptable answers, you should pick the one you think is best and accept that, and upvote anyone else you feel offered a useful answer.

*If you figure out your own problem before someone else does, answer your own question*

SO is a community resource: if you have a problem, chances are, someone else has it too. If you've figured it out, go ahead and answer your own question for the benefit of others.

If you enjoy helping the community, consider answering questions yourself: it's fun and rewarding, and it can lead to benefits that are more tangible than an arbitrary reputation score. If you have a question for which you've received no useful answers for two days, you can start a *bounty* on the question, using your own reputation. The reputation is withdrawn from your account immediately, and it is nonrefundable. If someone answers the question to your satisfaction, and you accept their answer, they will receive the bounty. The catch is, of course, you have to have reputation to start a bounty: the minimum bounty is 50 reputation points. While you can get reputation from asking quality questions, it's usually quicker to get reputation by providing quality answers.

Answering people's questions also have the benefit of being a great way to learn. I generally feel that I learn more from answering other people's questions than I do from having my questions answered. If you want to really thoroughly learn a technology, learn the basics and then start trying to tackle people's questions on SO: at first you might be consistently beat out by people who are already experts, but before long, you'll find that you *are* one of the experts.

Lastly, you shouldn't hesitate to use your reputation to further your career. A good reputation is absolutely worth putting on a résumé. It's worked for me and, now that I'm in the position of interviewing developers myself, I'm always impressed to see a good SO reputation (I consider a "good" SO reputation anything over 3,000; five-digit reputations are *great*). A good SO reputation tells me that someone is not just competent in their field, but they are clear communicators and generally helpful.

# Contributing to Express

Express and Connect are open source projects, so anyone can submit "pull requests" (GitHub lingo for changes you've made that you would like included in the project). This is not easy to do: the developers working on these projects are pros and the ultimate authority on their own projects. I'm not discouraging you from contributing, but I am saying you have to dedicate some significant effort to be a successful contributor, and you cannot take submissions lightly.

The actual process of contributing is pretty easy: you fork the project in your own GitHub account, clone that fork, make your changes, push them back to GitHub, and then create a pull request, which will be reviewed by someone on the project. If your submissions are small, or are bug fixes, you may have luck simply submitting the pull request. If you're trying to do something major, you should communicate with one of the main developers and discuss your contribution. You don't want to waste hours or days on a complicated feature only to find that it doesn't fit with the maintainer's vision, or it's already being worked on by someone else.

The other way to contribute (indirectly) to the development of Express and Connect is to publish npm packages, specifically middleware. Publishing your own middleware requires approval from no one, but that doesn't mean you should carelessly clutter the npm registry with low-quality middleware: plan, test, implement, and document, and your middleware will enjoy more success.

If you do publish your own packages, here are the minimum things you should have:

*Package name*
>While package naming is up to you, you obviously have to pick something that isn't already taken, which can sometimes be a challenge. Unlike GitHub, npm packages are not namespaced by account, so you're competing globally for names. If you're writing middleware, it's customary to prefix your package name with connect- or express-. Catchy package names that don't have any particular relation to what it does are fine, but even better is a package name that hints at what it does (a great example of a catchy but appropriate package name is zombie, for headless browser emulation).

*Package description*
>Your package description should be short, concise, and descriptive. This is one of the primary fields that is indexed when people search for packages, so it's best to be descriptive, not clever (there's room for some cleverness and humor in your documentation, don't worry).

*Author/contributors*
>Take some credit. Go on.

*License(s)*
>This is often neglected, and there is nothing more frustrating than encountering a package without a license (leaving you unsure if you can use it in your project). Don't be that person. The MIT license (*http://bit.ly/mit_license*) is an easy choice if you don't want any restrictions on how your code is used. If you want it to be open source (and stay open source), another popular choice is the GPL license (*http://bit.ly/gpl_license*). It's also wise to include license files in the root directory of your project (they should start with *LICENSE*). For maximum coverage, dual-license with MIT and GPL. For an example of this in *package.json* and in *LICENSE* files, see my connect-bundle package (*http://bit.ly/connect-bundle*).

*Version*
>For the versioning system to work, you need to version your packages. Note that npm versioning is separate from commit numbers in your repository: you can update your repository all you like, but it won't change what people get when they use npm to install your package. You need to increment your version number and republish for changes to be reflected in the npm registry.

*Dependencies*
>You should make an effort to be conservative about dependencies in your packages. I'm not suggesting constantly reinventing the wheel, but dependencies increase the

size and licensing complexity of your package. At a minimum, you should make sure you aren't listing dependencies that you don't need.

*Keywords*
Along with description, keywords are the other major metadata used for people trying to find your package, so choose appropriate keywords.

*Repository*
You should have one. GitHub is the most common, but others are welcome.

*README.md*
The standard documentation format for both GitHub and npm is Markdown (*http://daringfireball.net/projects/markdown/syntax*). It's an easy, wiki-like syntax that you can quickly learn. Quality documentation is vitally important if you want your package to be used: if I land on an npm page and there's no documentation, I usually just skip it without further investigation. At a minimum, you should describe basic usage (with examples). Even better is to have all options documented. Describing how to run tests goes the extra mile.

When you're ready to publish your own package, the process is quite easy. Register for a free npm account (*https://npmjs.org/signup*), then follow these steps:

1. Type npm adduser, and log in with your npm credentials.
2. Type npm publish to publish your package.

That's it! You'll probably want to create a project from scratch, and test your package by using npm install.

# Conclusion

It is my sincere hope that this book has given you all the tools you need to get started with this exciting technology stack. At no time in my career have I felt so invigorated by a new technology (despite the odd main character that is JavaScript), and I hope I have managed to convey some of the elegance and promise of this stack. Though I have been building websites professionally for many years, I feel that, thanks to Node and Express, I understand the way the Internet works at a deeper level than I ever have before. I believe that it's a technology that truly enhances understanding, instead of trying to hide the details from you, all while still providing a framework for quickly and efficiently building websites.

Whether you are a newcomer to web development, or just to Node and Express, I welcome you to the ranks of JavaScript developers. I look forward to seeing you at user groups and conferences, and most important, seeing what you will build.

# Index

## Symbols
302 redirect, 89
303 redirect, 89

## A
A records, 268
Accepts HTTP header, 94
Access-Control-Allow-Origin header, 174
action attribute, <form> tag, 88
admin interfaces, 161
aesthetics, 39
Airbrake, 142
AJAX, 280
    form handling, using dedicated URL, 90
    handling AJAX forms in Express, 92
    results of calls, receiving as JSON, 83
Amazon S3 account, saving files to, 147
Amazon Simple Email Service (SES), 120, 123
Amazon Simple Notification Service (SNS), 142
Amazon Web Services (AWS), Elastic Beanstalk (EB), 274
Amazon, cloud computing services, 270
analytics, 279
Angular framework, 3
Apache 2.0 license, 7
Apache, Node versus, 5
APIs
    csurf middlewae and, 218

    providing, 66
    third-party, integrating with, 235–252
        geocoding, 243–250
        social media, 235–242
        weather data, 250
app clusters, 134
    adding cluster support to the website, 134
    uncaught exceptions and, 138
app file, 21
    naming, 21
app.all, 112
app.configure, 5
app.defaultConfiguration, 260
app.get, 22, 112
app.get(env), 5
app.post, 112
app.render, 260
app.set, 131
app.use, 23, 111, 260
app.use(app.router), removal for Express 4.0, 4
application failures, monitoring, 142
assert function, 41
asset versioning, 186, 192
asynchronous functions, debugging, 259
attribution, 30
authentication, 218
    adding additional providers, 233
    HTTPS and, 209

*We'd like to hear your suggestions for improving our indexes. Send email to index@oreilly.com.*

Passport module, 222–231
     setting up, 226
passwords, problem with, 219
storing users in your database, 220
third-party, 219
versus authorization, 218
versus registration and user experience, 221
authorization
     role-based, 231
     verifying, 225
     versus authentication, 218
authorization filter, creating, 163
Azure, 270
     deployment to, 272
     Git-based deployments, 271

**B**

Basavaraj, Veena, 71
bash shell, 10
basicAuth middleware, 116
behavior-driven development (BDD)
     in Mocha, 43
Berkeley Software Distribution (BSD) license, 8
Berners-Lee, Tim, 159
Bert, William, 140
best practices, 29
binary downloads, 183
Bing
     geocoding service, 243
     Webmaster Tools, 278
Bitbucket, 272
blocks, 74
body-parser middleware, 4, 91, 116
boilerplate code, 19
Bootstrap, 20, 92
     alert messages, 107
     online documentation, 287
boutique hosting services, 270
breakpoints, 258
browserify, 189
browsers
     CACert and, 212
     caching, 184, 191
     headless, 45, 50
     information passed in request headers, 57
     plugin showing status code of HTTP requests and redirects, 22
     trusted root certificates, 210
     viewing cookies, 105

viewing response headers, 58
BSD (Berkeley Software Distribution) license, 8
bulk email, sending, 124
bundling, 192
     and minification, 192
     skipping in development mode, 196
     third-party libraries and, 197

**C**

CACert, 211
Cache-Control header, 191
caching
     browser, 184, 191
     refreshing server-side cache (example), 247
     templates, 76
call stack, 258
Campaign Monitor, 124, 280
catastrophic errors, 173
CDNs (see content delivery networks)
certificate authorities (CAs), 210
     commercial, purchasing a certificate from, 212
     using a free CA, 211
certificate insurance, 214
certificates, 210
     chained root certificates, avoiding, 212
     domain, organization, and extended validation, 213
     generating your own, 210
     single-domain, multisubdomain, multidomain, and wildcard, 213
Chai assertion library, 41
chained root certificates, 212
Chrome, 256
     Ayima's Redirect Path, 22
     Postman - REST Client plugin, 175
     viewing cookies, 105
     viewing response headers, 58
Chromium project, Blink engine, 256
CI (see continuous integration)
client errors, 174
client-side JavaScript, 183
     static resources in, 189
client-side templating with Handlebars, 83
client/server applications, web-based, 15
cloud computing
     and treating web servers as generic commodities, 5
     services, 270

storage services, 145
cloud hosting, 268
    SaaS, PaaS, and IaaS, 269
cloud persistence, 147
cluster.fork, 136
cluster.isMaster and cluster.isWorker properties, 136
CNAME records, 268
Coates, Danny, 255
code examples from this book, xviii
code reuse and refactoring, 281
    middleware, 283
    private npm registry, 282
code reviews, 277
Codio, 11
command prompt, 10
    (see also terminals)
comments in Handlebars versus HTML, 74
Comodo Group, 212
compilation of JavaScript by Google's V8, 5
compression, 184
ConEmu, 10
Connect library, 4
    common middleware in, 116
    contributing to, 290
    installing and having available in applications, 116
    installing for Express version 4.0, 4
connect-bundle module, 196
connect-redis package, 158
connect-rest plugin, 178, 218
consoles, 10
    (see also terminals)
    Node Inspector, 257
    using REPL and the console in debugging, 254
consumer key and consumer secret, 236
content delivery networks (CDNs), 185
content type, view engine returning text/html by default, 26
Content-Type header, 23, 57
    Internet media types, 58
context, view engine/Handlebars, 62, 73
    accessing current context with . (period), 75
    blocks and, 75
    partials, 79
    specifying a different template, 79
    specifying layout: null, 79

template engine combining view, layout, and context, 77
continuous integration (CI), 52
controllers (in model-view-controller pattern), 201
    creating, 205
Cookie request headers, 102
cookie secret, 102
cookie-based sessions, 105
cookie-parser middleware, 103, 117
cookie-session middleware, 117
cookies, 101–105
    examining, 105
    externalizing credentials, 102
    important points about cookies, 101
    in Express, 103
        names of, 104
        specifying cookie options, 104
    sessions and, 109
CORS (see cross-origin resource sharing)
createApplication function, 260
credentials
    externalizing, 102
    importing into your application, 103
Crockford, Douglas, 49, 172
cross-origin resource sharing (CORS), 174, 184
cross-page testing, 40, 44
cross-site HTTP requests, 174
cross-site request forgery (CSRF), 217
CRT file, 211
CSS, 183
    bundling and minifying files, 194
    online documentation, 287
    static resources in, 187
    static resources referenced in, 185
    styling file upload button, 98
csurf middleware, 117, 217
Ctrl-S on Unix-like systems, 11
currency conversions, 158

## D

Dahl, Ryan, 2
database persistence, 148
    adding data, 155
    creating schemas and models, 151
    database connections with Mongoose, 150
    for REST API, 175
    performance and, 148
    retrieving data, 153

seeding initial data, 152
setting up MongoDB, 149
using MongoDB for session storage, 156
database server, 7
databases
performance, NoSQL versus relational databases, 148
relational, 148
storing users in, 220
use with Node, 6
debugging, 253–262
asynchronous functions, 259
Express, 259
first principle of, 253
using Node Inspector, 255–259
using Node's built-in debugger, 255
using REPL and the console, 254
default layout for views, 25
delegated authentication, 219
DELETE method, 57
DEL endpoint, 67
dependencies, listing for a project, 33
deployment, 271–274
manual Git-based deployment, 273
to Azure, 272
using Git, 271
Amazon deployment with Elastic Beanstalk, 274
development and quality assurance (QA), 37
development mode
environment-specific configuration choices,
133
skipping bundling and minification, 196
using morgan for logging, 133
directory middleware, 117
distributed version control systems (DVCS), 30
DNS (Domain Name System, 264
document databases, 148
documentation, 30
online, 287
domain certificates, 213
domain names, 263
domain registration and hosting, 263–271
hosting, 268
traditional or cloud, 268
name servers, 267
security, 264
subdomains, 266
top-level domains (TLDs), 265

domains
specifying for REST API, 180
using to deal with uncaught exceptions, 138
Doyle, Arthur Conan, 253
dual licensed software, 8
Dust (template engine), 71
DVCS (distributed version control systems), 30
dynamic IP address, 268

E

EB (Elastic Beanstalk), 274
ECMA-262 ECMAScript language specification,
287
editors, 11
associating .handlebars and .hbs files with
HTML, 25
Elastic Beanstalk (EB), 274
elimination, 253
Emacs, 12
email, 119–129
formats, 121
headers, 120
HTML, 121
Nodemailer, 122
receiving, 120
sending
bulk email, 124
encapsulating email functionality, 128
HTML email, 124
images in HTML email, 125
SMTP, MSAs, and MTAs, 119
to multiple recipients, 123
using Nodemailer, 123
using views to send HTML email, 126
using as site monitoring tool, 129
using to monitor application failures, 142
Ember framework, 3
encapsulation, using Node modules, 35
encoding for forms, 88
encryption, 214
level of, certificates and, 212
endpoint, 66
entropic functionality, testing, 48
error-handling middleware, 112
errorhandler middleware, 117
errors
AJAX handler returning object with err
property, 281
failed tests in Mocha, 47

finding potential errors using linting, 40
in AJAX form handling, 94
invisible failures, 281
monitoring for your site, using email, 129
providing custom error page, 137
reporting in a REST API, 173
sending email using Nodemailer, 123
ESLint, 49
ETag header, 191
event-driven programming, 14
example website, xvii
exceptions, uncaught, handling, 137
execution environments, 131
expect function (Chai assertion library), 41
Expires header, 191
exporting functionality from Node modules, 35
Express, xv, 19–28
    brief history of, 4
    contributing to, 290
    cookies in, 103
    debugging, 259
    defined, 2
    disabling X-Powered-By response header, 58
    documentation, 288
    Express API documentation, 62
    form handling, 91
    form handling with
        AJAX forms, 92
    Handlebars support for, 76
    HTTPS, enabling for your app, 214
    installing, 20
    JavaScript revolution, 1
    licensing Node applications, 7
    Meadowlark Travel example website, 20
        ititial steps, 20
    model-view-controller (MVC) pattern, im-
        plementing, 201–207
    Node ecosystem, 6
    Node, a new kind of server, 5
    removal of middleware from, 116
    request object, 59
    response object, 61
    REST API, 177
    routing
        subdomains, 162
    saving time with
        scaffolding, 19
    source code, 63

static files and views, handling by middle-
    ware, 26
upgrading from version 3.0 to 4.0, 4
versions, 4
views and layouts, 24
views, dynamic content in, 27
express-handlebars package, 24
express-logger, 133
express-namespace, 169
express-resource, 169
express-session middleware, 106, 117
express.Router(), 162
extended validation certificates, 213
externalizing credentials, 102

## F

Facebook, 235
    purchase of fb.com domain, 266
Facebook app, 226
Facebook authentication strategy, 226–233
federated authentication, 219
Ferraiuolo, Eric, 24
file uploads, 95
    creating for Meadowlark Travel example
        website, 95
    jQuery, 97
file-based storage, problems with, 134
filesystem persistence, 145
    storing files from photo contest (example),
        146
fingerprinting resource bundles, 192
    bundled and minified CSS and JavaScript
        files, 195
flash messages, implemening using sessions, 107
flat files, 145
flexibility of Express, 3
FormData interface, 95
Formidable, 96
forms, 87–99
    constructing HTML forms, 87
    encoding, 88
    form handler for vacation photo contest (ex-
        ample), 146
    handling
        AJAX forms, 92
        deciding on response to send back to
            browser, 89
        different approaches to, 89
        file uploads, 95

jQuery file upload, 97
  with Express, 91
  processing, 65
  sending client data to the server, 87
fortune cookies for Meadowlark Travel example
  website, 27
  modularizing, 35
  unit testing the fortune generator, 48
forward-facing proxy, 140
fragment in URLs, 56
fs (filesystem) module, 145
fs.readFile function, 17, 259
Fuel, 278
fully qualified domain name (FQDN), 211
functionality of your site, quality of, 38

## G

-g (global) option, installing npm packages on
  Windows, 11
Gemfury, 283
geocoding, 243–250
  using Google API, 243
    displaying a map, 247
    geocoding your data, 244
    improving client-side performance, 249
    usage restrictions, 244
geographic coordinates, 243
geographic optimization, 185
GET method, 56, 87
  GET endpoints, 66
  in a REST API, 172
  in REST API tests, 175
Git, 30
  adding files to repository with git add, 32
  committing changes with git commit, 32
  creating .gitignore file, 31
  creating a repository, 31
  creating experimental branch, 33
  deploying your application with, 271–274
    automated deployments, 274
    manual Git-based deployment, 273
  how to use it in this book, 31
GitHub, 271
GlobalSign, 212
Go Daddy, 212
going live, 263–274
  deployment, 271–274
  domain registration and hosting, 263–271
    DNS (Domain Name System), 264

hosting, 268–271
nameservers, 267
security, 264
subdomains, 266
top-level domains (TLDs), 265
Google
  API key, 248
  authenticating with, 233
  cloud computing services, 270
  Geocoding API, 243
  PageSpeed, 279
  V8, 5
  Webmaster Tools, 278
Google Analytics (GA), 279
GPL (GNU General Public License), 7
  combining with MIT license, 8
Grunt, 41
  automating QA testing with, 50
  compiling LESS to generate CSS, 188
  grunt-lint-pattern module, 198
  Gruntfile.js, configure plugins section, 51
  Gruntfile.js, load plugins section, 51
  installing globally, using npm, 13
  plugins, 50
  registering tasks in Gruntfile.js, 52
  running, 52
  using for bundling and minification, 193

## H

Handlebars templating engine, 24, 71
  (see also templating with Handlebars)
HAProxy, 140
Haraka, 120
hash in URLs, 56
hashres task, 195
<head> element in main.handlebars, modifying
  to include test framework, 42
<header> element, 27
headers
  email, 120
  HTTP requests, 57
  HTTP responses, 57
headers property (request object), 57
headless browser, 45, 50
Holowaychuk, TJ, 4, 5, 24
hosting, 264, 268–271
  boutique hosting services, 270
  cloud hosting
    acronyms, 269

the behemoths, 270
traditional or cloud, 268
hosts file, 180
hosts, hostname in URLs, 55
HTML
    email, 121
        images in, 125
        sending, 124
        using views to send, 126
    files for static resources, 16
    generating using JavaScript, 69
    in Content-Type response header, 57
    online documentation, 287
    rendering with Handlebars, 73
    sending direct HTML response in form han-
        dling, 89
    views, 24
HTML Email Boilerplate, 121, 126
HTML5
    <header> element, 27
    local storage, 105
    online documentation, 287
HTML5 Boilerplate, 19, 82
HTTP
    port 80 as default, 215
    requests and responses (see request and re-
        sponse objects)
    stateless protocol, 101
HTTP module, 63
HTTP status codes
    browser plugin showing, 22
    error reporting in a REST API, 173
    view engine returning 200 status code by de-
        fault, 26
HTTP verbs, 22, 56
    in a REST API, 172
    method-override middleware, 118
    route handlers for, 112
    testing our REST API, 175
http.IncomingMessage object, 59
http.ServerResponse object, 61
HTTPS, 209
    enabling for your Express app, 214
    generating your own certificate, 210
    getting certificate from free certificate au-
        thority, 211
    ports and, 215
    proxies and, 216
    purchasing a certificate, 212

hybrid (multipage and single-page) web applica-
    tions, 3

**I**

IA (see information architecture)
IaaS (Infrastructure as a Service), 269
IIS (Internet Information Services), Node ver-
    sus, 5
ImageMagick, 97
images
    background image for a site, 188
    in HTML email, 125
    shopping cart, on the client, 190
    small, combining into a single sprite, 184
information architecture (IA), 159
    suggestions for designing lasting IA, 160
Infrastructure as a Service (IaaS), 269
installer (standalone) for node, 10
integration testing, 39
Internet Corporation for Assigned Names and
    Numbers (ICANN), 266
Internet media types, 58
invisible failures, preventing, 281
IP addresses, 263
    static and dynamic, 268
issue tracking, 277

**J**

Jade, 24, 71
JavaScript
    bundling and minifying files, 194
    client-side, as static resource, 183
    credentials.js file, 103
    failure of, fallback for, 280
    floating-point numbers and financial com-
        putations, 151
    generating HTML with, 69
    in Node, 6
    JavaScript engine used by Node (Google V8),
        5
    logic testing (fortune generator example), 48
    misconceptions about, 2
    online documentation, 287
    promise of all-JavaScript technology stack, 1
    resources for learning, xv
    server-side containers, 6
    specifying files to be linted for JSHint, 51
    static resources in client-side JavaScript, 189

static resources in server-side JavaScript, 189
static resources referenced in code, 185
utilities, installing globally, using npm, 13
JavaScript stack, 7
Jenkins (CI server), 53
JetBrain (CI server), 53
Joyent, 270
jQuery
    dynamically changing shopping cart image,
        190
    File Upload middleware, 97
        documentation, 99
    not included in bundles, 197
    online documentation, 287
    using to test assertions, 42
JSHint, 49
    Grunt plugin for, 50
    specifying JavaScript files to be linted, 51
JSLint, 49
JSON, 172
    configuration file for connect-bundle, 196
    receiving results of AJAX calls as, 83
    returning in AJAX form handling, 94
json (middleware), 116
Just in Time (JIT) compilation, 5

**K**

key-value databases, 148
keyword monitors, 141
Kovalyov, Anton, 49

**L**

LAMP stack (Linux, Apache, MySQL, and
    PHP), 6
Last-Modified header, 191
LastPass, 220
layouts, 24, 76
    adding header to every page, 27
    modifying to conditionally include test
        framework, 42
    referencing bundled and minified files, 195
    templating engine rendering view with a lay-
        out, 77
    using (or not) in Express, 78
lead tracking, prioritizing, 279
LESS, 187
    linking in static mapper as LESS custom
        function, 188

lib/application.js (Express source code), 63
lib/express.js (Express source code), 63
lib/request.js (Express source code), 63
lib/response.js (Express source code), 63
lib/router/route.js (Express source code), 63
libraries
    bundling third-party libraries, 197
    third-party, 41
licensing for Node applications, 7
link checking, 40, 49
LinkChecker, 49
    configuring grunt-exec plugin to run, 52
    no Grunt plugin for, 50
LinkedIn, templating language, 71
links, testing in page-specific test, 43
linting, 40, 49
    catching unmapped statics, 197
    specifying JavaScript files for JSHint, 51
Linux
    commands in background and foreground,
        256
    installing Node, 9
    Node on, 6
    package managers, Node installation and, 9
    shells, 10
Linux VM, using for development on Windows,
    11
Litmus, email testing, 121
load testing, 142
loadtest, 142
localhost, 13, 180
logging
    adding to an application, 133
    console, 255
    errors, 281
    logger middleware, 261
logic testing, 40, 48
    configuring Mocha plugin for Grunt, 51
logic versus presentation, 39
longevity plan, 275
loopback address, IPv4 or IPv6, 13
lossless size reduction, 184
lossy size reduction, 184

**M**

Mac OS X
    creating .gitignore file, 31
    installing Node, 9
    Node on, 6

running commands in background or foreground, 256
shells, 10
Mail Submission Agents (MSAs), 119
errors sending email, 123
Mail Transfer Agents (MTAs), 119
MailChimp
article on writing HTML email, 121
bulk email service, 124
main.handlebars file, modifying <head> element to include test framework, 42
maintenance, 275–285
code reuse and refactoring, 281
principles of
doing routine QA checks, 278
don't procrastinate, 278
exercising good hygiene, 277
longevity plan, 275
monitoring analytics, 279
optimizing performance, 279
preventing invisible failures, 281
prioritizing lead tracking, 279
using an issue tracker, 277
using source control, 277
maps, 243
(see also geocoding)
displaying geocoded dealers map (example), 247
Markdown, 35, 289
master pages, 25
MDN (Mozilla Developer Network), 287
Meadowlark Travel example website, xvii, 20
creating file upload for photo contest, 95
cross-page testing, 44
initial steps, 20
modifying to allow running tests, 41
meadowlark.js file (example), 21
defining array of fortune cookies, 27
linting with JSHint, 49
MEAN stack (Mongo, Express, Angular, and Node), 6
Mercurial, 30, 271
method-override middleware, 118
Microsoft
.NET, 2
Azure cloud storage, saving files to, 147
cloud computing services, 270
IIS (Internet Information Services), 5
model-view-view model (MVVM), 201

PowerShell, 10
Visual Studio, 12
middleware, 4, 111–118
adding in Express, 23, 260
common, 116
defined, 111
function exported by a module, 114
handling static files and views in Express, 26
important points about middleware and route handlers, 112
injecting weather data into res.locals.partials object, 80
jquery-file-upload-middleware package, 97
logger, 261
module exporting an object containing properties, 115
requirement to be a function, 114
reusable, packaging, 283
module exposing a function returning middleware, 283
module exposing an object constructor, 284
module exposing an object containing middleware, 284
module exposing middleware function directly, 283
route handlers, 162
session, 261
static, 261
third-party, 118
migration guide, upgrading Express 3.0 to 4.0, 5
MIME (Multipurpose Internet Mail Extensions) types, 58
minification, 192
skipping in development mode, 196
MIT license, 7
combining with GPL, 8
Mocha, 41
configuring cafemocha plugin for Grunt, 51
Grunt plugin for, 50
multiple interfaces controlling style of your tests, 43
using for cross-page testing, 47
using for logic testing, 48
model-view-controller (MVC) pattern, 24
implementing in Express, 201–207
controllers, 205
models, 202
view models, 203

model-view-view model (MVVM), 201
models, 150, 202
    creating, 151, 155
    creating for users, 220
    defined, 201
modules
    declaring routes in, 166
    exposing a function returning middleware, 283
    exposing an object constructor, 284
    exposing an object containing middleware, 284
    exposing middleware function directly, 283
MongoDB, 7, 148, 202, 221
    retrieving data from, 153
    seeding initial data, 152
    setting up, 149
    using for session storage, 156
MongoHQ, 149
MongoLab, 149
Mongoose, 149, 202
    creating dealer model, 244
    creating model for users, 220
    creating schema and model for REST API
        data store, 175
    creating schemas and models, 151
    database connections with, 150
    upserts, 156
monitor utility for automatic server restarts, 41
monitoring your website, 141
    application failures, 142
    third-party uptime monitors, 141
morgan middleware, 118
    using for logging in development environ-
        ment, 133
Mozilla Developer Network (MDN), 287
MSAs (Mail Submission Agents), 119
    errors sending email, 123
MTAs (Mail Transfer Agents), 119
multidomain certificates, 213
multimedia, 183
multipage web applications, 3
multipart form processing, 95
multipart middleware (deprecated), 117
multipart/form-data encoding, 89
    specifying for file uploads, 96
multithreading through server parallelism, 5
Mustache templating engine, 24, 69
MVVM (model-view-view model), 201

# N

name attribute in <input> fields, 88
nameservers, 267
next function, 112
Nginx, 140
    setting X-Forwarded-Proto header, 216
Ninjitsu, 283
Node, xv, 2
    app clusters, support for, 134
    apps, 5
    components of, 6
    Connect library, 4
    debugger, 255
    documentation, 63, 288
    filesystem persistence, 145
    getting started with, 9–18
        editors, 11
        event-driven programming, 14
        installing Node, 9
        npm package manager, 12
        routing, 15
        serving static resources, 15
        simple web server, 13
        supporting multiple versions of Node, 13
        using the terminal, 10
    licensing for applications, 7
    new kind of web server, 5
    param method of request object, 59
    platform-independence of, 6
    proxy servers, 140
    request object, 59
    response object, 61
    support for scaling out, 134
Node Inspector, 255–259
    available actions, 257
    setting breakpoints, 258
Node modules, 35
    exporting functionality from, 35
    importing, 35
    official documentation site, 36
Nodejitsu, 270
Nodemailer, 122
    HTML or plaintext email, 124
    sending email, 123
        to multiple recipients, 123
nodemon, 41
NODE_ENV, 131
node_modules directory, 20, 33
NoSQL databases, 6, 148

notification services, 142
npm (package manager), 12
    -g (global) option, 11
    install command, 13
    installing Express, 20
    managing Express project dependencies and
        project metadata, 20
    online documentation, 288
    packages your project relies on, 33
    private npm registries, 282
npm init command, 20

## O

object document mappers (ODMs), 149
online documentation, 287
OpenSSL, 210
    generating private key and public key certifi-
        cate, 211
Opera, 256
operating systems
    hosts file, 180
    installing ImageMagick, 97
    installing Node, 9
    Node on, 6
    ports, 215
    Unix/BSD system or Cygwin, modifying ex-
        ecution environment, 132
organization certificates, 213
OS X (see Mac OS X; operating systems)

## P

PaaS (Platform as a Service), 269
package managers
    installing Node via, 9
    npm, 12
package.json file, 20, 33
    main property, 21
    project metadata, 34
page testing, 40
    embedding tests in the page, 41
    global tests, 43
    Grunt and, 50
    page-specific test, 43
PageSpeed, 279
parameters, request object, 59
partials, 79
    organizing into subdirectories, 81
partials object, 79

Passport, 222–231
    setting up, 226
passwords
    problem with, 219
    third-party authentication and, 222
path in URLs, 56
PEM (Privacy-enhanced Electronic Mail) file,
    211
performance
    and handling of static resources, 184
    databases, NoSQL versus relational, 148
    optimizing, 279
    social media plugins and, 235
periodicals, 288
persistence, 145–158
    cloud storage, 147
    database, 148
        adding data, 155
        creating schemas and models, 151
        database connections with Mongoose,
            150
        performance and NoSQL databases, 148
        retrieving data, 153
        seeding initial data, 152
        setting up MongoDB, 149
        using MongoDB for session storage, 156
    filesystem, 145
    website designed to be scaled out, 134
personally identifiable information (PII), securi-
    ty for, 209
PhantomJS, 45
PHP, templating in, 69
Pilgrim, Mark, 287
Pingdom, 141
pipeline, 111
Platform as a Service (PaaS), 269
platform-independence of Node, 6
PNG images, 184
PORT environment variable, 22
ports, 215
    port in URLs, 56
POST method, 56, 87
    bodies of POST requests, 58
    in a REST API, 172
    specifying in the <form> tag, 88
    using for form submission, 87
Postman - REST Client Chrome plugin, 175
PowerShell, 10
presentation, logic versus, 39

private key, generating, 211
private npm registries, 282
process.nextTick, 138
processing forms, 65
procrastination, 278
production concerns, 131–143
    environment-specific configuration, 132
    execution environments, 131
    monitoring your website, 141
        application failures, 142
        third-party uptime monitors, 141
    scaling your website, 133
        handling uncaught exceptions, 137
        scaling out with app clusters, 134
        scaling out with multiple servers, 140
    stress testing, 142
production mode, NODE_ENV, 132
profile first, then optimize, 279
project dependencies, 33
project files, keeping separate from web app
    files, 20
project metadata, 34
promises, 241
protocol in URLs, 55
protocol relative URLs, 186
proxy servers, 140
    HTTPS and, 216
    informing Express of, 141
public key certificates, 210
    (see also certificates)
    generating your own, 210
PUT method
    in a REST API, 172
    PUT endpoint, 67
PuTTY, 11

**Q**

quality assurance, 37–53
    automating testing with Grunt, 50
    continuous integration (CI), 52
    cost of, and return on investment model, 38
    cross-page testing, 44
    doing routine QA checks, 278
    in small or budget-conscious organizations,
        37
    link checking, 49
    linting, 49
    logic testing, 48
    logic versus presentation, 39
    overview of techniques, 40
    page testing, 41
    QA department in large or well-funded or-
        ganizations, 37
    running your server, 40
    types of tests, 39
query middleware, 118
querystring in URLs, 56

**R**

random functionality, testing, 48
random password generator, 102
Razor template engine, 81
reach, 38
read-eval-print loop (REPL), 254
README.md file, 20, 34
recoverable server errors, 174
red light, green light testing, 47
redirects
    browser plugin showing, 22
    for flash message display, 109
    responding to form submissions, 89
        choices of where redirection points, 90
Redis, 158
redundancy, 280
registration, 221
regular expressions, route paths and, 164
relational database management system
    (RDBMS), 148
relational databases
    interfaces for Node, 6
    performance, 148
rendering content, 63
representational state transfer (see REST APIs)
req.accepts property, 94
req.body, 66
req.cookie method, 64
req.cookies, 104
req.query, 59, 63, 66
req.session, 63, 107
req.session.authorized, 163
req.session.flash, 109
req.signedCookies, 64, 104
req.xhr property, 94, 108
request and response objects, 55–68
    getting more information, 62
    HTTP request methods, 56
    Internet media types, 58

most frequently used functionality in Ex-
    press, 63
    processing forms, 65
    providing an API, 66
    rendering content, 63
parameters, 59
request body, 58
request extensions, 260
request headers, 57
request object, 59
response extensions, 261
response headers, 57
response object, 61
sending a response, 260
sessions and, 107
URLs, 55
requests, reducing number of, 184
require function, 35
require statement, running a script as a module
    via, 135
res.cookie, 103
res.format, 94
res.locals object, 42, 62
    function to inject special offers data into, 163
res.locals.flash, 109
res.locals.partials object, middleware to inject
    weather data into, 80
res.locals.showTests property, 42
res.render method, 63, 127
res.send method, 63, 113, 260
res.set method, 23
res.status method, 23
res.type method, 23
resources, additional, 287–292
response-time middleware, 118
REST APIs, 161, 171–181
    cross-origin resource sharing (CORS), 174
    csurf middleware and, 218
    data store, 175
    error reporting, 173
    JSON and XML, 172
    planning an API, 172
    testing our API, 175
    using a REST plugin, 178
    using a subdomain, 180
    using Express to provide, 177
REST functions, 179
rest.get, 176
rest.put, 176

RESTful services, 171
restler package, 175
reverse proxy, 140
role-based authorization, 231
route handlers, 112
    as middleware, 162
routers
    controllers (MVC) versus, 205
    explicit linking into the pipeline, 111
routing, 15, 17, 159–169
    adding routes in Express, 22
        order of, 23
    adding routes to new views in Express, 25
    automatically rendering views, 168
    declaring routes in a module, 166
    defined, 159
    grouping route handlers logically, 167
    lib/router/route.js in Express source, 63
    organizing routes, 165
    route handlers as middleware, 162
    route organization, other approaches, 169
    route parameters, 164
    route paths and regular expressions, 164
    routers versus controllers, 205
    routes and SEO, 161
    static middleware serving static files, 26
    subdomains, 161
Ruby, 2
    scaffolding, 19
    Sinatra framework and Express, 4
Ruby on Rails, scaffolding utility, 19


S

SaaS (Software as a Service), 269
same-origin policy, 174
Sass, 187
scaffolding, 19
scaffolding utility (Express), 19
scaling out, 133
scaling up, 133
scaling your website, 133
    handling uncaught exceptions, 137
    scaling out with app cllusters, 134
    scaling out with multiple servers, 140
scaling, filesystem persistence and, 145
schemas (database), 150
    creating, 151, 155
scope variables, 258

<script> elements in the <head>, putting HTML in, 83
scripts, running directly or included as a module via require statement, 135
search engine optimization (SEO), 38, 278
   routes and, 161
sections, 81
security, 209–234
   authentication, 218
      adding additional providers, 233
      Passport module, 222–231
      passwords, problem with, 219
      storing users in your database, 220
      third-party, 219
      versus authorization, 218
      versus registration and user experience, 221
   cross-site request forgery (CSRF), 217
   domain, 264
   HTTPS, 209
      enabling for Express apps, 214
      generating your own certificate, 210
      ports, 215
      proxies and, 216
      purchasing a certificate, 212
      using a free certificate authority, 211
   role-based authorization, 231
Selenium, 45
semver (semantic versioner) in npm, 34
SendGrid, 120
   limits on number of email recipients, 124
Sentry, 142
server errors, 17
server-side JavaScript, 1
   static resources in, 189
server-side templates, 76
servers
   continuous integration (CI), 52
   information passed in response headers, 57
   running in production mode, 132
   running your server, 40
serveStaticFile helper function, 17
session-mongoose package, 156
sessions, 105–109
   cookie-based, 105
   memory stores, 105
   middleware, 261
   preferring over cookies, 102
   storing, using MongoDB, 156

using, 107
   using to implement flash messages, 107
   when to use, 109
Set-Cookie header, 102
setTimeout, 137
shells, 10
   learning to use, 11
signed cookies, 101, 104
SimpleSMTP, 120
Sinatra framework, 4
single threading (Node), 5
single-domain certificates, 213
single-page web applications, 3
Sinopia, 282
Site24x7, 141
SMTP (Simple Mail Transfer Protocol), 119
social media, 235–242
   integration with
      social media plugins and performance, 235
      Twitter, 236–242
Software as a Service (SaaS), 269
source control, 277
spoofing, 120
SpritePad, 184
sprites, 184
SSL certificates, 210
Stack Overflow (SO), 288
stateless protocols, 101
static content, 183–199
   bundling and minification, 192
      skipping in development mode, 196
   changing, 192
   future-proofing your website, 184
      static mapping, 185
      static resources in CSS, 187
      static resources in views, 187
   performance considerations, 184
   serving static resources, 191
   static resources in server-side JavaScript, 189
static IP address, 268
static middleware, 26, 116, 118, 261
static resources
   serving with Node, 15
   views versus, 24
static-favicon middleware, 118
storage failure, total, 280
stress testing, 142
Stylus, 187

subdomains, 55, 161, 266
    using for REST APIs, 180
Subversion, 271
Symantec, 212

# T

technical debt, 278
templating
    defined, 70
    what it isn't, 69
    with Jade, 71
templating engine, 7
    choosing, criteria for, 71
    decoupled from programming language, 69
templating with Handlebars, 69–85
    basics, 73
    blocks, 74
    client-side templating, 83
        loading Handlebars, 83
    comments, 74
    perfecting your templates, 82
    server-side templates, 76
    using partials, 79
    views and layouts, 76
        rendering a view with a layout, 77
        sections, 81
        using layouts in Express, 78
terminals, using, 10
    Unix-like systems, Ctrl-S, 11
test-driven development (TDD) in Mocha, 43
testing, 277
    types of, 39
    writing tests before implementing features,
        47
Themeforest, 82
themes, third-party, 82
top-level domains (TLDs), 55, 265
Travis CI, 53
trusted root certificates, 210
Twitter, 235
    creating apps for, 236–239
    rendering tweets, 239–242
Twitter Bootstrap, 20, 92
    (see also Bootstrap)

# U

uglify task, 194

uncaught exceptions, handling, 137
    using domains, 138
uncaughtException event, 138
Underscore, 204
unit testing, 39
    unit test for fortune generator (example), 48
Unix-like systems, Ctrl-S, 11
upserts, 156
UptimeRobot, 141
URL encoding, 88
URL-encoded body parsing, 261
urlencoded (middleware), 116
URLs
    design suggestions for lasting IA, 160
    designing for website content, 159
    fragment (or hash), 56
    host, 55
    path, 56
    port, 56
    protocol, 55
    protocol relative, using to reference static re-
        sources, 186
    querystring, 56
    subdomains, 161
usability, 38
user uploads, never trusting, 147

# V

version control, 30, 277
versioning, semver in npm, 34
vhost middleware, 118, 180
vi (editor), 11
vi mode (editors), 12
view models, 154, 201
    creating, 203
views, 24, 76
    adding routes to, in Express, 25
    automatic view-based route handlers, 166
    caching, 76
    creating view pages for Meadowlark Travel
        website (example), 25
    defined, 201
    dynamic content in, 27
    handling by middleware, in Express, 26
    layout, 25
    modifying to conditionally include test
        framework, 42
    rendering automatically, 168

rendering using configured templating engine, 62
rendering with a templating engine, 77
rendering with Handlebars
    using layouts in Express, 78
    using partials, 79
    using sections, 81
static resources in, 187
static resources referenced in, 185
unmapped database objects and, 154
using to send HTML email, 126
vim editor, associating .handlebars and .hbs files
    with HTML, 25
virtual machines (VMs), 10
VirtualBox, 10
virtualization, 10, 269
Visual Studio as JavaScript editor, 12

## W

watch expressions, 258
weather data, current
    creating middleware to inject data into
        res.locals.partials object, 80
    function to get weather data, 80
    using partials for weather widget in Handle-
        bars, 79
    using Weather Underground API, 250
web application framework, Express as, 3
web applications
    creating with JavaScript, Node, and Express,
        xv
    defined, 3
    mltipage and hybrid, 3
    single-page, 3
web page for this book, xix
web servers
    Node versus other web servers, 5

writing with Node, 13
    "Hello World" example, 14
web services, 171
    (see also REST APIs)
WebFaction, 267, 271
Webmaster Tools, 278
websites
    launching (see going live)
    Meadowlark Travel (example), xvii
    stacks that they're built on, 6
widgets, 79
wildcard certificates, 213
wildcards in Express routes, 23
Wilson, Mike, 278
Windows systems
    editors, 12
    installing Node, 9
    Node on, 6
    OpenSSL on, 211
    using a terminal and shell, 10
WrapBootstrap, 82

## X

X-Forwarded-Proto header, 216
X.509 certificates, 210
xkcd password generator, 102
XML, 172
XMLHttpRequest Level 2's FormData interface,
    95

## Z

Zombie, 45
zsh shell, 10

## About the Author

**Ethan Brown** is a senior software engineer at Pop Art, a Portland-based interactive marketing agency, where he is responsible for the architecture and implementation of websites and web services for clients ranging from small businesses to international enterprise companies. He has over 20 years of programming experience, from embedded to the Web, and has embraced the JavaScript stack as the web platform of the future.

## Colophon

The animals on the cover of *Web Development with Node and Express* are a black lark (*Melanocorypha yeltoniensis*) and a white-winged lark (*Melanocorypha leucopter*). Both birds are partially migratory and have been known to range far afield of their most suitable habitat in the steppes of Kazakhstan and central Russia. In addition to breeding there, male black larks will also winter in the Kazakh steppes, while females migrate southwards. White-winged larks, on the other hand, fly farther west and north beyond the Black Sea during the winter months. The global range of these birds extends still farther: Europe constitutes a quarter to one-half of the global range of the white-winged lark and only five percent to a quarter of the global range of the black lark.

Black larks are so named for the black coloring that covers nearly the entire body of males of the species. Females, by contrast, resemble the coloring of the male in only their black legs and the black feathers of their underwings. A combination of dark and pale grays covers the rest of the female.

White-winged larks possess a distinctive pattern of black, white and chestnut wing feathers. Gray streaks down the white-winged lark's back complement a pale white lower body. Males differ in appearance from females of the species only in the males' chestnut crowns.

Both black and white-winged larks evince the distinctively melodious call that has endeared larks of all variations to the imaginations of writers and musicians for centuries. Both birds eat insects and seeds as adults, and both birds make nests on the ground. Black larks have been observed carrying dung to their nests to build walls or lay a kind of pavement, though the cause for this behavior has not been identified.

Many of the animals on O'Reilly covers are endangered; all of them are important to the world. To learn more about how you can help, go to animals.oreilly.com.

The cover image is from Lydekker's Royal Natural History. The cover fonts are URW Typewriter and Guardian Sans. The text font is Adobe Minion Pro; the heading font is Adobe Myriad Condensed; and the code font is Dalton Maag's Ubuntu Mono.

# Have it your way.

# Get even more for your money.

**Join the O'Reilly Community, and register the O'Reilly books you own. It's free, and you'll get:**

- $4.99 ebook upgrade offer
- 40% upgrade offer on O'Reilly print books
- Membership discounts on books and events
- Free lifetime updates to ebooks and videos
- Multiple ebook formats, DRM FREE
- Participation in the O'Reilly community
- Newsletters
- Account management
- 100% Satisfaction Guarantee

### Signing up is easy:

1. Go to: oreilly.com/go/register
2. Create an O'Reilly login.
3. Provide your address.
4. Register your books.

Note: English-language books only

**To order books online:**
oreilly.com/store

**For questions about products or an order:**
orders@oreilly.com

**To sign up to get topic-specific email announcements and/or news about upcoming books, conferences, special offers, and new technologies:**
elists@oreilly.com

**For technical questions about book content:**
booktech@oreilly.com

**To submit new book proposals to our editors:**
proposals@oreilly.com

**O'Reilly books are available in multiple DRM-free ebook formats. For more information:**
oreilly.com/ebooks

# O'REILLY®

CPSIA information can be obtained at www.ICGtesting.com
Printed in the USA
BVOW09s2256060416

443212BV00005B/40/P

9 781491 949306